T0245656

BUSINESS
SECRETS
FROM THE
BIBLE

BUSINESS SECRETS FROM THE BIBLE

SPIRITUAL SUCCESS STRATEGIES
for FINANCIAL ABUNDANCE

Second Edition

RABBI DANIEL AND
SUSAN LAPIN

WILEY

Library of Congress Cataloging-in-Publication Data Is Available:

ISBN 9781394215881 (Cloth)
ISBN 9781394215904 (ePDF)
ISBN 9781394215898 (ePub)

Cover Design: Wiley
Cover Image: © Polyanska Lyubov/Shutterstock

SKY10069992_032024

To All Our Happy Warriors
wherever you may be.

Contents

Introduction

We don't need the gift of prophecy to state that most people picking up this book or doing a search for the word *business* are interested in increasing their income. As we work on this second edition of *Business Secrets from the Bible*, inflation is eating away at the fruits of people's labors, and many young people are giving up on the idea of working productively and may have despaired of gaining an income that will yield them an equal or better financial life than their parents enjoyed.

We doubt if you would read a book on business by someone who limited their research to companies founded in the last two years. We all know of seemingly roaring successes that crash down only a few years later. This book is not going to direct you to start a crypto-coin or electric vehicle company, nor is it going to direct you to get back to the land and grow organic parsley. Perhaps you will do one of those things, but you might just as well develop a graphic design business or become an electrician. Your path to financial improvement might include getting a medical or law degree. This book shares more than 3,000 years of wisdom that can be applied in almost all times and places. It has been tested and guided by millions of ordinary people to build wealth in both good and bad economic times. That wisdom stems from the Bible, and specifically from a faithful rendering of Jewish transmission.

You might be wondering, *Why Business Secrets from the Bible? Why not Tennis Secrets from the Bible,* or *Car Racing Secrets from the Bible,* or *Beauty and Makeup Tips from the Bible?*

One can find pretty much whatever one seeks within the pages of that mysterious and majestic volume that has had so much influence on the story of civilization. Over the years, many have projected onto its pages their own visions, fears, and hopes and have subsequently seen it reflect back confirmation of their convictions. Unfortunately, this has led to all kinds of misguided and invalid biblical proclamations. The Bible can tell us much, but if we impose upon it whatever we wish, we destroy its usefulness. The original meaning of the Bible must be preserved.

But how to know the difference? Let ancient Jewish wisdom be your guide.

Meticulous meanings, diligent intergenerational transmission and specifics laid out in the Oral Torah have helped preserve the original meaning of the Bible. There is magic in what we call the Lord's language—Hebrew. Teachers of the Torah must impart a deep adherence and responsibility for original meaning on the next generation of faithful students of the Torah. Teachers should faithfully transmit to their students exactly what they learned from their own teachers. This has been the case for generations. Thus, within the authentic chain of transmission, there has been very little distortion and almost no imposition of personal agenda. So long-standing are these ideas that they have become embedded in Jewish culture. Even when some Jews reject God and His Bible, they often retain these principles for a number of generations, often unaware of their biblical source. One example of these principles would be reverence for learning and respect for books.

Fortunately, you don't have to take our word for any of the axiomatic propositions you will encounter in this book. We ask you to unshackle yourself from the dreadful intellectual prison of "expertitis"—trusting others who are deemed "experts"—and allow room for your own powers of observation and deductive reasoning. If many of this book's propositions were already widely published, you'd be wasting your time reading our repetitive account. Instead, you will gain enormous value from many of the premises presented within this book. You may wonder if they are in fact true. This is allowed—again, use your own powers of observation and reasoning. Reflect upon what you read here, perform diligent research, and arrive at your own conclusion. Don't surrender your discernment to others, regardless of how qualified they may be. Remember, nobody else cares as much about your money as you do.

For some—particularly for those who are not familiar with the Bible—your initial instinct may be to reject this material because of its deistic or religious source. We have come to expect this too. Many have been trained and schooled by the educational bureaucrats and propaganda professors of the academy to accept as true only what originates from the modern, academically anointed. Do not misunderstand us: we have the greatest of respect for authentic scholarship. But we also have disdain for the scam scholarship and bogus education masquerading as truth that is so common on campuses these days. We have a sneaking suspicion that any course of university study that needs the word "studies," such as Gender Studies or Religious Studies, is most likely a waste of students' time and their parents' money. Have you ever heard of "physics studies," "mathematics studies," or "computer science studies"? No, of course not—because those are real fields. We reject the political correctness, bigotry, and prejudice that have taken an undeserved prominence in our secular-only education system.

We witness prejudice within academia against all things nonmaterialistic, which is to say, nontangible. Most universities today have adopted a blind and baseless hostility toward anything connected to religion or the Bible. This is usually because of the mistaken belief that science answers all questions and modern thought always reflects positive progress. This is certainly not education. Teaching students to utterly ignore a text so preeminent as the Bible, a text that has shaped the outlook and beliefs of countless generations of wise and accomplished people over two millennia, is doing a colossal disservice. Furthermore, many people growing a business, whether they are aware of it or not, will be interacting with serious Bible enthusiasts in their personal and professional life in the form of customers, vendors, fellow travelers, and so on.

This book focuses on ideas that emerge organically from the Bible in that area of the human experience having to do with finance. Could someone attempt to derive principles of victory on the tennis court from Scripture? We don't doubt it, but the result would lack credibility and possess the thin unsatisfying consistency of improperly strained spinach soup. The same would go for car racing, cosmetology, and television production—the Bible has nothing specific to tell us about these subjects.

However, business secrets from the Bible is quite a different story, and that is what this book explores. Even a cursory study of history reveals that the Jewish people have, over many centuries, lived in many countries and have been summarily expelled from many countries with nothing but what they could carry. Frequently, their activities were severely restricted and regulated, curtailing the fields they could pursue. When expelled yet again, as they were from England in 1290 or from Iraq in 1952, with scores of other instances in between, they needed to start all over in new locations as penniless refugees. They did this again and again in places where they did not know the language or have a social network. Amazingly, a surprisingly large number of them persevered, not only surviving but also building great financial enterprises and accumulating wealth.

It is notable that in the first four months following the mass invasion of Israel by thousands of armed Palestinian terrorists in October 2023 that resulted in the worst single-day massacre of Jews since World War II, that small country experienced a high number of business start-ups and an unusually high number of Israeli couples got engaged or married. Both starting a new home and starting a business reflect hope and confidence in the future. Both actions, starting a business and getting married, are quick, easy, and pleasant. But both actions tacitly acknowledge that one is committing oneself to weeks, months, and years of hard work, heavy responsibility, and even frightening times. Yes, this book reminds us that starting an independent business is the action of an optimistic and confident soul. But it also reminds us that operating a business, being in business (regardless of what you do, as we explain later in the book), is an ongoing source of optimism and confidence.

The bottom line is that unlike many books on starting, building, and growing your business, this one is not based on the experience and knowledge of one person. It is based on a vast system that has helped the many and diverse Jewish people thrive and prosper for centuries, in good times and bad, in hospitable countries as well as in tyrannical regimes. Regardless of your personal background, it can help you, too.

God Wants Each of Us to Be Obsessively Preoccupied with the Needs and Desires of His Other Children

If we are going to transform our financial lives with 40 Bible-based success strategies for business, we must first ask ourselves, what is business? Simply put, business is the most effective process of specialization and exchange by means of which humans can wrest a living from an often-reluctant earth. Business is one of the most important ways in which we connect, communicate, and collaborate with each other and our environment. It is thus a timeless linchpin of civilization.

As long as we all grow our own wheat and herbs, stitch our own clothes, bake our own bread, and cobble our own shoes, we need nobody else. We aren't even thinking of anyone else. We're only thinking of how to find enough time in the day to grow vegetables, feed the goats, shear the sheep, and shoe the horses. This is no way to live if you don't have to, and in the modern world, we do not have to.

Most humans, when given the chance, have discovered that life is easier and more pleasant when we abandon complete independence for interdependence, specialization, and exchange. Independent homesteading is terribly inefficient when compared to a system of specialization and exchange. If Anthony grows wheat and Juan grows corn; if Tim grows fruit and Wanda grows vegetables; if Madison raises chickens and goats while Kirk keeps cows; if Lewis turns cotton into fabric, and Michael does so with wool, and Charlie sews those fabrics into clothing and then Anthony, Juan, Tim, Wanda, Madison, Kirk, Lewis, Michael, and Charlie all meet once a week to exchange these goods with one another, astonishingly, all have more of all these things with far less time, not to mention energy expended on acquiring them, than if each person was doing everything for him- or herself.

When Anthony, Tim, and friends all specialize, they are able to focus on how to better serve one another, and in doing so, they gain more in return. The good Lord incentivizes us to increase our dependency upon each other by offering the blessing of financial abundance for those of us who comply. In other words, we each win more of a living with less effort when we specialize and trade. This process is called *business*.

This relates to everyone, whether or not you homestead. Do you prepare your own taxes or hire a specialist? Sell your own house or use an agent? Embedded in Jewish tradition is this idea of specialization and cooperation. You will rarely find Jews tinkering with their cars in their driveways on weekend afternoons or even mowing their own lawns. Why? Because we understand the power of specialization. If I pay my incredibly competent mechanic to maintain my BMW automobile and if I pay the ambitious youngster down the block to mow my lawn, I thereby purchase valuable hours in which to practice and perfect my own craft or trade. Each of us accomplishes our task far more quickly than we could do individually, because we have acquired proficiency at our particular skill and are able to apply efficiency by not spreading ourselves thin. By hiring others, I have more time and attention to devote to becoming better at my own trade, and I will certainly gain more by working in my own specialized trade than I will trying to save a dollar by tinkering with my car rather than paying a proper mechanic. The difference adds to my wealth. It adds to the mechanic's wealth, too. Everyone wins.

This is the power of specialization and exchange. In the late eighteenth century, Scottish philosopher and economist Adam Smith, who was a Bible-believing Christian, popularized this understanding of the efficiencies of a specialized market economy, but Jews had already known this for millennia. But from where did they learn it? From the Bible, of course! Jews have always understood specialization, as it is described in both Genesis and Deuteronomy. In chapter 49 of Genesis, verses 1 to 28, the elderly Jacob blesses his 12 sons. He could simply have gathered them and said these few words: "I am about to be gathered to my people; I bless you all with everything good. May God take care of you always, and please bury me in the Cave of Machpelah, which my grandfather Abraham prepared. Good-bye." But that's not what happened. Instead, there are 28 verses that record the distinct and separate blessings that he gave to each son.

Similarly, in Deuteronomy 33, before ascending the mountain to be shown the Land of Israel before his death, Moses spent 29 verses blessing the individual tribes. Again, he easily could have issued one comprehensive blessing to the entire children of Israel and promptly taken his leave.

The idea behind both Jacob's blessing and that of Moses was unity with diversity. Each tribe was to have its own unique niche in the rich tapestry of a durable nation. Each tribe was to have its own specialty and to become dependent upon their brethren for everything else. If one thinks about it, isn't this what all parents would like to ensure for their children? Some way of guaranteeing that they remain united, each as concerned with the welfare of his siblings as with his own. The same is true for our Father in Heaven. In desiring to unify His children, He created a world that rewards those who specialize in some area of creative work and then trade their efforts for everything else.

Of course, each of us could declare ourselves independent of all other people and live in isolation on a remote piece of land. We could grow our own herbs and spices. We could milk our own cows and clean our own homes and knit our own sweaters and brew our own beer. And many of us do some of these things for pleasure. That is wonderful. To a degree, some weary urban dwellers yearn for this sort of existence, which they fondly imagine to be idyllic. But this is pure nostalgia. Almost everyone who has tried their hand at such a life has discovered that when it is a necessity rather than a choice, it is grueling and punishing, offering very little quality of life.

Such nostalgia makes a mockery of those who are truly trapped in such a life. True subsistence farmers and hand-to-mouth peasants typically cannot escape such a life quickly enough. In developing countries, such individuals gladly flee the grueling existence of trying to eke out a living and a life from a small plot of land as soon as they can. They flock to cities where they can sew clothing or stitch shoes in factories. Not that the life in those hot and crowded factories is delightful—it isn't—but trading their specialized skill of sewing and stitching gives them a far superior lifestyle to the alternative of stitching, sewing, planting, milking, threshing, harvesting, milling, baking, churning, and making everything else the solitary human needs to survive. In a true subsistence life, one must do almost everything by oneself. Specialization allows these individuals to throw off the shackles of the subsistence lifestyle, and business allows them to ply their trade for profit.

Compare the outlook of the solitary survivalist with that of the business professional. The former views other people as competitors and threats. By contrast, the business professional's life is intricately linked to many other people. He has to be concerned with providing goods or services at sufficient quality and at a reasonable price in order to attract and serve his customers. He has to be concerned with his employees and associates because only if they are happy and fulfilled will his enterprise prosper. Finally, he needs to be concerned with those vendors who supply him with the raw material of his production because without them he is incapable of operating. Now whom do you think God prefers: the lonesome isolationist whose slogan is "I need nobody," or the business professional active within a complex matrix of connectivity and interdependence in which he is preoccupied with making life better for so many of God's other children?

We all sometimes think we just want to get away from everyone else. We may daydream about some calamity sweeping away everyone in the world except ourselves. We think, finally, we will be able to get a parking space downtown. There will be no traffic on the freeway. At last we'll be able to watch television without fighting with our family over who gets the remote.

This is silly daydreaming, though. Imagine if it actually happened! What if everyone did disappear? Who would be operating the television station? That remote won't do you much good if there is nothing to broadcast, no news anchors, no actors. What good is that parking space downtown if there is nowhere to work? And with nobody operating gas stations or oil refineries, parking will be the least of your problems! Good luck trying to capture a wild horse or donkey once you have used up all the gas in your tank! Time for dinner? Feel like a restaurant meal? Out of luck—no cooks, no wait staff. In the grocery stores, food is rotting on the shelves. At home, your heat and electricity have gone out because no one is running the utility company.

The truth is that without other people, your life becomes even worse than that of impoverished third-world subsistence-level peasants—at least they have one another to depend on!

Are you beginning to see why specialization and exchange are the foundations for God's plan for human economic interaction? If you care about your customers as people—if you like, appreciate, and desire to serve them—you will be rewarded. However, if you prefer to spurn others in favor of making yourself utterly independent of all other humans, your life will be considerably less pleasant. Thomas Hobbes, the seventeenth-century British political philosopher and author of *Leviathan*, a Bible-believing Christian, once wrote that when we are alone, "the life of man [is] solitary, poor, nasty, brutish, and short."

We've already told you what business is, but not what the definition of *a business* is. This need not be made more complicated than it is. Some define a business as any organization or individual engaged in commercial, industrial, or professional activities. Others define a business as any organization involved in the trade of goods or services to consumers. While these definitions are not wrong, they are overly precise. The truth is simply that a business is any person or group of people who have customers. If you have someone willing to pay you voluntarily for the work you do, products you produce, or service you provide, then you're in business.

Everyone who works for compensation can be considered "in business." If City Transit pays you for driving a bus, you're not an employee—you're in business. Admittedly you're in business with only one customer—City Transit—but you're in business, nonetheless. If you knit scarves for fun and agree to make a few for your friends in exchange for some dollars for your time, guess what, you are in the fashion/clothing business.

The difference between the bus driver and the person who occasionally knits scarves in this example is that the bus driver makes more, in part because he has specialized. If the person who knits scarves quits her part-time retail and food service jobs to focus on growing her business, she too might make more money by specializing. By specializing in a trade, rather than doing a little of everything, she can enjoy better efficiency and more disposable income rather than spreading herself thin. If she goes into her own business, she will find that her customers become valuable human beings to her, and she will desire to please them.

There is much to digest in Secret #1 and we know that you will frequently review it because, like being an airplane pilot, much in life works best when we operate on absorbed instinct rather than by constantly needing to hurriedly look up the checklist or the directions. In other words, we need the knowledge we absorb into our heads to make the difficult 13-inch journey from our heads to our hearts. Most circumstances both in the flight deck and in life don't allow the time to slowly decide how to react. By reviewing the principles, they will become a part of your being. Then you will be ready to find out in what distinctive way you can best serve God's other children and obsessively preoccupy yourself with doing just that.

An Infinite God Created Us in His Image with Infinite Imagination, Potential, Creative Power, and Desires

Though God placed Adam in the Garden of Eden in which all was provided, He nonetheless insisted that Adam was to work (Genesis 2:15). Adam could have lived an idyllic and idle life drinking from the bountiful rivers of Eden and plucking luscious fruit as he desired from all but two trees. We shall soon see that God's plan is for man to strive to achieve more. Ambition is a good thing. We all were created to desire as much as possible, but we also wish to expend only the least possible effort. Discontentment and unhappiness are wrong, but this in no way contradicts our legitimate desire for more.

Most of us have had the experience of being teenagers and thinking, "If only I could lay my hands on a thousand dollars, I'd be so happy." As we get older, a thousand dollars is no longer so unattainable for most, but we are still discontented because now we want more. The target has moved. The target, it seems, is always moving.

This may seem like greed, and taken to excess, it can be a bad thing. But it is actually a powerful motivator and drives us to do God's work, the work of living that we all depend on each other to do.

Imagine what would happen if tonight at midnight, all other humans decided that they already had enough of everything they need and no longer needed to work. From now on, they decide, they will stay home. Picture your own life in this scenario. You get up the next morning unaware that your fellow citizens have abandoned all ambition and are sleeping in. There goes your day! Good luck trying to get milk for your morning coffee. The dairy farmer and the delivery-truck driver are home in bed rather than producing and supplying fresh milk to your grocery store. It won't much matter, of course, because the grocery store will be shut down—the manager who ordinarily works the morning shift is also still at home contentedly asleep. The same goes for getting gasoline for your car, gas or electricity to cook your meals, or a new suit of clothing. The economy and all it provides has come to a screeching halt. Your fellow citizen's innate desire for more is what makes it possible for your own life to function as smoothly as it does. Likewise, your decision to work makes life easier for everyone else.

Back in 1980, about 85% of 25-year-old men worked at a full-time job. By 2023 that number had shrunk to about 70%. There are many theories as to why so many men are not working or how they are sustaining themselves, but we know that far fewer men are chafing to work. This is not a good sign for our civilization. In your personal life, make sure that you surround yourself with ambitious peers. In that way you will spur each other on to achievement.

As a student, I [RDL] once spent a long but rewarding summer selling fine English bone china door-to-door in Europe. After a rigorous and immensely valuable training period, before being let loose to sell, all of us rookie trainee sales professionals were gathered together, and the manager announced that we were each to choose our preferred compensation plan. Choice A was that we would receive a guaranteed base salary, or draw, of $250 a week in advance against our sales plus 10% commission on all sales. Choice B provided zero base salary or draw, but we would receive a 40% commission on all sales.

For a while I pondered what to do. Not knowing how effective I would be at selling, I figured I could at least count upon a few thousand dollars by the end of the summer if I took Choice A. This was reassuring. I was about to sign up for Choice A when, suddenly, I had an epiphany. If I turned out to be unsuccessful at selling, why would they continue to pay me $250 a week merely for trying? And if I did find myself successful at selling, why would I want to earn only a small commission of 10%? I thought this through again, and I could think of no reason why the company would keep paying me if I failed to sell. They might pay me for a few weeks but would then surely dismiss me. On the other hand, if I developed any aptitude for sales, I could do far better with Plan B. I worried about the "sure" $1,000 a month I was perhaps giving up, but surely it was not really guaranteed if I did poorly, so I went with Plan B.

We had to write our choice on slips of paper along with our names and pass them to the front where the manager's assistant quickly divided them into two piles, which I assumed to be a tall pile of As and a much smaller pile of Bs. Picking up the larger pile of papers, he asked everyone whose name he called out to go into the next room. That was the last I ever saw of my former fellow trainees.

To the rest of us, he spoke warmly and congratulated us on successfully completing our training. He welcomed us into the company and explained that he wanted only ambitious men and women who yearned for unlimited potential working for him. He wanted people interested in infinite possibilities. Anyone seeking the security of a minimal $1,000 a month was not nearly as interesting to him as those of us who had ambition for considerably more. And considerably more was exactly what I did earn that summer.

It is the exciting possibility of the infinite that drives medical research to come up with life-enhancing and life-extending drugs and devices. It is the exciting possibility of the infinite that drives all technological advances. It is the exciting possibility of the infinite that drives the business professional to find ever better ways of serving more customers more effectively. It is what drives progress in the world and according to ancient Jewish wisdom, it is God's will.

On some subconscious level, we humans are always trying to emulate God. One reason that technology so fascinates us is that it allows us to enjoy a taste of God's omnipresence. While God can be everywhere at once, the closest we come to achieving that is being able to sit in our living rooms and observe the activities of our fellow human beings half a planet away. Technology grants us the illusion of almost godly power.

This is also true with regard to air travel. Travel by ocean liner is far more comfortable and less expensive than by jet. Yet by the 1960s, most transatlantic ocean liner services were being discontinued. Why would people forsake a leisurely, comfortable, economical three-day journey from New York to Southampton in favor of being squeezed into a long aluminum cylinder and being hurtled across continents within only a few jet-lagged hours? Again, one explanation is our deep desire to try and overcome human limitations of space and time just as God does.

God created us with an urge for the infinite. We need to embrace it and never surrender to the seditious and spurious summons of contentment cowering in the sanctuary of security. Accepting our desire for the infinite doesn't condemn us to misery and unhappiness. On the contrary, rejecting contentment doesn't mean being unhappy. In a green and lush meadow on a sunny afternoon, a cow can be content. A human should never be content. Happy—yes, always. But content? Never!

Humans Alone Possess the Ability to Transform Themselves

T he reality of animals is that they are what they are and will always be so. A cat, a cow, a camel, or a kangaroo will always be a cat, a cow, a camel, or a kangaroo. But a homeless person can transform himself into a published author and successful motivational speaker. This is just what Richard LeMieux did. As he describes in his personal odyssey, *Breakfast at Sally's: One Homeless Man's Inspirational Journey*, he went from sleeping in his car and eating at the Salvation Army (Sally's) to an eventual middle-class lifestyle. An aimless teenager can get a grip on her life and become an accomplished academic, professional, or businesswoman. An immigrant can arrive in a new land with nothing but the clothes on his back and ultimately achieve greatness without ever feeling imprisoned by the promise of permanent poverty, or even worse, the belief in perpetual victimhood.

In his book, *The Wealth Choice: Success Secrets of Black Millionaires*, courageous author and motivational speaker Dennis Kimbro insists that wealth has little to do with birth, luck, or circumstance, but everything to do with choice, commitment to change, discipline, self-improvement, and hard work. We could not agree more. His sentiment echoes this Jewish theme: No shame is attached to starting out poor, but remaining that way is a different story.

We have known Jewish men and women who didn't have a fraction of what most others have going, and yet these individuals have prospered beyond anyone's wildest dreams. This is clearly not a case of "where you come from" or of "what you've got." It's a case of a deep visceral commitment to change.

In every industry, you see Jewish men who have made indelible marks on history and the economy. A man named William Konar lived near Rochester, New York. Have you heard of CVS Pharmacy? He started that and owned most of it, and as you may have guessed, did pretty well for himself. Nathan Shapell was one of California's largest homebuilders. Jack Tramiel, way back in the dawn of the computer age, founded Commodore Computers, which he grew into a substantial company. And how about Fred Kort, who invented those little bouncy rubber balls that every kid in the world seemed to have a few years back? Fred Kort made the bubble machine and the stuff from which legions of kids make soap bubbles in the summer. He marketed these and other toys under the brand of Los Angeles Toy Company. Felix Zandman started Vishay Intertechnology, a major electronics firm supplying the computer and aerospace industries.

These are not people who became internationally known billionaires. They are people, however, who each donated millions of dollars to charity. They have all made serious money.

But something else unites these people, something harrowing and nightmarish. They were all Holocaust refugees. William Konar was 12 years old when his family was uprooted from their small Polish village and carted off to the Auschwitz death camp. The last time he saw his mother and siblings was in July 1942, shortly before they were murdered by the Nazis. He witnessed more horrors than any adult, let alone a child, should ever have to endure before arriving in the United States on a refugee boat in 1946. He was a 16-year-old orphan. He ended up in a foster home in Rochester, which, as a result, now boasts the William and Sheila Konar Center for Digestive and Liver Diseases in the city's Strong Memorial Hospital.

Nathan Shapell fled from the Germans and lived in hiding until he was finally captured and brought to the Auschwitz concentration camp in the summer of 1943. He was a teenager and, like all other inmates, destined for death. His arm was tattooed with a registration number by the meticulously bureaucratic Nazis. He bore that number, 134138, quite clearly on his forearm until the day he died in Beverly Hills in 2007. When the war ended, he was a shattered refugee and spent a few years as a DP, a displaced person, as they called it back then. He arrived in the United States in the early 1950s, and starting from scratch, he built a few houses at a time, eventually becoming a real estate tycoon.

In April 1945, Jack Tramiel, the emaciated and beaten 16-year-old lone survivor of his entire family from Lodz, Poland, was liberated from Auschwitz by American forces. He found part-time work with the U.S. Army in Poland and eventually made his way to New York, where he worked as a janitor for a Fifth Avenue lamp store. He joined the Army, which is where he learned to repair office machines. Upon his discharge several years later, he bought old and broken typewriters, which he repaired and sold. By the 1960s and 1970s, he was moving from office machines to computers, and he is now part of the history of the personal computer. Over the years, Tramiel and his wife, Helen (herself a survivor of the notorious Bergen-Belsen concentration camp), gave away vast sums of money.

Fred Kort was one of only nine survivors of the hundreds of thousands of Jews who were exterminated at Treblinka concentration camp. He lost his entire immediate family and 60 relatives there before arriving in the United States, penniless and destitute. He took a job at the Bendix Company. This is how he got into the toy business where he later made his fortune.

Felix Zandman initially survived the Holocaust in a tiny hole cut in the ground beneath a peasant's hut. He lived there for several years, foraging for food in the nighttime. One of the few Jews of Grodno who survived the war, he was eventually caught and enslaved in a Nazi factory, where he witnessed the massacre of family members. After being freed by Allied forces, he immigrated to America.

All of these people survived the unimaginable. They arrived as young refugees with scarred souls and broken bodies, but they knew one fundamental Jewish principle: The way I am today has nothing to do with what I'll be tomorrow.

The Jews knew this secret when few others did. For centuries in Britain, the socioeconomic class into which you were born was where you lived and died. In Europe, peasant girls never married princes regardless of what fairytales would have you believe. The situation was no different in most of Asia and all of Africa. The early Greeks saw destiny as a function of birth; Plato and Aristotle believed that some were born to rule while others were born to be ruled. The Romans also lacked any mechanism for anyone to rise in rank socially or economically.

These beliefs stunt people emotionally and intellectually. If you don't know and believe that human beings have the power, unique within nature, to utterly transform themselves, then you are fatally handicapped. How did Jews know and believe that change, growth, and transformation are the natural legacy of humans? From the Bible, of course, where there is account after account of people becoming better, kinder, stronger, more effective, more powerful, more successful people than they were before.

The Bible is full of such transformations. Consider Abraham, the first Hebrew. Wait! Before looking at Abraham, let's find out what the word *Hebrew* means. The original word for Hebrew is *Ivri*, which means "one who crosses over." In other words, Abraham's badge of pride, his very identification meant his willingness and ability to transform himself from someone who stands on one side of a matter into someone entirely different who takes quite a different approach. This classic term for Israelites or Jews, *Hebrew* identifies the children of Abraham chiefly as possessing this characteristic to recognize that their destiny is not engraved in stone.

Now back to Abraham, who earlier in his life was known as Abram:

And God said to Abram, "Leave your country, your family, and your father's house, to a land that I will show you." (Genesis 12:1)

Ancient Jewish wisdom posits a very important question here: Why did God choose to issue his famous command, "Leave your country . . ." to this man rather than to anyone else? There is nothing in previous passages to suggest his special suitability. We're told almost nothing of his life, certainly not anything that would explain his lofty qualities. Why, then, did God choose Abraham? The answer is that God did *not* choose Abraham. The command was offered to everyone, but only Abraham responded. Abraham thus chose himself.

God continues to offer this command to each one of us today, if only we will take heed. The command is not a historical order intended exclusively for Abraham to depart his homeland and family, although for Abraham it did mean just that. It means just that for each of us. We should not leave and destroy everything in our past. If our morals and ethics align with those from the Bible, we must cling to those with all our might. Knowing our history is imperative. But each of us is invited by God to depart from bad circumstances or from comfortable situations to which we've become accustomed and to move and grow. It is up to us to take heed of this invitation.

You can see, here and elsewhere, that the Torah is not a historic account of long-forgotten people and anachronistic events, but it is a handbook to life. It is the foundation of ancient Jewish wisdom. Yes, everyone in Abraham's generation could have heard God's call to reinvent himself or herself and redirect their footsteps, but only Abraham seized upon the challenge. Similarly, each of us today has the opportunity to clearly hear God's clarion call: "Leave your country, your family, and your father's house, to a land that I will show you." Each of us has the opportunity to seize the challenge. Move into a new zone in which you can fully fulfill the potential God planted into you. You might not yet know the destination, but rest assured God will show it to you, though He will not do so until after you have commenced the odyssey.

Today, there is an added challenge. Once again, in the third decade of the 2000s, we are being told that our birthplace, or race or gender or any uniqueness we might have, is our destiny. Society is raising victimhood as the banner under which each of us is directed to march. This is in complete opposition to God's message to Abraham and to us. Be an Ivri—cross over and reject that dreadful dead-end message.

We see this vitally important directive to do things a little differently today from how we did them yesterday not just in Genesis, but also in Exodus, where a similar message is offered to us:

> And an angel of God appeared to him [Moses] in a flame of fire from inside a bush; and he looked, and the bush burned with fire, but the bush was not consumed. And Moses said, "I will now turn aside to see this great sight, why the bush is not burnt." (Exodus 3:2–3)

Again ancient Jewish wisdom poses a question here. Why Moses? Like Abraham, he chose to listen to God. Dozens of people went by the burning bush that morning, and nobody else stopped to look. Nobody else was perplexed enough to ask why the bush wasn't being consumed by the fire. Moses alone was transfixed by an event that appeared to contradict his vision of normality. This mindfulness and openness toward God is what opened up Moses' life, and it is what can open up our own life as well. If we are open to an alternative vision of normality, our lives can develop in amazingly unexpected ways.

We implore you to be open to the monumental significance of what you're reading now. Just think for a moment about what your most important external organ for the purpose of increasing your ability to generate income is. Well, unless you're a swimsuit model, wouldn't you agree that it is your mouth—your ability to speak and communicate effectively?

From time-to-time software engineers and app creators, researchers of various kinds, and Amazon resellers reach out to us with the argument that they make their money sitting in front of a computer and don't use their mouths at all. While we don't doubt that there are many introverts who do very little communicating with others, we are pretty sure that, with a few exceptions that make headlines, they are not making as much money as they could. When the software engineer negotiates an equity share in lieu of his services, he uses his mouth and communicative abilities—and makes money. Similarly with researchers and everyone else, the difference between making a living and making money often depends on how well you communicate with others.

This is one of the great things about business. You can be tall or short, male or female, black or white, splendidly hirsute or bald, it all makes very little difference. Your business success will depend upon how well you can communicate and how well you understand *what* to communicate.

Of all the handicaps Moses could have been inflicted with, he suffered from the one condition most likely to diminish his chances of success:

> And Moses said to the Lord, "My Lord, I am not a man of words, neither yesterday nor the day before, nor since you have spoken to your servant; for I am heavy of speech, and heavy of tongue." (Exodus 4:10)

You may not know this, but Moses suffered from a speech impediment! He really did. God accepted this as true. God didn't respond to Moses impatiently by saying, "Oh, come on, Moses. You speak perfectly well, stop making excuses!" No, instead God said, "Look, if you accept this commission and do something that is as different from being a mere shepherd than you can ever imagine, if you go ahead and transform your destiny, I, who gives man the power of speech, will ensure that you will be able to communicate more than adequately."

Sure enough, Moses goes ahead and rescues the Hebrews from Egypt, leads them through the desert for 40 years, teaches them the Law that God gave him on Sinai, and speaks out the entire text of Deuteronomy during a month of nonstop talking. During all this we never again hear of Moses' speech impediment. As you can see, often the obstacles we see obstructing our progress vanish once we accept God's invitation to resculpt our lives.

Nobody is saying change is easy. The Bible also provides examples of those who were simply incapable of bringing about change in their lives. For example, in chapter 19 of the first book of Kings, we encounter Elijah. God wants Elijah to transform himself from a zealous prophet constantly criticizing Israel into a gentler prophet who guides Israel. God shows Elijah spectacular pyrotechnic signs and soft, quiet ones, yet Elijah's response remains the same: he shows no ability to change his path, style, or life. Finally, God recognizes that Elijah is incapable of developing himself into the kind of person who can lead going forward, so God tells him to appoint Elisha as the new prophet to replace him.

Often, remaining just where you are and just who you are isn't really an option. It is true that animals possess no ability to change, but humans often have no alternative but to change and grow. In fact, the alternative does not allow us to remain where we are. Often, reluctance to transform ourselves condemns us to slide backward.

Sometimes change is painful, which accounts for the reluctance most people feel toward change. For example, few changes are more painful than ending a long-standing friendship. And as anyone who has loved and lost knows, losing a loved one is indeed trying. If friendship serves as a metaphor for productive human partnership, then its breakup can also teach us something. My wife and I often nursed young congregants through the heartbreak of romantic relationships coming to an end. Indeed, we often encouraged and hastened the good-bye, assuring our tormented friend that only by suffering the tears of breakup now could the joys of tomorrow arrive.

Henry Ford's Model T automobile first arrived in 1908. By 1914, a quarter million autos were being built each year. This was truly terrible for people who had spent years in the horse-wagon business. In the year 1900, about 110,000 people were employed building or repairing carriages and harnesses. Nearly 250,000 blacksmiths lived and worked in America that year fitting shoes on countless horses. And thousands more earned a living by sweeping tons of horse manure off city streets.

But the coming of the first mass-produced automobile meant that jobs in the horse-driven transport business quickly vanished. The end of the horse-drawn era was tough on many, but those who simply couldn't divorce themselves from the past deprived themselves of the blessings that were rolling down the new highways. There were soon far more automobiles than there had ever been horses and carriages, and along with the cascade of cars came not thousands, but millions of new jobs. All those wagon builders, harness makers, wheel makers, horseshoe smiths, and manure street sweepers who were capable and accepting of change now had exciting new possibilities at their disposal.

The ending of a business partnership, the breakup of an empire that allows the newly sovereign nations to thrive, the demolition of a building that has fallen into disrepair so that a new building may rise in its place, the smashing of an atom releasing unimaginable amounts of energy and freeing humans from drudgery—all of these things share a common thread. Every justified act of breaking, changing, or separating, as painful as it always is, can launch us into something new that carries us further down the path of our own development as individuals, as a nation, and as the human family of God's children.

The Universe Was Created for Connection

Rolling a 50-gallon drum of water downhill is far easier than lugging it uphill. The reason for this asymmetry is a powerful force in nature—gravity. Preventing a parked car from rolling downhill takes far less work than bringing a fast-moving car to a standstill. This is due to another powerful force in nature—inertia. Now you may certainly choose to try rolling the heavy drum of water uphill. You can even try to stop a moving car with a weak parking brake instead of the power-assisted foot brake. You're free to attempt whatever you want; just know that fighting forces larger than yourself is likely to end in failure.

Perhaps you may choose instead to use a winch to haul the barrel up the hill. Perhaps you engage the foot brake to stop your speeding car instead of futilely yanking on the hand brake. You will probably be far more likely to succeed. But a wise and experienced bystander could have confidently predicted these very outcomes without having to test out lesser tactics. The lesson is this: success is always more likely when you are swimming with the current rather than against it. In other words, don't waste time and energy fighting reality.

Needless to say, sometimes we must emulate the indefatigable salmon that relentlessly fights its way upstream. In matters of principle and honor, we often must fight our way upstream. However, when it comes to finding the best way to serve our fellow humans and earn their trust, going with the stream is nearly always more effective and efficient. Trying to overcome the spiritual laws of reality is just as futile as fighting the physical laws of nature.

Connecting with other people makes for a better life—this is a law that is inextricable from the natural world. Trying to achieve happiness and fulfillment while remaining isolated from others is as futile as all other attempts to defy nature's laws. God clearly wants us to connect with one another. He wants us each to be obsessively preoccupied with serving one another. He wants us to provide for one another's needs and desires. Cynics may denounce monetary motivations as greed, but this is false thinking. The virtue of service is in no way compromised or diminished by the monetary reward received for doing so.

Just consider the case of poor "Godfrey," who is beset by seemingly insurmountable problems. Godfrey is in desperate need of a leg up. He needs some money to get himself out of a fix and start himself off on some successful path. Now we introduce him to two different people. One is a struggling good man who at considerable self-sacrifice has come up with $100 to give to Godfrey. He loves all needy people and is genuinely happy to have $100 less this month if the money can help Godfrey escape his painful predicament.

The other would-be benefactor is a prosperous financier who is offering gifts of $1,000 to needy folks like our Godfrey. Because of his high tax bracket, this financier receives a tax write-off of $600 for each gift of $1,000. Thus, his large gift to Godfrey ends up costing him only $400. Lastly, we must honestly report that unlike our first benefactor who is sacrificing to make his gift, our affluent philanthropist will lack nothing on account of his gift.

Godfrey asks you for advice. Should he accept $100 from the kind, compassionate, and caring donor, or should he go for $1,000 from the second man who will derive some benefit from the transaction? Surely you would not hesitate to recommend that he accept the larger gift. Now, looking at the circumstances from the other angle, which donor is able to be more helpful to Godfrey? Yes, of course it is possible that the former might be a better human being, though not being God, we cannot be sure of this. However, our question concerns which benefactor is being more helpful. We hope that as humans with no ability to peer into the hearts of other people, we can agree that the man who is making the sum of $1,000 available is, strictly speaking, helping Godfrey more.

It is hard to dispute that he who helps more people is doing more practical good than he who helps only a few. Though we mean no disrespect to the venerable and beatified Mother Teresa of Calcutta, we do ask ourselves this: Who provided more help for more people— Mother Teresa or Holocaust refugee William Konar, the creator of CVS Pharmacy and generous philanthropist whom we mentioned in a previous chapter? We assume that most people who have purchased anything from a CVS Pharmacy did so because the products they bought enhanced their lives in some way. CVS Pharmacy products made their lives healthier, more productive, or somehow more satisfying or they would not have made the purchase. In addition, Konar gave tens of thousands of people jobs at which they were able to earn their living and support their families. It can safely be said that William Konar improved the lives of many millions of people even *before* he started giving away large sums through his charitable foundation.

Now let's ask ourselves, how many people's lives were helped by Mother Teresa? Between those who found solace in her hospices and other institutions, those she cured, and those whose poverty she eased, what might the total be? We don't know the exact number, but whether it be a hundred or thousands, or even slightly more, the fact remains that William Konar, to name just one prominent business professional, added value to the lives of far more people than Mother Teresa, and this can be measured quantitatively. It is true that numbers are not the only important factor. But neither are they a completely unimportant one.

Why then, do so few religious people sing his praises compared to Mother Teresa? Certainly there is no talk of beatifying William Konar. But why not? He did so much good!

People have adopted the mistaken view that benefiting from the good one does somehow diminishes the virtue of your good deeds. And certainly William Konar benefited from his good work. But why should this diminish the virtue of his deeds in the eyes of his fellow man? From a biblical perspective, win-win situations are the best all around. The measure of how much you do for people should naturally be how much you do for people, not some other concern. The goal is to try to be as helpful as you can be for as many other people as possible. If you also benefit from doing good, well, that is icing on the cake. It allows one to earn a living and continue doing more. It is self-perpetuating.

From time to time, individuals who have enjoyed spectacular financial success have consulted us on the best way to commence a career in philanthropy. While many of us think we'd enjoy the problem of how to distribute $5 million to charitable causes, the reality is that much work is required to distribute money philanthropically, and the results, because they are not driven by the hand of the market, are often imperfect.

Imagine that you had only one week in which to distribute $5 million. How would you go about doing so without harming the very people you hoped to help? Just think of what happens to the lives of most people who win fabulous sums of money in state lotteries. Suddenly receiving a large sum of money they did not have to work for doesn't necessarily improve people's lives. It undoubtedly provides a period of intoxicated disbelief in which all seems possible. The evidence, however, suggests that for most people, a lottery windfall turns into a curse within a short period. People tend to squander the money on their worst vices. Knowing this, is it wise to give away money for free? Perhaps not. So what would you do if you had only a week in which to choose how to give away $5 million?

To put this into perspective, in order to maintain its charitable foundation status, the Ford Foundation must distribute an average of more than $1 million per day. The Bill and Melinda Gates Foundation must distribute more than $3 million per day. No wonder these organizations and others like them employ hundreds of highly trained professionals. And even so, their giving might do more harm than good. Giving away money is no simple matter.

An unusual young couple we know recently consulted us. They live in a relatively small town in quite a small country. Until recently, like their neighbors, JB and Nora lived modestly on JB's salary and regularly donated 10% of their income to their little local church. With Nora's enthusiastic support for his hobby, JB had been doing exciting microbiological research on his own time. Suddenly his results attracted international attention along with a mind-blowingly large financial offer for his patent. Nora and JB accepted the offer and were suddenly multimillionaires! Their problem was that their regular tithe would now utterly distort the church's finances. They wisely decided on several strategies to diminish possible harmful effects of their charitable giving, including disbursing their gifts over time.

When people ask us how they should best use their money to create a greater good for mankind, our usual response is to recommend that they put that money back into the source that created the treasure in the first place—their talent for business. They should reinvest in their own skills and expand or start a new business. This will invigorate the economy, sending ripples of benefit throughout society. A new business will benefit the employees who will be employed in the enterprise. It will also benefit the suppliers of raw material, office goods, furniture, tools, and anyone else who provides the goods and services necessary to the success of a profitable company. These people are very grateful to have a new customer in you, and they will benefit from the exchange. Last but not least, this reinvestment in business will benefit all of the customers who will purchase the goods or services you provide. Your customers' lives are obviously enhanced by your goods and or services, or else why would they make the company profitable by purchasing them?

We am sorry to report that few of the entrepreneurs to whom we have given such counsel have followed it. We are also sorry to have to tell you that we are not surprised. Their explanations are usually the same. "We want to be acknowledged for doing good," they proclaim, and few of their friends and associates will praise them for doing good if "all" they are doing is making more money. What they do not realize is that making money is far from "all" they are doing for the world. That is not all they are doing—they are creating valuable and useful goods and services. Granted, they are making more money in the process, but how exactly does that diminish the good they are doing for their employees, their vendors, and their customers?

The answer is that it does not.

We cannot stress this point sufficiently. Regardless of whether or not you subsequently give away to charity any of the money you make (and God does want you to do so), the very act of creating wealth in a free and transparent market in which nobody is forced at the point of a gun or by the heavy hand of the government to purchase your goods, services, labor, or skills, is, *in itself*, virtuous.

Wealth is God's way of incentivizing you to do exactly what He wants you to do, which is to care obsessively about satisfying the needs and desires of His other children. Should you live your life either ignoring others or else filled with disdain toward them, the likelihood of you prospering is very low.

Why would God want us to be so committed to connection? Most parents would be thrilled to see their children utterly devoted to one another's welfare. A husband and wife become one in the conceiving of those children, and they see the unity of the family as a reflection of their own unity. Our Father in heaven is no different. To God, all humans are His children, and our unity echoes His own. Furthermore, to God, the entire world becomes a mirror of His unity by connecting, joining, and bonding.

For this reason, though the good Lord created 92 elements, we use very few of them just as they are. For instance, among those elements is iron. Yet, other than cast-iron pans and lawn ornaments, we make very little out of pure iron. We must blend it with carbon, another element, to make steel. Throw in a few more elements, and we get stainless steel, useful for everything from cutlery to surgical instruments and beyond. We breathe air, a mixture of two elements, oxygen and nitrogen. We drink water, a compound made of hydrogen and oxygen. We enjoy furniture made of wood, a complicated blend of several elements, and we use plastic extensively, which is a complicated hydrocarbon blend. The elements themselves seem to be God's eloquent call for connection within nature. It is as if He is saying there are 92 basic substances, but to get anything useful, you're going to have to learn to connect and bond them to one another. It is true that the periodic table today lists 20 or 30 additional elements, but these all must be synthesized in the laboratory, and few last much more than a few seconds before breaking down through nuclear reaction into one of the basic elements. These "new" elements themselves require the hand and manipulation of man to bring them together.

In 1886, scientists invented a new electrolytic process that would become the basis for all aluminum production today. This process allowed for aluminum to be combined with other elements, such as iron, silicon, zinc, copper, and magnesium, which yields useful alloys. Prior to this, aluminum was quite useless, but now we use these alloys to create materials that are used in airplanes, corrosion-free materials for use in building bridges and boats, and many other products. Aluminum was thought useless for so long. And it is, until we combine it with other elements to create materials of value.

This is true of most other elements as well. Very little is made from the approximately 92 basic substances that God created as the building blocks of creation. We see an absolutely amazing example of how God included a blueprint to reality in the Bible concerning this very topic. How many Hebrew words do you think are used in Scripture to describe Creation? Would you be shocked if we told you there are precisely 92 Hebrew words? Many of them, of course, are used more than once, but in terms of how many discrete, separate elements are used to recount the story of Creation, which involved creating 92 elements, there are—92 words. This kind of structural integrity is part of ancient Jewish wisdom and gives an example as to why the original Hebrew text of Scripture is so important.

Man has had to learn to combine the elements God gave us in order to make them more useful. There are countless products that make your life easier, healthier, longer, more comfortable, and more enjoyable and almost none are made from pure elements. Elements include things like iron, carbon, hydrogen, oxygen, sodium, gold, copper, chlorine, and many others. When was the last time you picked any of these up from the store? Most of the things we actually need and use are made of wood, plastic, steel, glass, alloys, and other complex elemental compounds. Even water and air are made up of multiple elements.

God is giving us a message here. He is telling us to combine things to produce utility and value. This is the basis of manufacturing and invention. There has never been a better way to sell milk and eggs than by combining them into ice cream. Meat has been around for quite a while, as has bread, but someone made a fortune putting them together and calling it a sandwich. Rubber is collected from the latex sap of rubber trees, but it wasn't much good for making wheels until we learned to blend rubber with sulfur in a process called vulcanization. Presto—we have tires. We could go on and on. Unless you are in the business of selling helium for balloons or gold bullion, chances are you make or sell something that requires combining elements and ideas.

Cement is strong enough to carry a very heavy load. It becomes even stronger when aggregates like sand and crushed rock are added to form concrete. But even concrete still crumbles quite easily when pulled on. This is because concrete is strong in compression but weak in tension. Concrete isn't terribly useful in real-world construction because of that weakness of tension—it does not bend, but it breaks.

Concrete is used in construction, though. How? Engineers learned to combine steel and concrete to make steel-reinforced concrete. Steel is strong in tension, though weak in compression. Concrete is the opposite. Combine them, and you get a material strong enough to hold up a skyscraper but flexible enough to sway without breaking. Steel and concrete compensate for each other's weakness.

Steel and concrete were literally made to complement each other. This is no coincidence, for no such thing exists in God's creation. Not convinced? Consider this: concrete and steel have identical coefficients of expansion. This means that, when heated or cooled, they expand and shrink at the exact same rate. In the jungle or the Arctic or anywhere in between, steel-reinforced concrete holds up for generations because both materials expand and contract in unison. If they did not have exactly the same expansion and contraction rate, they would warp and break over time. These two materials don't just go together—they seem made to be combined. And indeed, they were. God intended humans to continue His act of creation by connecting steel and concrete, and He made it possible by giving them the exact same expansion characteristics.

To be a successful entrepreneur, useful to millions of people and able to get rich, you don't need to invent anything new. You just need to think of yet another useful way to blend, mix, combine, or connect two or more existing things. God intended for us to find ways to bond, combine, and connect.

There can hardly be a more compelling indication that connections are integral to creation. In striving to connect with others, we are riding nature's wave of intent.

Letters, syllables, and sounds join into words that join into sentences in order to create communication. Notes, beats, and rhythms leap into harmony with one another to make music. "It is not good for man to be alone," God said early in Genesis. This is far more of a sweeping Divine pronouncement than merely a precursor to Adam meeting Eve. After all, though very busy people living frenetic lives can be forgiven for suspecting that solitary confinement is a reward, the truth is that it is torture. We humans simply do not thrive alone. People have been known to take leave of their senses when alone for too long. Regardless of how overwhelmed we sometimes feel when surrounded by throngs of people, connections don't ultimately drive us crazy. Being alone, on the other hand, very much can and does.

Some young people in the West used to feel drawn to escape to quiet ashrams high in the remote Himalayas and sequester themselves in solitude in order to do what they called finding themselves. This is nearly always counterproductive. The truth is that in order to find oneself most effectively, the best circumstances are in close contact with other people. It might be in proximity to a loving family or within the embrace of a positive work environment. Whatever the case, our best mental balance can be found when connected to others in our day-to-day lives.

The connectivity principle is built into the world. Living successfully requires that you be attuned to the manifestations of this principle. You want to internalize this principle into your worldview so that you may raise your connectivity quotient. The connectivity principle is built into the world and firmly implanted in God's blueprint for reality, the Bible.

The Torah cannot be sliced and diced, and neither can life. You may not pick and choose which verses you want to abide by. They are all essential. For instance, you cannot keep the rules forbidding incest, which you find distasteful, while tossing out the rules about honesty in business because you would rather make some easy money by cheating the system. It doesn't work that way. The Torah is a package deal. There is a continuity to the Torah and the book is one comprehensive entity that cannot be subdivided. You do not get to keep the parts you like and extirpate the passages you find difficult to live by.

A proper Torah scroll is generally written in 248 columns and every single column must start with the letter *vav*, the sixth letter in the Hebrew alphabet. This letter is imbued with special meaning because it serves as the ultimate connector letter that bridges other words and letters. *Vav* serves a similar function to the English conjunction "and." Conjunctions are connector words, such as *but, with, and, therefore,* and other similar words. When one of these conjunctions follows a phrase, it signals that another phrase is to follow and that both will be connected in some way.

Starting every column of the Torah with a *vav* may sound difficult, but in fact it is not. This is to indicate the connectivity built into the book and that the Torah is of one piece. It is one long unbreakable story.

Not every section of the Tanach has the same proportion of verses that start with a *vav*. The frequency of this is about 65% of the verses in the Five Books of Moses. Once you move onto the prophets and the other books of the Tanach, such as Ecclesiastes, Esther, and Daniel, the proportion of verses that begin with *vav* (or "and" in English) drops to about 40%.

There is one conspicuous exception to this trend of decreasing appearance of the *vav*. The book of Ruth has about 90% of its verses starting with the letter *vav*. Yes, 90%! Why does the book of Ruth alone seem to disrupt the pattern? We find a clue in the fact that the book of Ruth is read on Shavuot, the feast of Pentecost, 50 days after Passover. Pentecost or Shavuot falls on the sixth day of Sivan, the day on which the Torah was given to Moses on Mount Sinai. In a breathtaking display of synchronicity, the book that is read on the day of receiving the Torah best encapsulates the connectivity characteristic by starting the vast majority of verses with "and," with the *vav*.

The book of Ruth is replete with instances of spiritual connectedness. It reveals an utterly disconnected Elimelech. We do not know much at all about his father, family, or other connections. He seems not to care about those connections since he abandoned them to the famine and moved to Moab. But by the end of the book, we see many connections highlighted. Powerful father-son connections that link King David through many generations all the way back to his great-great-great-grandfather, Judah. Ruth will never abandon her mother-in-law, Naomi, come what may. Boaz does not abandon his distant relative Ruth. All of this is highlighted by the lyrical repetition of the *vav*—and, and, and, and. . . .

Naturally it makes sense to read the book of Ruth, which is all about connection, on the day that the ultimate Book of Connectivity was given to humanity. This day has become a symbol for connectedness. It might surprise you to know that the telegraph—that instrument that would beget the telephone, radio, television, and the internet, in a long lineage of increased human interconnectedness—was introduced on May 24, 1844, when Samuel Morse turned on his new invention, the electric telegraph, and tapped a few words from the book of Numbers (23:23), "What hath God wrought," which then traveled down copper wires from the capitol in Washington, DC, to Union Station, Baltimore.

There is a biblical significance to this date. May 24, 1844, fell out in the Hebrew calendar exactly on the Feast of Pentecost, the sixth day of the month of Sivan, in the Hebrew year 5604, the holy day of Shavuot. Of course! When else would have made so much sense? The biggest modern moment in human connection occurred on the day when God gave us the book that is the key to human connection—the Torah. You could rightly say that the Torah is the Book of Connectivity, and that it proves that you and I, and all children of God, were indeed created for connectivity.

Secret #5

Making Money Is a Spiritual Activity

ll human activities can be located somewhere along a spectrum that is anchored on one end by spirituality and on the other by physicality. Praying is near the spiritual end; reading and writing as well as composing music are its neighbors. As the source both of great sensual pleasure and also of all new life, sex might be somewhere near mid-spectrum, while eating and all other bodily functions belong over toward the physical end.

So where do commercial transactions fit? When a human being exchanges coins in his pocket for goods he desires, is he performing a physical act or a spiritual one?

One way of identifying a spiritual act is by determining whether a chimpanzee would understand the action. When we return home from work and slump into comfortable armchairs, our pet primate undoubtedly sympathizes. As we move to the dinner table and begin eating, he certainly knows what is going on. When we open a newspaper, however, and hold it motionless before our face for 20 minutes, he becomes quite confused.

Another criterion for the spiritual is whether the action can be replicated by a machine. If a human soul is indispensable for a certain process, that process is at least partially spiritual. Only a human soul can

31

compose original music intended to inspire men to march to war or to evoke a poignant sense of nostalgia, for instance, without reference to existing work.

Machine-composed music has been around for a while. One example of artificial intelligence (AI) put to work in music making is known as AIVA, artificial intelligence virtual artist. Say its creators, "We have taught a deep neural network to understand the art of music composition by reading through a large database of classical partitions written by the most famous composers (Bach, Beethoven, Mozart, etc.). AIVA is capable of capturing concepts of music theory just by doing this acquisition of existing musical works." Of course, that is quite different from what a human composer does. It is doubtful that machines will ever be able to obey the instruction "write a happy tune that makes people want to dance" without reference to an existing body of "happy tunes" as a talented human composer would do.

No machine exhibits loyalty, persistence, or resourcefulness nor can any machine reliably test whether an individual possesses those qualities. We therefore know these attributes to be spiritual.

These tests suggest that a business transaction is more spiritual than physical. A chimpanzee would not have the slightest idea of what is transpiring between proprietor and customer at a store counter. No machines exist that can independently affect transactions, nor can they predict whether a customer will buy something or for how much. Economic exchange takes place only after two thinking human beings will the exchange into existence. The process is spiritual.

It is important to analyze actions because we human beings are always slightly uneasy with pursuits that lack spiritual overtones completely. When necessary, we superimpose spirituality just to avoid being exclusively physical because it makes us feel uncomfortably animal-like. We apply ceremony and ritual to our actions that are also animalistic.

Only people read books or listen to music; hence, these activities require no associated ritual. On the other hand, most living creatures eat, defecate, engage in sexual activity, give birth, and die. If we do not confer a uniquely human ritual upon these functions, we reduce the distinction between humans and creatures in the animal kingdom. Therefore, we celebrate the birth of a child, often by a naming ceremony—no animal does this. We prefer to serve food in dishes on a tablecloth rather than straight out of the can, although doing so does not enhance the physical or nutritional qualities. We even say a grace or a benediction before eating, and according to ancient Jewish wisdom, afterward as well.

After encountering an attractive potential partner, psychologically healthy people did not used to proceed directly to physical intimacy. An engagement announcement followed by a marriage ceremony served to accentuate that all-important distinction: marriage. No animal announces its intention to mate and then defers gratification for a year or more while it calmly prepares its wedding and future home. Having abandoned this uniquely human waiting period over the past number of decades does not seem to have added happiness to most men's, and particularly not to most women's, lives. Ignoring our spiritual needs has not served us well.

Burials traditionally are similarly full of ritual. After a long and good life, the mortal remains of elderly Aunt Agatha are not simply left out in the alley for the city to pick up on Tuesday. There is mourning and a burial ceremony, followed perhaps by annual visits to the cemetery. The more physical the activity, the more awkwardness and subconscious embarrassment surround it, the more we need ritual to give our lives purpose and spiritual meaning.

Nudism is practiced with a certain bravado in order to conceal the underlying tension between healthy animals and people trying to escape the dignity of human uniqueness. Famous photographer Richard Avedon shattered a barrier by capturing images of people as they ate. Frozen in the act of chewing, humans resemble apes rather than angels. Similarly, we express a normal and healthy reticence about bathroom activities. In fact, it is the bathroom that is often the most adorned and decorated room in the house. At the moment of urination and defecation, when we are perhaps at our most animal-like appearance, we take deep comfort in reflecting upon the little soaps cast in the shape of seashells and upon the monogrammed hand towels and the other handicrafts with which we adorn our restrooms. They remind me that although I am doing in private exactly what most animals do in public, it would be a mistake to think of myself as an animal. No animal decorates the room in which he relieves himself. I am a human being, and I exult in my specialness.

On the other hand, as purely spiritual occupations, reading and art evoke no discomfort. We need no act of ritual here to dress up that which is already so spiritual.

Our entire approach to manners is based on this aspect of biblical tradition. Any child born in the English-speaking world before 1980 probably had a mother or grandmother who, following some egregious breach of manners, would ask, "What are you doing? What is the matter with you? Were you raised in a barn?"

This wasn't a slur on farmers; in fact, my [RDL's] mother was a farmer's daughter. It was a suggestion that your behavior was reminiscent of the barnyard and therefore unacceptable among humans. When your mother told you, just as mine told me, not to comb my hair in public, she was in essence reminding us that we are not animals. Baboons groom themselves in public; humans do not. How many times did your father object to you making animal noises at the dinner table? Mine did so frequently, always explaining that people must not let their bodies sound like animals. Even allowing our bodies to emit involuntary animal sounds is a source of embarrassment, as well it should be.

Emphasis on manners is the way civilized members of a Judeo-Christian society remind one another that our entire culture is founded on the conviction that we are not merely animals, but that we are so much more. We are unique creatures touched by the finger of God. Forgetting this fact dooms our society to descend into an abyss of animalism, economic failure, and ultimately barbarism.

Economic activity is another way in which we satisfyingly distance ourselves from the animal kingdom and draw closer to God. Revealing his own brand of genius in *Paradise Lost*, John Milton (1608–1674) etched the Bible's indelible centrality into man's literary consciousness. He reflected everyone's subconscious awareness that the opening chapters of the Bible focus on the eternal tug of war for man's soul between the angels and the apes. There is a titanic struggle between the divine aspirations of a person's nobility and his basest indulgences. Whom would Adam obey, God or the serpent personification of the animal kingdom? After thousands of years of human history, the lingering memory of that tussle still resonates in the human soul. All heirs to the Judeo-Christian tradition feel the need to distinguish themselves from animals and to unequivocally demonstrate who won that primeval conflict. Seizing another's property by force is animalistic and a victory for the serpent; purchasing that property voluntarily for a price negotiated with the seller finds favor in God's eyes.

That relationship between currency and God's favor springs from the Bible and the Hebrew language itself, in which the Hebrew word for God's favor or grace is *cheyn*. This word's meaning includes God's plan for human economic interaction. It is not only the etymological origin for the English words *coin* and *gain* but also for the Chinese word for coin, *ch'ien*, and similar words in many other languages. The word *cheyn* also serves as the root of the Hebrew word for store or shop as well as for a market-based economy. A store or market is a place for people to interact and make voluntary exchanges, leaving both parties happier and better off than they were before.

Even Ayn Rand, author of *Atlas Shrugged*, observed that when extracting specific performance from people, the only alternative to a gun is money. No wonder then that God smiles upon the marketplace! Freedom from tyranny is a necessary precondition for both worship and trade, and money paves the way for this freedom.

One of the Hebrew words for a business professional is *ohmein*, which means "a person *of faith*," and shares the same root with the liturgical *amen*. With no verifiable information that he will be successful in selling his wares, the merchant nonetheless purchases inventory. He then delights in selling out his entire inventory, even vital commodities like food or clothing, in exchange for little metal discs. Instead of despairing about how he will now feed and clothe his children, he has complete faith that whenever he wishes, there will be someone who will gladly sell him food or anything else he may need for those very metal discs. It is that faith that converts metal discs and printed paper into money. This faith gives currency value. Were he to trade on the basis of doubt and suspicion, he would contract no business at all. It is chiefly his faith that makes his profits possible.

It is therefore not surprising that economics used to be a field of study that belonged within the realm of religion and theology. Adam Smith, as well as many other eighteenth-century economists, were religious philosophers first, economists only second. Smith wrote his book *Theory of Moral Sentiments* before he wrote the better-known *Wealth of Nations*.

When the great universities moved the study of economics from their religious departments to their science departments, they actually were driving a wedge between capitalism and the moral arguments and spiritual dimensions that underpin its validity. Faith is the fuel that drives both commerce and religion, despite what secular academia would have you believe.

It is difficult for a successful business professional to remain self-centered. It is precisely a preoccupation with the needs of others that characterizes the entrepreneur. Concern for customers is the hallmark of a business professional. This is where the phrase "the customer is always right" comes from: business professionals putting the customer before themselves. This is not necessarily always the best practice, but the concept is based in reality.

Business professionals also must value their employees as well, for these employees are among their most valuable assets. They must attend to their welfare, recognizing them as spiritual beings with their own divine aspirations. Not only must employees be compensated competitively but wise employers also help those who work for them find transcendent meaning in that work. Ancient Jewish wisdom prohibits an employer from instructing a worker to perform meaningless work. For example, he may not hire a worker to dig a hole one day, fill it the next, and thereafter repeatedly dig and refill it. This prohibition applies no matter how generous the pay may be because it leaves the worker with no sense of accomplishment and, therefore, no sense of the value of his contribution. The business professional whose own selfish wants and needs constantly fill his mind is doomed. Thus, both business and religion discourage selfish and narcissistic behavior. Thankfully, there is synergy between business and religion because, as we have discussed, business transactions are spiritual actions.

Knowing that a close relationship exists between God and the marketplace helps us in three crucial areas. First, this fact helps to explain why atheism and business are not natural allies. One would have supposed that a philosophy of secular humanism, recognizing no authority and sanctioning all behavior, would be naturally drawn to the world of money and power. One would have expected the political left to excuse what it calls the "greed" of capitalism and to recognize it as nothing other than Darwinian law applied to the life of modern man. Yet, this is not possible; something as truly spiritual as commerce simply cannot

coexist with socialism. The atheist himself recognizes that, to be true
to his credo, he must reject the free market because of its godliness. It
is hard to think of an atheistic tyranny that built a successful and durable economy. It goes without saying that Communist China, certainly
an officially atheistic regime, was an economic disaster until it began
operating under an unusual hybrid of free market and centrally controlled society. Not only did the government tolerate a departure from
Chairman Mao's doctrinal rigidity and obliteration of China's traditional
values but, though few are aware, there are more practicing Christians in
China today than there are members of the communist party.

Secondly, belief in the relationship between God and the marketplace helps us integrate our career into our greater life so that we need
not regard those 8 or 10 hours a day that we spend at work as a faintly
distasteful and isolated part of life. "Business is business" cannot serve
as a convenient explanation for moral departures in the marketplace
because business is tied to life by overall spiritual awareness. Immorality
in business is as repugnant as immorality in marriage. Business success
is secondary to our private relationship with God. It is precisely that
relationship that makes sense of everything else.

Finally, recognizing the congruence between work and spiritual
reality, the business professional is all the better able to sell himself
and his product. His work is creative and therefore a legitimate way
of emulating God and His infinite creativity. Anyone with a sneaking conviction that socialism has a point—that man and his abilities
are as finite as the economic pie and that he who brings that pie to
the market and slices it for customers exploits both the baker and the
public—is forever handicapped as a business professional. Nobody
throws himself wholeheartedly into an endeavor he secretly considers
demeaning and unworthy. The difference between the animal instinct
of a squirrel gathering nuts and the inherent nobility of a human being
earning a living becomes clear when you perceive economic enterprise
in its correct position, at the spiritual end of the spectrum.

Everything Important and Joyful You Have Achieved Has Been in Partnership with at Least One Other Person

Consider your best moments and greatest accomplishments. Have they not always been the product of participation or cooperation with at least one other person? Of course, they have! Your most memorable moments, your most significant achievements, many of your most joyful and jubilant experiences occur when at least one other person has been there to assist and take part in them. The myths about lonely artists creating magnificent and unforgettable classical masterpieces alone in their attic studio are just that—myths. Even great artists and musicians did not spring grown from the earth. They were kept alive by parents or other adults; they often apprenticed and learned skills from mature artists. They saw, heard, and studied the works of previous generations. The isolated human alone can create a masterpiece about as well as he can create a baby, which is to say, not at all. At the very least, someone must see or hear that piece of work. If a person paints a picture and then destroys it before anyone else lays eyes on it, what has he created of value?

Science is no different. The myth of the brilliant, obsessed scientist alone in his laboratory creating marvelous things in the dead of night is just that, a myth. Far closer to the truth is Thomas Edison's headquarters in New Jersey in which dozens of scientists and engineers labored alongside the master. Like the artist, the scientist does not start from scratch.

In a letter to fellow scientist Robert Hooke in 1675, Isaac Newton made one of his most famous statements: "If I have seen further, it is by standing on the shoulders of Giants." The biblical depiction of Adam and Eve is much more than a description of humanity's start on earth. In the perspective of ancient Jewish wisdom, the Bible is not a history book. The Bible is an instruction manual. It provides a blueprint for successful living on this planet. The Bible instructs us on business and money because these activities are essential to successful living. Success in business is an end in and of itself, but that aside, how can one support any activity without making a living for oneself? Clearly, you cannot! All creation must include the act of making money, making a living.

The Bible is the ultimate guide to creativity. It allows us to ask the question: What is the ultimate creation of which humans are capable? The beginning of Genesis gives us our answer.

The ultimate act of creativity that any human being could be involved in is the creation of a baby. We know this, right? That baby could start a scientific revolution. After all, I don't know who they were, but I think you'll agree that there was a certain man and a certain woman who were the parents of Albert Einstein. There was a certain man and a certain woman who were the parents of Henry Ford and of James Watt and of Marconi and Edison and thousands and thousands of other scientific innovators and medical minds, people who changed the world. It's possible your baby might grow up to have a baby who discovers the cure to a terrible disease. Clearly, we can do little that is more creative than bringing a baby into the world and raising that baby to become a happy and successful human being.

There are, of course, many other acts of creativity. We can paint a beautiful piece of art. We can write a novel. We can discover a miracle drug. We can invent something. If you were to ask us, we would say that one of the best acts of creativity is creating a business. This allows us to enhance the lives of untold customers, employees, shareholders—the good done reverberates through the economy and world.

All of the many acts of creativity that a person may engage in can be modeled after that ultimate act of creation as outlined in the Bible: the creation of a baby. We can use this ultimate act of creation as a metaphor for all of creativity and, by extrapolating from the advice given in the Bible, apply the same wisdom about creating a baby to all other acts of creation.

The Bible tells us that there are three things needed for an ultimate act of creativity.

First, it requires at least two people. Oftentimes, creativity requires far more, as in the case of business, but always at least two people are needed.

Secondly, the two people need to be different from one another. Just as mother and father must be different in order to create a child, so must any two creators be. Imagine yourself trying to create something with a clone of you—you and your clone would obviously agree on everything! There would be no mingling of minds, no give and take, and no integrating different perspectives. That's not a very good way to be creative because a creator needs somebody who helps them to become and do more, not who simply nods in agreement. This is the reason for Genesis 2:18—a helpmate *opposite* him. What is the value of a wife who always agrees with her husband? Now no man wants to be publicly humiliated by his wife, but wise men value their wives' input. The interests of no two people are more aligned than those of a husband and his wife. Similarly, imagine trying to start a business with a clone. What could you learn from each other? What have you to offer each other? Nothing. Working with a clone makes no sense. There can be no creativity.

Male and female partners, mother and father—these are a metaphor for giver and receiver. When sitting down with a partner to discuss a business proposal, the listener assumes the role of the female, regardless of the person's biological gender, and the talker is the male, again, regardless of true gender. The "male" puts out a "seed" of an idea and hopes for a conception. (Jewish wisdom bears out this idea, and even in English, we speak of "conceiving" of a plan or idea.) At this point, the "female," which is to say, the listener of the first exchange, responds. Note that during the part of the discussion in which one is listening, that listening is far from passive. It is listening as an act of receiving, which is why people often say something like this: "So to make sure I understand, are you saying that...?" Being a good listener takes skill, and it is so important because a good listener stimulates the speaker to greater creativity. In a business connection the individuals exchange roles in being the male and female—putting out an idea and responding. If all works out, after much give and take, we may see a conception—a viable idea born into fruition. It may take days, weeks, months, as with the ultimate act of creativity. The story of Adam and Eve is a model for the act of creativity, and one of the greatest acts of creativity is entrepreneurship, building a business.

The third thing that the Bible tells us about the act of creation, with the creation of a child as our model, is that—and we are not being coy or suggestive here—creating anything is one of the most exciting and pleasurable things that people can do.

Creating anything, whether it is a novel, work of art, invention, or a business, is both fun and rewarding. This creation involves interacting with others in creative pursuits that we find immensely satisfying. You cannot do this by yourself.

Perhaps you are again thinking of the myth of the "solitary artist" working all by himself to create a masterpiece. But does he really work alone? Who provided his food while he painted? Who provided him with paint in the first place? Where did the canvas come from? As you can see, nobody creates anything alone. It is not possible.

Have you ever wondered why bread is sacramental in faiths that are based on the Bible of the God of Abraham, Isaac, and Jacob? A sacred sacrament involving bread is common to many churches. Each week I (SL) prepare two special Sabbath breads for each of our Sabbath meals. The meals don't start until we make a blessing over the bread. What is so special about bread, you may ask?

The answer can be found in the beginning of Genesis when Adam and Eve sinned by eating the fruit of the tree in the Garden of Eden. They were upset, they prayed, and they atoned for their sin. As part of this atonement Adam wailed to God about how much he regretted lowering himself to the animal level by failing to exercise his will. After all, animals eat whatever they see; humans are meant to choose what and how to eat. Finally, God said, "By the sweat of your brow, you will eat bread." This is often erroneously believed to be part of their punishment for eating the forbidden fruit. Not so. The punishment was eviction from the Garden of Eden and the ushering of death into the world.

God's compassionate response was to grant Adam a new food, unique to humans—bread. Eating bread is no punishment. Bread is delicious! "By the sweat of your brow, you shall eat bread." This is God's mercy. Adam and Eve have sinned, and they are now being shown mercy. God is telling them from now onward they will eat that which they have worked for by the sweat of their brows. He does this because he knows they will find satisfaction in reaping what they have sowed. They will better savor that bread which they have earned. God invents a food that only human beings are going to eat—bread.

Bread is a special food because, unlike carrots, cucumbers, and cauliflower, bread can't just be grown, it takes cooperation between people. Someone must farm the wheat. Someone must grind the wheat into flour. Someone must bake the flour into bread. Here we see cooperation among at least three separate disciplines, usually three different people. (In modern times, it also requires agricultural workers, an industry to build the farm equipment, trucks and truckers to haul the bread, and vendors to market it.) All of these people cooperate, and the result is a delicious, crusty, warm loaf of bread.

Prior to bread, whenever Adam or Eve felt hungry, they simply reached up for the nearest plum or apple and ate whatever was on hand. But from here on out, they would have to plan in advance. The moment when you feel like some bread is not the time to start planting wheat for flour—that must be done in advance. Making bread requires faith. There is no guarantee that when you put wheat seeds in the ground, the crop will grow. Flour must be mixed with other ingredients and made into dough. That must then be baked. Cooperation and time are needed to create anything of true human value—that is the lesson of bread, and it's an absolutely essential lesson.

There is more, however, to the ritual. After making the blessing on the bread, we sprinkle the bread with salt, and not because it tastes good or because salt is a nutrient for the body. The Bible is not a handbook for our bodies. God assumes that human beings will develop medical science and medical science will tell us what our bodies need. If the salt in the sacrament was for health reasons, we might also sprinkle a little potassium and iron filings over our bread as well! We do not do that.

We sprinkle salt over the bread because in the book of Leviticus, chapter 2, verse 13, it reads, "You shall salt every meal offering with salt. You must not stop the salt of your God's covenant from upon your offerings. On every offering you must offer salt."

The Sabbath table is a miniature temple in our own homes. Salt is required to complete this analogy and create an environment of holiness. In the sacramental moment, salt has a very important role to play. Adding salt to our Sabbath bread, known as challah, is nothing other than a capturing of a primeval human memory that the sacrifices in the temple in Jerusalem used salt.

This, of course, begs the question: Why salt? Why not iron or potassium? The answer is that salt is special and metaphorical. Salt is the combination of two elements: sodium and chlorine. It takes an atom of each to make a molecule of salt. One of these atoms is a positive ion and the other a negative ion, that join to form salt. It is important to know that, prior to joining, sodium is terribly toxic and chlorine is poisonous. But together, they become something the body needs and craves. They become something good.

And so it is with people.

The message here is that you can take two separate human beings who may be no good, useless, or even toxic alone, but when you merge them together, they can become more than the sum of their parts. This merger may be a marriage, or it could be a business partnership. This is what salt in the temple reminds us: that when you bring people together, the result is something so much more creative, so much more powerful than individuals could ever do or be alone.

Have you ever stopped to wonder why so many expressions for money involve bread? Will you lend me some *bread?* Got any *dough?* Many languages engage in this metaphorical association because there is a primeval recollection of bread's capacity for bringing people together to bring about creativity and wealth. In the Bible, every reference to bread can be read on a deeper level as a reference to money. For instance, Deuteronomy 8:3 ("Man does not live by bread alone") is telling us that while financial transactions are vital for people to live together in harmony, money is not everything.

Bread connects us to God through the power of creativity. We are reminded that, in emulation of God's ability to create the universe, we too have the collective power of creation. We create babies. We create art. We create inventions, medicine, and bread. And, yes, of course, we create business enterprises. Just remember that the creativity, this wealth, is only possible when we join together. Collaboration requires at least two people who are not identical working together. And while collaboration brings about joy and gratification, the third tenet, creation, requires a deferment of gratification.

If you understand that creativity requires you to join with others, it should be obvious that other people are the key to your success. You must begin to look at them with warmth. You can express that positive outlook by looking for ways to serve and do favors and treat others with respect and appreciation. This can be as simple as smiling and silently admitting your need for others to yourself. Try this: Before job interviews, phone conversations, business meetings, or any other interaction with another human being, put a smile on your face and tell yourself that you really care for this other person. You must show authentic warmth to others, even if they do not visibly reciprocate. Force yourself to do this, if need be. Over time, it will become natural and feel and be genuine. Over time, your words and actions penetrate your soul and your soul believes and adopts them. Don't worry that you should not say or do things (assuming they are good things) that do not feel true in your heart, out of fear that will make you a hypocrite. You are, instead, training yourself. Act in a certain way and your thoughts will follow your actions.

There are many instances in which we should and must say things we don't believe, both to ourselves and to others. Consider a friend who asks for your advice about a new suit only after they have purchased it and removed the tags. Though you might well believe the suit to be a sartorial disaster, they can no longer return it, and your advice is moot. In these cases, God wants us to respond only with warm enthusiasm so that we may add to their joy of their new possession. Obviously, if they ask your opinion prior to purchase, your honest assessment is probably being solicited, and you should offer it. But if they are simply seeking affirmation of their choice, why would you not find something in the purchase that allows you to rejoice with them? The relationship is paramount.

Coming full circle, we see that if we wish to prosper in the wonderful world of business, we need other people. Not only do we need other people, but we need warm and strong connection to other people. We need other people to know us, like us, and trust us. Now the reason for why God wishes us to prosper in business becomes clearer. In order to succeed we need to form those interpersonal connections, which is exactly what God wants us to be doing in the first place. Hence His first Biblical expression of disfavor: "Not good for man to be alone." A very helpful perspective is that business and the wealth it creates is God's way of incentivizing us to connect with His other children.

Focus on Other People's Needs and Desires and You Will Never, Ever Be Short of What You Yourself Desire and Need

Does God want you to be rich? How about this question: Does God want men and women to enjoy physical intimacy? People are sometimes made uncomfortable by this question, but we ask it to draw a parallel. We cannot tell you with any certainty that your pleasure is one of God's top concerns. But what we do know is that God wants men and women to live together as couples in the exclusive and holy covenant of marriage. It should not surprise us that a loving and gracious God would reward couples that follow His will with the greatest sensual pleasure available to humans. Similarly, we cannot assure you that God wants you to be rich. However, this we can tell you: God does want us to be obsessively preoccupied with one another's needs and wants, and if a good and loving

God should reward those who follow His wishes with the incredible blessing of financial abundance, why should that surprise us?

There is only one way to make money with integrity: find out what other people want or need and then provide those things to as many of our fellow humans as possible. No matter what your occupation is, whether you are providing lollipops or legal help, this is the only way to make money. To do this effectively, you need to establish meaningful connections with your customers. This is no accident: God has designed money to be an instrument that both rewards and motivates us to do His will.

Earning a living requires *making* money, not *taking* money. We literally bring money into existence by making another human being happier. As long as you haven't robbed, defrauded, or coerced someone into giving you money, or taken advantage of a weakness of theirs to harm them (for example, pushing drugs or porn), then every dollar in your pocket was given to you by people you made happy enough to reward you with their money. Maybe it was a boss, a customer, or a client. They willingly gave you money because you gave them something they wanted in return.

Have you ever wondered how so many companies can afford to offer money-back guarantees? Shouldn't they be worried that people will return the merchandise? Some might, but by far the majority of shoppers are happier after purchasing a wanted or needed product or service. The company is standing behind what they know to be a useful and good product. If we wanted our money more than the product or service, we wouldn't have made the purchase in the first place. Willful transactions are proof that you have created happiness by fulfilling someone's wants or needs.

Making money is not something we do surreptitiously when we think God is not watching. Making money is not the result of an occupation that we reluctantly undertake just to pay the bills. Making money is not an unworthy and selfish activity, and you need not be ashamed of engaging in the making of money. On the contrary, making money—when done in an honest manner in an open and transparent marketplace—is dignified and moral and the consequence of carrying out God's will. In other words: money is the consequence of working, not the goal. Profit comes from connecting with God's other children and serving them. We were in fact created for this very purpose—to connect with one another.

Do you speak to the people seated next to you when flying? Conversation invariably turns to what we each do for a living. Train yourself no longer to think of it as making a living, but as serving humanity. Ask people, "How do you serve humanity?" At first, people won't tell you about their occupation. They won't say that they sell insurance, teach classes, or broker real estate deals. Instead, they will tell you about the work they do at the soup kitchen, their pro bono clients, or the time they spend volunteering at the animal shelter.

After you commend their compassion, explain to them that supplying other people with goods and services in exchange for pay and profit is no less an act of serving humanity than their volunteerism. Chances are the work they do for profit does more total good than the few hours they spend helping for free. Requiring and obtaining reward for a service rendered does not corrupt the service itself. Money is what comes to us when we focus on serving all God's other children. To think of your occupation and work as only "making a living" suggests that you are only interested in what you get out of work. There is nothing wrong with wanting to make money but make serving (the process of making money) your goal. If you consider your work to be a calling, your way of serving humanity, then you both make money and serve. This is the correct way to approach work. Work is your calling. Align your work with your values, align your values with your work, and you will see the innate purpose and worth of all compensated work.

The money is what happens as a result. It is your reward. But the reward does not negate the value or sanctity of the work. In fact, the money you make substantiates the fact that you have done good for others. Making money proves to yourself and others that you are serving God's other children. To serve them, you must first get to know them. You must understand their wants and needs. You must earn their favor and trust. This is what making money is all about.

Have you ever wondered why a worship service is called a *service*? The phrase uses the same construction as another phrase: *customer service*. This is no accident. Consider what goes on at the shoe store. When you sit down at a shoe store to try on a shoe, a salesperson goes down on one knee in front of you and takes your shoe off for you. And what if you do not like the new shoes and instead want to try a pair of fancy sneakers that are the hot new item this year? No problem, the salesperson says, as he or she runs off to find it for you.

The customer service you see here is not that dissimilar to what happens at worship service. People are again down on their knees. This is one of the reasons that the Hebrew word for blessing is the same as the word for knee: B-R-CH. Hebrew uses the same word because going down on your knees is a way of serving God. This is no different than the service given by a salesperson who understands that the customer needs new sneakers. It should not be considered a menial or degrading gesture. It is one we can take joy in because we know that we are serving another one of God's children. The salesperson understands that he fulfills this desire. This is beautiful harmony. The salesperson is happy to serve God by making His other children happy, and the customer is happy to walk out of the store with the perfect new sneakers on her feet. These feelings are inherently rewarding, but our good and loving God and our fellow man provide us with further rewards in the form of a salary or a commission or both.

When I [RDL] was 16, I got my first car, which I remember as clearly as if it were yesterday. I had saved my money for years and spent all of it on this one purchase. I was in love with this car the first time I drove it. Learning to smoothly work the clutch together with the stick shift was joy. I would drive with one hand on the wheel and the other arm resting on the open window ledge. I was in heaven. But then the car began to make a horrible grinding noise, and my heart sank. I went home to tell my father, the rabbi of a large congregation, that there was something seriously wrong with my car. My father referred me to Sam Goldberg, a member of his congregation who ran an auto repair shop. I drove to see Mr. Goldberg at his shop and told him that my father had recommended him to me. Mr. Goldberg opened the hood and asked me to start the engine and give it some gas. He then made the sound you never want to hear from your mechanic. He let out a long, low whistle that descended in pitch. My heart sank . . . I knew there was something significant wrong and that it was going to be expensive. That whistle meant lots of money. And I realized that I didn't have lots of money because I'd spent all my money on the car. I was very unhappy.

Mr. Goldberg told me to sit in the waiting room while he took my car out back to the shop. I tried reading magazines while I waited, but I was too distracted wondering how I would deal with this. Finally, he brought the car back around. The grinding sound was gone. It was as if he put in a whole new engine! I'd never heard a car sound so good. It sounded better than my mom's sewing machine. It was smooth. It was softly musical. It was beautiful.

Only now I was torn. I was happy the car was fixed but scared to get the bill, for which I had no money. Mr. Goldberg handed me the keys and told me I was good to go. When I asked him how much it was, he said, "No charge." I must have looked pretty confused. He explained that my father had once done him a huge favor. Mustering every bit of character that I could, I confessed to him that the car was mine, not my father's.

And he said something to me that I've never forgotten: "When you get older and have your own children, you will discover that the best thing somebody can do for you is to do something good for your kids."

This person honored his debt to my father by doing something for me. When someone does something for your children, it is just as good or even better than if they had done it for you. Consider the opposite. If you had to choose someone doing something horrible to you or to your children, what would you choose? Most parents would say, "Do it to me instead!" This works both ways, and most people would, if pushed to choose, rather see goodwill and favors showered upon their children than upon themselves.

Now consider our Father in Heaven. Think about how He feels when you do something to please His other children. He smiles upon those who smile on His other children. He wants us to be kind and serve one another. Loving other people is the key to both spiritual happiness and wealth. Do not forget this: by loving and serving others, you are turning the key to unlocking wealth and happiness.

You must surround yourself with other people if you want to make money and be happy. This is why, for all their problems, people still flock to cities. If you were going to open a jewelry store, where would you open it? Most cities have many jewelry stores, and they are often located in the same part of town. This is very common. Similarly, often you will see furniture stores or clothing stores all clustered in the same part of town. Why? How can all of these stores compete with one another? Perhaps to avoid competition, a new jeweler should go across town, or way out into the country where there are fewer jewelry stores? Better yet, what if he opened a jewelry store in Death Valley, California, where there are no jewelry stores for hundreds of miles! He'd make a killing, right?

Of course not.

If this was you, the place you should put your jewelry store is right next door to the other jewelry stores. You will benefit from your competition. Everyone who wants to buy engagement rings or jewelry knows exactly where to go to get it—that same area. Some of them will shop at your competitors, but you know what? Some of them will come to your store as well. What is more, your competitors will send a customer to you for a product that your store stocks and his doesn't, just as you will send customers to another store in the same way. Everyone does better when stores are near similar stores. This clustering is not the result of a city's government dictating that all jewelry stores must be on the same road; no, it happens by itself. It is built into the system that God created that rewards those of us who get together and connect with other people. This is why you see such distinct business districts in every town and city. It is also why, since time immemorial, that Middle East peculiarity, marketplaces or "shuks," those cramped concentrations of narrow alleyways jam-packed with stores and haggling shopkeepers, came into existence in ancient cities.

Business begets more business. The winemaking industry in Napa Valley, just north of San Francisco, spurred an entire subindustry of hundreds of smaller companies that supply the vineyards and the winemakers with everything they needed at prices and service levels they could never expect to receive if they were alone and isolated. Likewise, high-tech areas always sprout up in clusters; proximity breeds the connectivity and constant cross-pollination of ideas. This is why tech companies flock to Silicon Valley. It is why there are areas with outdoor cafes in Rome rather than having one café every few blocks, and why there is a fashion district in London.

One of the reasons for both Israel's and Singapore's extraordinary economic success is that both nations are small and compact. This keeps the entire nation well connected. People know each other.

Knowing everybody and being known by everybody is the ultimate recipe for success, though this is, of course, impossible. You cannot know everyone. But you can dramatically increase the number of people who know you, the number of people who like you, and the number of people who trust you simply by remaining in proximity to them and being a good neighbor.

Malcolm Gladwell's best-selling book, *The Tipping Point*, posits that a person's financial success is directly correlated to the number of people he or she knows. This is not arguable. It's not up for debate. It is not an opinion. It is a quantifiable fact: The more people you know, the more they like and trust you, the better you are going to do in life and business. Cynics may argue that people flock to those who have money, and not necessarily because they are friends. This is true, but not the driving factor. People with many friends often make their friends first and their money later. Successful people have usually worked on developing relationships first. Wealth followed, just as it can and it will, for you.

Is this principle found in the Bible? Consider Cain, the first child of Adam and Eve. Remember, when we speak of the Bible, we're not talking about a history book here. We're not talking about some obsolete account of some long-forgotten people in anachronistic accounts. We're looking to the Bible as a blueprint of how to live. Ancient Jewish wisdom tells us that every name in Scripture has a specific meaning. Cain's name means "acquisition," which refers to a desperate eagerness to accumulate stuff. This was the entire essence of Cain's identity.

Genesis 4:8 does not report what Cain said to his brother, Abel, shortly before killing him. We only are told, "And Cain spoke to Abel." But what did they speak about? The weather? Football? Not likely. Nothing in Scripture is irrelevant. Nothing in Scripture is accidental. We know Cain spoke to Abel, but we do not see what he said. Why?

The Bible doesn't have to tell us what he said because, as ancient Jewish wisdom tells us, it is so obvious that we can figure it out for ourselves. If we are willing to "read between the lines," we can answer the mystery. Adam and Eve are getting old and after their sin, there is death in the world. Cain approaches Abel and says, "Hey, Dad's going to be on his way soon. Mother's going to be on her way. That means we inherit the earth. I just want to be clear that since I'm the oldest son, I will be getting everything, and you may live wherever you like but you will have to pay me rent."

In return, Abel says, "Cain, no, I don't think you understand. It's not going to be like that. As a matter of fact, we're going to be splitting it in two."

How does Cain, whose name literally means acquisition and whose only one purpose in life is taking, react to Abel's refusal? He kills his brother, of course. This is his natural choice because he sees other people as the obstacle to his wealth. Cain has it exactly backward. Cain's folly is that he thinks that the fewer other people who exist in the world, the better off he will be. He thinks that if he can get rid of everybody else, then he will have everything to himself. Abel wants half, and Cain's response is, *This Abel has got to go.*

God punishes Cain in a way that makes him appreciate and understand the error of his ways. Cain finally understands. Having other people around is good.

What is the next step? Cain has a baby. He calls the baby Enoch, or Chanoch in Hebrew, which means "educated." The birth and naming of his child shows us that Cain has caught on; he understands. Before, he thought that having other people around was counter to his own interests, but he now understands that people do not detract from your life; they enrich it. The very next thing Cain does is build a city, which is surprising when you consider that, at this point, there are only about half a dozen human beings on the planet. Why would he need a city? This question misses the point. The Bible is showing us here that cities are good for people. Cities produce people. People flock to cities because it is a place where everyone can live better with less effort. You can extract a living from the often-reluctant earth more easily in a city than in remote isolation.

We know what you may be thinking. As we write this, many cities aren't doing so well. In fact, some major cities around the world, and certainly in the United States, are losing their population of workers and producers as crime rises, homelessness abounds, and there is a breakdown of civil society.

In the 10 years that separated the 2000 census from the 2010 census, the percentage of Americans who moved from living rurally to the cities was 2%. That is more than five million people in only 10 years.

This trend, what was evident since the founding of America and happened just as reliably in most other countries, is changing. Not only are many major cities on a downward population trajectory, but technology allows many people to work remotely. We can sell our jewelry online, prepare someone's taxes without ever meeting them, and teach over Zoom. Even some medical diagnoses and surgeries can be performed from far away! Who needs to be near other people anymore?

This is one of the greatest benefits of studying the Bible. The Bible deals in long-term truths, not in only looking at the here and now. And in the larger picture, cities are where wealth is made. Even now, companies are grappling with the problem that remote work doesn't spur the creativity that abounds when employees see and interact with each other. Teaching over Zoom proved to be a disaster for thousands of children when schools were shut down during COVID-19. Many people are suffering from loneliness and isolation, and the number of prescriptions being given for emotional and mental health is multiplying meteorically.

A sine wave is a mathematical curve that has highs and lows. In many areas of life, great positive potential is matched by great negative potential. An airplane allows one to travel a much greater distance than can be covered on a bicycle. It can take you places that a bicycle cannot reach at speeds the cyclist can only dream of. At the same time, if a bicycle falls over, it usually results in the rider getting a few scratches. If an airplane falls out of the sky, the passengers will usually die. The airplane's potential is greater and so is its potential for damage when things go wrong.

Cities have the potential to harness the energies of multitudes of people and produce great wealth. When they go wrong, they go very wrong. To paraphrase poet Henry Wadsworth Longfellow, when cities are good, they are very, very good—But when they are bad, they are horrid.

Right now, in many places, many of the people governing cities and living in them have abandoned God and His principles. We are seeing the results, and indeed, people are moving away. The story of Cain, along with other biblical messages, tells us that this change won't last. Perhaps new cities will arise, perhaps older ones will hit rock bottom and bounce up again. But scattering away from each other and disconnecting from one another will not produce the wealth that cities have produced.

People, collectively, are our wealth. Our ability to make money depends on how well we connect and communicate with others. In 2007, *Scientific American* published an article detailing what would happen to New York City if all humans were to vanish from the earth. Over the course of only decades, cities crumble without human maintenance. Abandoned cities become overrun by nature. Skyscrapers topple, and bridges collapse into the water. Mountains, rivers, and deserts do not need people. But cities do. And we need cities. A special relationship is here, but it is less between city and man than between man and man. Man needs cities because they allow people to be in proximity so that they can communicate, collaborate, and create.

Start by giving other people the respect they deserve as individuals created in the image of God. Respect them. Value them. If you can, love them. Every single one of them. No matter how irritating or inconsequential a person may seem, you need them.

Notice that the focus here is not on how to make more money, but how to better and more frequently serve more human beings. You should not ask yourself how best to get rich, but rather, what do people around me need done? How can I fill their needs or their desires? How can I improve their lives? Focus on service, and wealth will follow. How can I improve a lot of other people's lives? That's the big question. The money follows . . . you don't have to worry about that; it will take care of itself.

Become a People Person

What psychologists call the intelligence quotient (IQ) is, as the name suggests, an attempt to quantify human intelligence. However, a very high IQ correlates poorly with wealth. There is evidence that people with a very high IQ tend to be less successful at making money. Highly intelligent people gravitate toward academia more than the general population. Almost any financial planner will tell you that few demographics are as bad with money as members of university faculties.

There are exceptions, of course. Bill Gates, founder of Microsoft, and Warren Buffett of Berkshire Hathaway are both exceptionally brilliant businessmen, and they both happen to have super-high IQs. But they are in the minority. Most people with high IQs are not outstandingly successful, either financially or socially. Many people with very high intelligence do not have a lot of friends because they have trouble befriending those they consider less intelligent than themselves. Furthermore, people are often uncomfortable around those who seem to be too smart for their own good. Extremely intelligent people can come across as aloof and not completely forthright. They are not necessarily dishonest; there is simply a big cognitive gap between them and the average person, and this can alienate the general population.

While a super-high IQ is poor at predicting success in life, a high connectivity quotient (CQ) is very positively correlated with success. Your CQ is a measure of your ability to establish connections. People with a high CQ are likely to have many friends and large professional and social networks, which do make you happier, healthier, and, yes, wealthier. These things depend upon your ability to make connections. This is confirmed by Scripture when God declared: "It is not good for man to be alone." This is as true for you as it was for Adam. The fewer people you are involved with, the more disconnected you are, and the less healthy, happy, and wealthy you will be.

In 2019 the U.S. National Center for Health Statistics published a study entitled "Mortality Among Adults Aged 25 and Over by Marital Status: United States, 2010–2017," showing what has been widely accepted for decades. Namely, that people in close connection with others, primarily through marriage and family, enjoy significantly higher health outcomes and significantly quicker recovery from illness and surgery. Many similar studies have been performed both before and since and in none has this basic reality been challenged. People in close real-life (as opposed to digital or online) relationships enjoy far better health. It is hard to ignore the inevitable conclusion: we humans are hardwired for connection.

Dr. Irving Janis, author of *Air, War, and Emotional Stress*, described the positive impact of military camaraderie on the medical outcomes of wounded soldiers. The Medical Department of the U.S. Army has reported that a soldier's willingness and ability to endure the severe stress of combat was primarily dependent on how close a soldier feels to the rest of his unit. We can thus see that friendship aids not only health, but also happiness. Princeton professor and Nobel laureate Daniel Kahneman did research into what he called "hedonic psychology"—the study of what gives people pleasure and happiness. Dr. Kahneman found that having strong friendships with many people is one of the primary factors positively affecting our sense of satisfaction and happiness.

If close relationships and friendships can make such a difference in your health and happiness, imagine what those relationships and friendships can help you achieve in your business. Every major economic expansion in history arose from some dramatic breakthrough in our ability to connect with one another. The expansion of railways in the early 1800s was followed by an enormous explosion of wealth. The invention of the telegraph, telephone, radio, and television all led to booms in prosperity. The advent of the internet at the start of the twenty-first century ushered in an age of wealth such as had never been seen before.

The explosion of online businesses along with social media has led to two parallel phenomena. On the one hand, opportunities for an individual to create wealth by buying and selling internationally with little more physical infrastructure than a computer abound. At the same time, the internet has led to a lack of connection. We can ruin someone's reputation with the click of a mouse and confuse real relationships with virtual ones. Not seeing a customer makes it easier not to care about that person. Like every powerful invention, the internet can be a source of both good and evil. This was true of railways, telephones, and the telegraph as well.

God created a world in which the economy rewards positive human interconnectedness. Why? Because, from His point of view, that is the purpose of the economy: to encourage and cultivate human connections. We were made by Him to be connected. You ignore this truth at your own personal and professional risk.

We have already established that anyone who works is technically in business, whether they are a bus driver or barista, coffee shop owner or CEO. It is easy to see that a business owner and a senior executive are in business. However, should hourly employees consider themselves in business? Yes. They are in the business of providing services, even if at that moment, they might only have one customer, their employer. This is not a matter of semantics, but an important distinction that requires you to change the way you think. The company that writes your paycheck every two weeks should not be seen as your employer but rather as your customer. Adopt this mind-set and everything changes. You are free from the daily grind—free to grow your business and serve your customers, your fellow man.

How does this play out in daily life? As an employee, it is easy for our focus to be on our coffee breaks and the end of the workday. Especially for those of us who were not raised with a strong work ethic, work is nothing more than a means to a paycheck. If, instead, we are actually in business for ourselves, then our work is an opportunity for us to do our absolute best, to gain skills, and constantly improve. With this mind-set, we either become more valuable and have tangible reasons to ask for a raise and advancement, or we recognize that we want a different "customer" who will choose to pay more for our services.

So often we forget that our employer really is our customer. Remember, everyone is in business, even if their one and only customer is their boss. Successful employees view their bosses the same way successful shopkeepers treat the people who patronize their establishments. When you realize that your boss is really your customer, you will have an easier time asking for a raise because it is just a case of you raising your prices.

A good analogy is the difference in the way we treat rental cars and our own cars. You seldom take a rental car to a car wash. You take it back dirty. What do you care? It doesn't belong to you! I am not saying this is the way we *should* think, but it is the way many of us *do* think. It is the same with work. Are we invested in seeing ourselves as individual business owners or as cogs in the machine? If I am an employee of a small gift shop that closes each day at 5:00 p.m. and a customer comes to the door at 4:55 p.m., I tell them that they had better hurry if they want to buy something. As a business owner, I stay 10 minutes late and make their experience a pleasant one.

One recent change in medicine is that many hospitals have been bought out by corporations and private equity funds More experienced doctors tell us that this, along with changes in medical school, is producing a new generation of doctors who lack professionalism. While the older doctors would never casually call in sick and would stay well past the end of their shifts if they were in middle of a case, the newer crop of doctors see it as a job, not as a calling. They are employees and nothing more.

Thinking this way will lead to poorer medical care and less fulfilled doctors. The same idea leads to poorer care from everyone from our plumber to teachers. To do the best possible job, everybody in business should see what they do with a sense of pride and ownership.

We can hear you saying, "But what about work–life balance? What if staying late means missing supper with the family or a child's soccer game?" The conundrum of how to do everything well—earn a good living while also being a good spouse, parent, and friend—all while taking care of your own physical and spiritual self needs a book of its own. (In fact, we wrote a book on that topic: *The Holistic You: Integrating Your Finances, Family, Friendship, Faith, and Fitness.*) However, for this discussion, let's look at the message you give your children when you regularly favor their activities over your customers. Do you really want to instill in your child the idea that it is okay to abandon a customer in need so you always can be there for their games? Of course not. You want your children to see you putting the needs of another human being before your own personal wants. Life requires this kind of balancing act of your personal and professional lives. We want our children to be happy, yes, but first and foremost we want to instill in them proper values. Ignoring other people's needs and seeing themselves as the center of the universe are not the lessons we want to pass on.

There are so many fascinating people in this world, and through our work we are privileged to meet a good number of them. One was a harried-looking mom attending a personal finance seminar we were engaged to conduct for a Dallas church. She told us that she was a cashier for a large supermarket whose name we instantly recognized. She was puzzled about how she could possibly apply these principles to her particular line of work, which she saw as rather mechanical. We role-played how she might relate to customers were this her own store and were they her personal customers. She would engage with each one by looking directly at them. She would try to remember and recognize each regular customer and try to discover individual interests or personal facts. In other words, she was to try and get each customer to know her and like her.

Six months later, we were invited back to the same church to speak. Sure enough, she was sitting in the audience, but this time she was dressed quite differently. Neither of us are masters of women's fashion, by any means, but we can tell the difference between an inexpensive dress from Walmart and a well-tailored outfit from a designer brand. Six months earlier she had been wearing a nondescript tunic, and now she looked more Ann Taylor or Eileen Fisher. We sat down with her again after the service. She told us a story that brought much joy to our hearts.

"I started doing everything you taught me," she said. "And for the first time in my life, I actually started enjoying work. Before then, my head was always down on the cash register, pushing things past the scanner. Now I began to look at customers and smile and engage them. I treated them like real people." I started thinking of them as if they were my own customers. I told myself that every item they purchased improved my own bottom line.

And this was how she was "discovered." By engaging people. Her line at the supermarket had become the longest because regulars wanted to say hello to her as they checked out. One day a person came in whom she had never seen before and asked when she got off work. At first, she thought he was hitting on her and she spurned the advance.

"You misunderstand me," he said. "I don't want to date you. I want to hire you."

He gave her a business card from his real estate company. She didn't understand but agreed to meet later at a local coffee shop. There he offered her a job. He needed someone to work the front desk and serve as the face of first contact with potential clients. He had been watching how she treated people in the checkout line and decided she was perfect for the job. He offered her a salary and benefits that far surpassed the wage she was making as a checker. This has completely turned around both her life and the life of the child she supports.

And how did she accomplish this? By chasing wealth? No, though she seized upon an opportunity at hand. But that opportunity was only at hand because she first put in the effort to communicate and collaborate effectively with the individuals already around her.

The lesson here is important for all people in business. It is relevant to entrepreneurs and incipient entrepreneurs. It is relevant to those who are frustrated with where they are working and want to start their own business. It is relevant to employees simply seeking better employment. Even the unemployed should take note. All of these people need to understand this one thing: no matter how many people you know now, you will always benefit by knowing more. You want to connect with as many people as possible to increase your chances of serving more human beings and interacting with people who might change your personal and professional life.

But you cannot just stand there waiting. You must work to be seen. And that requires making changes to yourself as necessary. To succeed at making money, it is not enough only to learn new techniques and skills. Those things are important, but they are not enough. You must become a new person who is open to the world and all of its possibilities. Doing so is almost like being reborn. You cannot fake this—lack of it is more easily spotted in business than almost any other endeavor. Your customers and partners will want to know and see that a coherent and genuine structure of integrity rules your life. To succeed in making money in business, you need many people who know, like, and trust you. Even for those not in what is traditionally thought of as business, this still holds true. Consider a researcher who works alone in a laboratory. That researcher will perform much better if he begins to see himself as someone in business, producing research for his customers—the laboratory, the chemical company he works for, and the ultimate customers of his employer everywhere.

We understand that this does not come naturally for everyone. Some people find that cheerful bonhomie and gregarious camaraderie are just not their strengths. Plenty of people just don't see themselves as "a people person." They may have issues with shyness, social anxiety, or self-confidence, and they find it hard to talk to new people. What do you do if you are that person?

The answer is this: if you're that person, you have to learn to change. Before you say you can't, let us promise you that you can. One of the main things that separates humans from the animal kingdom is our ability to induce change in ourselves. Is it easy? Not always. Is it possible? Definitely.

Jews have always understood the importance of and mechanisms for change because we see change as the root of human fulfillment. By contrast, the feeling of stagnation is one of the worst feelings a human can feel. Birthdays, New Year's Day, and any other annual marker can make us feel depressed because they remind us that another year has gone by, and if we feel that nothing has changed, then we feel we are going nowhere. It is not enough to tread water, to stand still; we must constantly grow to feel happy and healthy.

Growth produces human happiness, but growth never comes without pain. There used to be a saying in the fitness community: no pain, no gain. This may be a clunky cliché, but for our purposes, it is a perfectly true sentiment. Growing requires us to do things that we are unaccustomed to, which frequently hurts. Growth is difficult, but when achieved, the result is joy and happiness.

We remind you of this if you are one of those who claims not to be a people person. You may not believe this, as we have our own podcast, we co-hosted a TV show for many years, and we lecture regularly, but we are both naturally shy. We sympathize and understand how you feel. But you can change.

There is no magic pill that will make the discomfort of experiencing new company and overcoming shyness any easier, but we can promise you that you do have it in you to change. How do we know? Because you are a human being. You are not a beaver. You are not a camel. You are not an otter. You are not any other animal. You're a human being. While this fact doesn't mean change is easy, it does mean that change is possible.

You're going to have to overcome your tendencies. It will be difficult and possibly painful at first, but it will get easier with time, and eventually—and this is what is meant by true change—your new habits will become innate. You will realize that other people are nice and interesting, and there was no reason to be nervous in the first place. But before you get there, you must leave the place you're at and move to a new one. You must accept the journey. It is a great journey, and at its end lies your new destiny. You will eventually find a place where you no longer hold yourself back, and you are now able to meet and befriend new people. You will make new friends and more people will know you, more people will like you, and more people will trust you. You will build a network that will allow you to achieve great things, personally and professionally.

While the internet has been revolutionary in connecting us online, be wary of online friends. Online friends can give us a false feeling of interconnectedness. People on social media sites often boast about having thousands of "friends" or "followers" or "connections." Just because some random person accepts your connection request on a social media site does not mean they are really a friend. Generally speaking, if someone won't take your personal phone call, they do not belong on your special list of authentic connections.

These so-called "friends" that we make or declare online are not equivalent to real friendships that we make and maintain through face-to-face interaction. The incredible popularity of internet applications that allow people not only to talk to one another but also to see one another's faces while they talk helps to make this point. Companies that provide face-to-face communication have proliferated and grown. This trend took off during the COVID-19 epidemic and provided social relief, educational opportunities, and enhanced business communication. Even so, after a couple of years, it has become clear that as helpful as this technology is, real human face-to-face connection still remains superior. Parents have realized that their children's education was not really well served by at-home learning, and companies are doing their best to bring workers back to the office. In spite of the wonderful internet connection technologies, business professionals still get on airplanes for in-person meetings.

Scripture reveals the enormous importance of face-to-face connection by highlighting the special relationship between God and Moses. Scripture is replete with references to Moses and God speaking face to face, such as Exodus 33:11: "And the Lord spoke to Moses face to face, as a man speaks to his friend." Do you see that language? Friends speak face to face in order to nurture their friendship.

The Hebrew word for "face" is *PaNiM*, which is also the Hebrew word for "inside," which is *PeNiM*. In Hebrew, these are actually the same word with the same spelling; they simply have a slightly different pronunciation. The Lord's language reveals a connection between these two words. The face reveals what is going on inside of us by providing a window into our souls. God gave our faces more than 50 muscles because control of the face is the key to effective communication and human connection. People can sense when your interest in them is insincere based on what your face reveals.

I [RDL] was once introduced to a candidate in a presidential primary who went on to win his campaign for the presidency of the United States. His countenance was animated and intense, but somewhat mechanical. His eyes darted around the room while he talked. I could tell that his interest in me was mechanical. It was as though he was talking to me only until he located a more rewarding guest upon whom to lavish his attention. He was busy, and I do not blame him.

In fact, he is still regarded as one of the very best "people persons" to occupy the Oval Office. But I do think my experience taught me that we can all tell when someone feigns interest in us.

The thing to take from this anecdote is that interest is not easily faked. You need to be sincerely interested in the person with whom you are speaking to avoid offending them. You also must learn to make your face reveal the sincere warmth and interest that turns strangers into friends. Making your face more expressive is a skill that can be practiced. Some of us are cursed with lazy faces that do not show a deepness of expression, which can make one come off as muted, cold, or disinterested. But practice can remedy this. Have you ever studied actors practicing their craft? Note how good actors are careful to emote clearly and distinctly. Watch accomplished actors interact with talk show hosts. Their faces are animated. You may not be able to be as good at this as a world-class actor, but we all can make improvements through practice.

We can train our facial expressions in the same way we can train our voices. Stand in front of a mirror and smile. What does your smile say about you? Do you have a ready smile? Or does your smile look more like a menacing grimace? Move your face around until you can smile the way you want—warmly and sincerely. A camera can also be useful so that you can compare different facial poses. Try to show surprise. Now concern. Practice a gamut of expressions. Do this for a few minutes a day, and you will see improvement. It will make your face nicer to behold and much easier for others to interpret.

Try to look animated when it is your turn to speak. The human eye is attracted to movement. People will converse in a far more focused fashion with you if you have an animated face. Learn to focus intently on whoever is speaking to you. Give them your full attention. Don't just act interested—be interested. Use your face to convey that interest while the other person speaks. When others are speaking, you should be listening. Appear focused and be focused. Do this well, and you will find that your face will bring you fortune. It need not be a pretty face or a young and fresh face. It just has to be a real and reactive face.

What matters is expression and focus. Use emotive expressions to make it easier for others to focus on you when you speak; when it is the other person's turn to speak, give them the same focused, undivided attention. Your face is the window into your soul. Use it properly.

When seeking out new friends, be open to those who are different from you in some ways. You do not want all of your friends and associates to be your clones. You can't share and trade anything with someone who is your clone. As long as you share a core value system, the more different you are, the more you will be able to benefit from one another. Differences allow us to trade and exchange knowledge and wisdom. Differences allow us to do business; for if we had nothing to learn and receive from one another, what would there be to exchange? Nothing. The only reason we can do business is because we are different. Celebrate that difference.

This is why it is so glorious to be human. Animals do not have this power of exchange because they are all identical. Dogs do not engage in exchange because, in many ways, all dogs are the same. All dogs enjoy a good bone and are indifferent to a good book. Therefore, a bone is of the same value to each of two dogs, and they will not, for example, trade it for a bag of carrots, or books, or currency. They have pretty much the same desires and nothing to trade. Humans, on the other hand, have different desires. One person may prefer a vacation at the beach, while another loves the mountains. One person appreciates modern décor while another is passionate about traditional furniture. One individual is meticulous about small details while another is a big-picture aficionado. That human beings are all unique and different is not a small matter—it is fundamental. In fact, our differences are what allow for exchange, commerce, and collaboration.

No two humans are identical, not even identical twins. Science proves it. Consider fingerprints. All human beings have different, unique fingerprints. Identical twins, who have the exact same DNA, have different fingerprints. Even though they are born with the exact same genetic material, their fingerprints are unique.

How can this be? Modern science has no definitive answer, but we can infer the answer from ancient Jewish wisdom. Fingerprints are not just biological; they also are spiritual. Fingerprints are not just your handprints but also the prints of your soul. They are one way in which God puts a mark of uniqueness upon you. Note that God did not put this mark of my uniqueness on our elbows or on our knees. He put this mark on our fingers. And why? Because our fingers are metaphors for creating, constructing, making, and doing. The phrase "the work of our hands" does not refer only to carpentry. It describes an author crafting a book or an actuary compiling statistics as well.

Fingerprints are not the only difference, nor are they the most important; they are just one of the most physically undeniable, and a spiritual metaphor for our uniqueness. We each have our own skills, talents, abilities, and ideas. This is why business is so important— because it allows us to exchange what is different between you and me. I can do things you can't do and desire things you don't care about. You can do things I cannot do and desire items and events that leave me cold. But we can trade and thus enjoy each other's bounty.

In this way, we are able to help one another as we help ourselves while bringing connection, collaboration, and peace to our community.

Secret #9

We Love the People Whom
We Help More Than We Love Those
Who Help Us

ncient Jewish wisdom makes a point that the following example illustrates. A judge was once waiting for a bus in the rain
when another man walked up to the bus stop. The man had
been caught in the deluge and was soaking wet. The judge asked the
man if he would like to stand next to him under the umbrella. The man
thankfully accepted the shelter, and when the bus came, they both
climbed aboard. The next day the judge went to work as usual. The first
case he saw involved two people. One was a stranger, but the other was
the fellow whom the judge invited to stand under the umbrella. Immediately, the judge recused himself from the case, saying that he must
since he had offered this man shelter from the rain the day before; he
could not sit on this case. The judge who was being reassigned to the
case did not understand the first judge's reasoning.

"I don't understand. Had he let you under his umbrella, I would
understand you recusing yourself because you might treat him favorably
for the favor he did you. But why does it matter that you did a
favor for him?"

This second judge did not understand the following biblical business secret: doing a favor for somebody causes you to love him or her more. The first judge was well aware of this principle of ancient Jewish wisdom. He understood that he would, probably subconsciously, be inclined to show favor to the man whom he had helped. Because the truth is, when we do something for another person we become invested in them. We love those whom we help even more than those who help us.

Consider the parent-child model for more insight into this principle. Who should love whom more, parent or child? Parents do much—and in the early years, everything—for their children. Shouldn't children love their parents more than parents love their children? This seems logical. We would not even be here were it not for our parents. We would not be successful had they not raised us, clothed us, put a roof over our heads. We would not have been able to play soccer, or football, or go to ballet rehearsal, or anything else when we were young were they not there to drive us to practice or rehearsal. We would not have an education were it not for their care and support; nor would we have good jobs. Think about how much you owe your parents for room and board, dental work, nice vacations, your college education—for anything they ever did for you. It adds up to an incalculable figure.

And yet all around the world, thousands and thousands of therapists make a very good living listening to people complaining about how their parents destroyed their lives. This refrain is repeated again and again. Now we don't know about you, but in our family, if anybody wanted to claim that their lives were "destroyed," it would be the two of us, not our kids. We had a happy-go-lucky existence pursuing hobbies like sailing when we were younger. But when our first child was born, suddenly our lives weren't our own anymore.

We would not, of course, say that our children wrecked our life, because they did not. Our life would be far less rich without our children, and we love them and know they are a tremendous blessing, but they sure did change our lifestyle. At the very least our provisioning changed immensely as we loaded dozens of diapers on board! The point is this: if anybody has the right to tell a therapist that their life was ruined, it is parents, not children. The parents are the ones who make all the sacrifices. And yet, we know quite a few therapists who do pretty well listening to people complaining about their parents.

A few years ago, I [RDL] checked the Los Angeles County records to see how many cases there had been of parents evicting their children for not paying rent. It was an experiment I was running to confirm something I feared to be true. I couldn't find one case. I then did a search for cases of children evicting their parents. I found 11 cases, all of them in a short span of time, a four-year period. The record specialists allowed me to look through the transcripts of the court proceedings and filings where these landlords were trying to get a judge to evict their parent. In one case, the judge flat out accused the plaintiff of being a disgusting human being for throwing his father out of an apartment. The son responded by saying, "Your honor, you've got to understand, he hasn't been paying rent for the past three months!"

What did he expect the judge to say? "Oh, okay, now I understand why you want to throw your dad out on the street! Well, if he's late on the rent, by all means!" The judge was right: The plaintiff was a disgusting, ungrateful human being.

As you can see, the love of children for their parents isn't nearly as great as the love of parents for their children. This illustrates the truth of this biblical business secret: we most love those for whom we do things, far more than we love those who do things for us. We love most those in whom we invest.

The painful truth is that most people feel resentful when they are the recipients of benevolence from others. Consider those who receive government handouts. You might expect citizens who are on public welfare and supported by their fellow citizens to be the most patriotic citizens out there. You might expect them to be thankful and full of love for those who give them so much. But in fact, those citizens who receive regular weekly or monthly payments at the expense of other taxpayers are, across all societies and people, generally quite resentful and negative.

As human beings, we find it difficult to be grateful when we receive things for free. This is why expressions of gratitude are difficult. Expressing gratitude goes against our nature. Our instinct is to feel some level of discomfort about people doing things for us. One reason why so many children are often ambivalent about their parents is precisely because they owe them so much. On the other hand, parents have been doing nothing but giving to their children for years, instilling in themselves a sense of deep commitment to their children.

Paradoxically, parents can engender love in their children by demanding more from them. Children will love their parents more if the parents give them more responsibility and allow the children to be givers as well as takers. This is one principle behind the Fifth Commandment. God tells children to honor their father and mother because doing so allows children to discharge their debt and thereby feel less resentful toward their parents. Sharing in household chores is but one very important way to honor parents. Households in which parents have their children help with chores are more harmonious than households that employ outsiders or where the parents do all the work. When children do chores, they feel like, and are, an important and contributing part of the family. They become more invested in the family and love their parents and siblings more. It is important that everyone in a family helps and serves other family members. This keeps the family bonds strong.

This principle does, of course, transcend family dynamics. It also applies to business relationships. We must be ever vigilant to help our fellow man as much as we can. Often, we are the recipients of help. Yet, you may find that you begrudge people who have done many things for you if you have not helped them in return. Why? Because these people remind us of our own inadequacies. It takes great character strength and much goodness to love those who benefit us. However, there is a way to make this easier to do: simply pay back favors. Also, pay them forward to others. Do not let yourself be a burden on your fellow man.

If every one of us seeks opportunities to do favors for others, we need not feel bad when people do favors for us. This is also the best way to build your personal and professional network: seek out new friends by doing favors and allowing others to do favors for you. God looks favorably upon such behavior for it is His plan for human and economic interaction: building relationships between others and us by doing things for one another. If you begin to implement this strategy and technique today, it will pay infinite dividends in your personal and professional life.

The very first verse of the Bible, Genesis 1:1, reads: "In the beginning, God created the heaven and the earth." From the very first verse of Scripture, we see that heaven and earth, the spiritual and the physical, are linked. A principle that is true for heaven is also true for the earth and vice versa. For instance, a pile of uranium needs to be a certain size for a nuclear reaction to take place. This is what is known as critical mass. Critical mass applies not only to physical objects, though. On the spiritual level, a group of people gets a certain magical energy when it reaches a certain size.

As we have seen, bonding is how the physical world works. Bonding is also crucial to the spiritual world. Just as the element aluminum works best when bonded with other metals, so too do human beings perform best when bonded to other humans. Living life without spiritual connections is just as drab, brutal, and impossible as living life without physical connections. We need other people just as much as we need water, air, and food. We must increase our connectivity to really thrive.

How many different patterns can a single coin make when flipped? Two, right? It can land either heads or tails. Now, how about if we toss two coins simultaneously. Those two coins can produce four combinations: H-T, T-H, T-T, or H-H. It is fairly easy to see that if we added another coin to make three coins tossed together, we'd arrive at a total of eight different ways those three coins could fall. Now, what if instead of coins we used dice, each offering six options? Two dice thrown simultaneously could land in 36 different possible arrangements, and three dice would produce 216 possibilities. The more possibilities each unit has, the greater the consequence of throwing a few together.

Think of humans now, each with our own infinite list of possibilities and ideas. Throw us together, and the number of possible outcomes is almost limitless. Connectivity and constant cross-pollination drive the progress made by tech companies clustered in Silicon Valley or Boston's Route 128 high-tech corridor. These clusters exist because proximity promotes interconnectedness. As we previously mentioned, one explanation for Israel's extraordinary economic success is that the entire nation is so small and well interconnected that, as people say, "Everyone knows everyone here." Geographic proximity means that people more easily meet up casually at local restaurants and coffee shops, not to mention deliberate, planned get-togethers. If one person who can conceive of, say, 10 ideas in an hour of constructive thinking teams up with another person capable of the same creativity, in unison they don't come up with 20 ideas; they give birth to more like a hundred ideas.

Increasing your interconnectedness is the primary way of increasing your income. Spending time and energy building social connections is a vital step toward financial prosperity. You can adopt some simple strategies today that we absolutely guarantee will help you build wealth and improve your life. Increase the number of people in your life. Make new acquaintances. Develop your existing acquaintances into full-fledged friendships. Deepen your relationship with existing friends. In other words, devote some time each day to expanding and building upon your connections.

In order to know that you are improving an area of your life, you must be able to measure that improvement. You cannot effectively undertake a weight-loss program without a scale with which to measure progress. Making money and budgeting requires keeping financial records. Likewise, you will never improve your connectivity if you cannot measure it. You must track your connections.

Make a list of all the people you know well enough to telephone out of the blue. You probably have innumerable Facebook contacts and numbers saved to your phone, but you are only allowed to include people who would accept a phone call or call back if you left a message. Online-only friends don't count, unless you are housebound. Over the course of the next month, add new names to the list as you actively seek out new friends. Do this each month to keep a record of your progress. This monthly tally will allow you to gauge how well you are making new friends.

Making new friends is not something you do once and then forget about. Like hygiene and exercise, expanding your social network is an ongoing process. It requires maintenance and sustained effort, just like weight loss or any other healthy activity. You don't coast along on that wonderful meal you ate four years ago. Neither do you coast along on the friends you made back in kindergarten, high school, or college. Those friendships must be maintained, and new ones forged. The act of meeting new people and converting them into friends is an ongoing effort, but it will contribute to your health and wealth. Both doing for and accepting favors from others is an important way to foster those relationships.

Life Isn't About What You Know—It's About Who You Are

ociety has adopted the mistaken belief that knowledge can solve all problems. We are led to believe that young girls become pregnant because they lack sex education or that criminals commit crimes because they don't get a good education. The government mandates that the dangers of smoking be printed in great big letters on packs of cigarettes under the faulty notion that if people just knew the dangers of smoking, no one would smoke. When immoral doctors are charged with molesting patients, we bemoan the fact that they did not receive more continuing education courses on ethics, as if this would have prevented them from following their harmful desires. We are told that if everyone attended college, no matter their levels of literacy, work ethic, or preparedness, we would have no economic inequality.

On the face of it, all of these assertions and assumptions are patently false. The dangers of smoking, of not working productively, of abusing the doctor-patient relationship are all well documented and understood by most. These are not failures of knowledge; more often than not, they are failures of behavior. They are moral failures.

Even when we have perfect knowledge of the problems that we face, that knowledge does not relieve us of the problems without our own commitment to actions that can change our situations and ourselves. Knowledge alone is not the answer to anything. Knowledge will not make better choices for us.

Imagine for a moment that we had perfect knowledge of a societal ill. We know, for example, that alcohol and certain psychotropic drugs have the potential to create dangerous chemical dependencies and addictions that can ruin one's life. We know this is reliable information borne out as fact by countless scientific studies and empirical observation. Knowing this, what if we were to launch a public information campaign? Suppose we gathered funds and disseminated these facts about addiction by using billboards, television commercials, speaking tours at high schools and college campuses, and other means, sparing no expense when it comes to marketing. Perhaps you have seen some of these things done—they are quite common tactics. And yet, now that people everywhere know the grave facts about addictions, have we managed to eradicate alcoholism and drug abuse? Of course not. But many people believe that this will work, even though we have tried it repeatedly in utter futility.

The reality of our modern world is that knowledge and information are now more accessible than ever before. Look at the internet— knowledge has never been so cheap and readily available. And yet, have we seen improvements in our moral behavior? Do we make better choices for ourselves? No. Overall, we do not. The problem is that knowledge alone does not alter our behavior. The only thing that will change our behavior is making the right decisions, and the only way to ensure we do that consistently is to build up the strength of our characters.

We could very easily instruct you in what you should do to be healthy, just as we could instruct you in all the practical things you should do to amass wealth. But most people already know what they should be doing; they just fail to follow through. We know how to exercise. We know how to get a job and show up on time every day and constantly aim to do more than is requested. The hard part is not knowing what to do, but in doing it, day in and day out.

This is why our goal with this book is not just to tell you what to do to succeed in business—our goal is to arm you with the Bible-based techniques handed down by ancient Jewish wisdom that will allow you to build yourself up as a person and take ownership of your own character. Only then will you make the right choices, personal and professional, that you might already intellectually know you should make.

At the end of the day, what we know means little; it is who we are and what we do that matters. This is true in all aspects of life, but it is especially true in business. It is one of the great secrets of business that will lead you to success. Your teachers may have cared about what you knew, but your customers, employers, partners, and shareholders are not going to quiz you at the end of each financial quarter or at your annual performance review. They are simply going to look at what you accomplished.

The myth of knowledge solving all problems is repeated like a mantra in our culture. That many people believe something so erroneous is no reason for you to believe it, too. Do not buy into what is not true, especially when it inhibits your capacity to move forward, improve yourself, and increase your income. Repetition of a statement does not make it true. When assessing what we believe to be true, we must realize that there are multiple ways of looking at things. We must be sure that we are evaluating facts accurately and realistically, not based on popular opinion or assumption. Ancient Jewish wisdom is our guide here, as in all areas of life.

The Bible lays out all of this for us in many places, but one of the most famous examples is in the Ten Commandments, which are, of course, foundational, but increasingly less well known by most people in Western societies. The Ten Commandments are presented in chapter 20 of the book of Exodus and later recounted in Deuteronomy, where Moses reviews all that has befallen Israel during the past 40 years and discusses the moral implications of each event.

What matters to us here is that there is an important discrepancy between the Ten Commandments as they appear in Exodus and later in Deuteronomy. Namely, in Exodus 20:8, the Fourth Commandment says, "Remember the Sabbath Day." This is straightforward. Later, when Moses recounts the Ten Commandments in Deuteronomy, chapter 5, he proclaims the Fourth Commandment as "Guard the Sabbath Day."

Why this discrepancy? Does Moses have a bad memory? Is it possible that Moses thought that, at the time of the giving of the Ten Commandments, God said to guard the Sabbath Day? No, in Exodus, God clearly said "remember," not "guard," and Moses well knew that.

Moses did not have a faulty memory. Neither did all the people who listened to him recount the Ten Commandments. Why did they not "correct" him? Surely, they noticed the discrepancy.

So, which is it? How does the Fourth Commandment really read? The answer is that it reads both ways. Both ways are "right."

You may ask, how is this so? We'd like to suggest an analogy. Imagine that we ask someone to draw a teacup. Perhaps this person thinks of a teacup sitting in a saucer, and he sketches out his picture and hands it to you. He gives you a picture of two concentric circles, one inside the other. The drawing is from a perspective above the teacup. The outermost circle represents the rim of the saucer, and the inner circle is the rim of the teacup.

Overhead
view

Now imagine that we ask another person to draw the same thing—a teacup on a saucer. The second person gives you a side view. The drawing is of a vertical rectangle sitting atop a horizontal line, the ends curving up slightly as a saucer does. From this angle you can see the teacup handle.

Side view

Here we have two conflicting sketches of the same teacup. Which one is correct? You might say that since they don't match, one must be wrong. But they do not match only because they are from different vantage points. They are indeed drawings of the same teacup, but you need both perspectives to assemble an accurate image of a three-dimensional teacup in your mind. Even if you had never seen a teacup, by looking at both drawings and understanding that both were accurate, you could begin to form an image of one in your mind's eye . . . but only if you have multiple perspectives to study.

If you thought solely in two dimensions, you would say one drawing is wrong, but teacups exist in a complex, three-dimensional world. In fact, it is difficult to fully convey a three-dimensional shape on two-dimensional paper without using more than one drawing. If you are limited in dimensions, you need more perspectives to see the whole picture. If you are limited in a Godly dimension, as we mere mortals are, then you need more than one "drawing" on an earthly level to understand God's word.

Clearly both perspectives of the teacup are valid, and both are needed. So, it is with the Fourth Commandment.

It does not make sense to wonder whether God meant "remember" or " guard" regarding the Sabbath Day. The two perspectives given, one in Exodus and one in Deuteronomy, tell us that He meant both.

You might ask yourself how God could use two phrases at the same time. God lies beyond our abilities of full comprehension and conceptualization. Trying to concretize a concept that defies being pegged down or quantified or defined eliminates its usefulness as a concept.

Here is a more earthly example as an analogy. In mathematics there is a concept represented by the symbol i (like the letter of the alphabet) that equates to the square root of negative one. The square root of something is a value that when multiplied by itself is equal to the value of that something. So, for example, the square root of four is two. The square root of nine is three. The square root of 25 is five. And so on. What is the square root of negative one—the actual value? The square root of one is one, because when you multiply one by one, you get one. Simple. But what about the square root of negative one? What do you have to multiply by itself that will give you negative one? Take a moment to think about it, but if you want to save the pain. . . .

The answer is that there is no answer—or rather, there is no tangible answer, no exact answer, no quantifiable answer. In literal terms, there isn't such a thing. There is nothing that you can multiply by itself that will yield the answer of negative one because a negative multiplied by a negative, as any elementary math student used to know, gives you a positive. Therefore, it doesn't exist. This is why we have the concept of "i": to define and speak about a concept that is indefinable and, in a way, does not really exist. Because while the thing itself doesn't exist, the concept of it does.

You may wonder why we need a name for something that doesn't exist. Without getting too technical, it is because i is a very useful concept in mathematical computations. However, as soon as you try to visualize it, as soon as you concretize it in your mind and you say to yourself, "Now what does i actually look like on the number line?" you can no longer see it in your mind's eye. For some, this destroys their willingness to entertain that concept. If they cannot visualize something, trying to do so causes them to shut down the process. They can't comprehend such a thing, and so they insist it has no use when, in reality, it does if they would only look at it in a different way.

The problem with this way of thinking is that it limits you to the bounds of your own imagination. We don't all have equally strong imaginations, and closing off our minds to that which we cannot visualize limits our possibility for thoughts. Sometimes we do this because a thing is too hard or painful to imagine—for example, many cringe at the thought of eternity, which we cannot fully visualize and thus it frightens us. But eternity does exist as a concept, even if you cannot visualize it. You can think of eternity; you just cannot pin it down and see it in your mind. Doing so causes us to lock up and not try. It is beyond the power of the human mind.

It is sad but true that while reading or listening improves our minds, video entertainment suppresses our cognitive abilities. Naturally, those who spend unimaginable sums of money advertising on video media want us to spend as many hours a day as possible watching amusing videos on TikTok or YouTube. They even install brilliantly designed algorithms tailored to our interests to lure us. That this entertainment wastes our valuable time is bad enough, but it inflicts even more harm. It reduces our ability to remember information and process it quickly. It diminishes our powers of imagination and our ability to think abstractly but trains us to need to see things in visual form.

If you try to visualize or concretize God's word, you fail to see His word in its entirety—as concepts. God's word transcends the capacity of our minds. Our bodies have limitations, which wise people recognize. You are never, for example, ever going to be able to jump over a house no matter how hard you try because the acceleration required is beyond the ability of humans—even the best athletes can't come close. It's physically impossible. Our minds have limitations as well. There are some things we simply cannot fully conceive. We can't concretize them. However, if we leave them as theoretical constructs, we can still work with them. Just as with *i*, we can use them as reference points. We can accept their multifaceted meanings.

"Remember the Sabbath Day" or "Guard the Sabbath Day"? Exodus or Deuteronomy? Which is it? It's both. The truth is a synthesis of the two. How did God say both? Stop worrying about that. God does not speak in words with lips from clouds on high. God's words transcend the confines of written language. If you try to picture God, you limit your perception of Him. So don't try; it's a futile and worthless endeavor. All you must focus on is what ancient Jewish wisdom tells us about these two messages and how they synthesize, and how we should integrate them into our daily lives—you can't and don't need to pin them down to an easily visualized reality.

For 3,000 years now, Jews have guarded and remembered and held sacred the Sabbath Day by not working on that day. This is extraordinary: more than 3,000 years ago, God told the Israelites not to work on the Sabbath and still we hear His words and obey. Of course, not all Jews do this, but many do, in all countries, across all generations, after all these millennia, and overall, the chain of those who remain Jewishly connected through the generations runs through those families.

And they do so at great financial sacrifice, or so it would appear.

It is family knowledge that my [RDL] own grandfather had a business partner who was not Jewish, and who burst into the synagogue on Saturday telling my grandfather that they had a business opportunity to acquire the patent for an invention that would sell very well, but they had to move on the deal immediately. My grandfather told him that he would be available that night after the sun had set to work on the deal. His partner was furious, but my grandfather would not budge.

My grandfather did go seek out his partner after sunset, but it was too late. "You've blown it!" his partner said. "It's too late. The deal is gone!" It later turned out that the deal went sour, and investors lost a lot of money. But no one knew that at the time, and my grandfather truly believed he was turning his back on an opportunity. Remembering and guarding the Sabbath was more important.

It is extraordinary that people would do something for 3,000 years that, on the surface, is quite illogical by human standards. They take one day a week, and they quit working. So how did observance of the Sabbath remain so important all this time? The answer is, again, binary. There are two main aspects to understand. First, there is the instruction, plainly seen in Deuteronomy ("guard"). God is telling us what we must do. On that one special day a week, we do not expand our capabilities by artificial means. We don't drive or write or use our computers. We don't conduct business or travel. We have special prayers and meals and spend the day with God, our families, and our communities. That is how we guard the day. But, there is another aspect. We must remember the Sabbath Day, we are told in Exodus. *Remember* it. God is telling us to consider its context. He is telling us to remember the creation of the world in Genesis. God worked for six days and rested the seventh. If we want to emulate God, we must do the same. It isn't just following the rules of the day; we must remember the larger picture.

Observing God's word here brings us closer to the ultimate Creator. It allows us to be creators ourselves. We all know that sleep recharges us for the next day. In the same way, resting on the Sabbath recharges us for the following week, so that we can commit ourselves fully to our business enterprises. By observing the Sabbath, we can create, on our own mortal level, things such as a successful business, or an invention, or a work of art. For us to be creators, we must emulate Him, the ultimate Creator. We must remember that at the beginning, God sent us a message about creating for six days and pulling back from action for one.

You see, God is not just stepping out and issuing an order, but He is also giving us an internal philosophical structure and narrative so that we understand the entire picture of the Sabbath. In order to "guard," we must first "remember." Furthermore, by guarding the Sabbath each week by changing our normal activities, we are also simultaneously remembering. It is not enough simply to know what we should be doing; we must understand the context and fully internalize it so that we may build up our character in a way that allows us to really integrate His will into our lives.

Do you now see how knowledge alone is not enough?

The knowledge of what to do ("guard") is not enough; we must also remember so that we can know the context for what we are supposed to do. We do this by developing the character necessary to do it. We cannot just say to ourselves that we must lose weight; we must exercise and eat well and make it happen. We cannot just say to ourselves that smoking and drugs are harmful; we must take steps to move away from them. We cannot just say to ourselves that we want to make more money; we must take concrete steps to do so.

Secret #11

In Order to Achieve Success, We Must and Can Build Up Our Self-Discipline, Integrity, and Strength of Character

L et's consider weight loss. Why do so many of us who decide that we want to lose weight, simply not do so? Because very real pain is involved in adopting a new lifestyle that holds more sway over us than the imagined—the visualized—gain of future health, vitality, and improved appearance. We want these results, but they aren't real to us. We must imagine them. On the other hand, we strongly feel the pain of turning down dessert. When we pit real pain against imagined gain, real pain wins most of the time. We set ourselves up for failure when we ignore the way the human mind works. When we face immediate pain, we usually need more motivation than simply imagined gain.

We encounter a similar dilemma when we try to make more money. Earning money involves real pain. We know that going into work delivers us a paycheck or builds our business that will allow us to gather savings and create the lives for ourselves that we want. But the promise of accomplishing future financial goals is more distant than the fact that I must wake up when my alarm goes off, get dressed, and spend the day working. The payoff is distant and gradual and requires our imagination. On the other hand, distraction is right in front of us, often right in our hands. Ignoring those distractions to do something more productive causes real and immediate pain. Imagined gain is not the best self-motivator when change is so painful and immediate.

We need to find strategies that will allow us to overcome the pain of taking action. One way or another, we must equalize the struggle— our success as business professionals in any professional endeavor depends on it. But how do we do this? How do we overcome our human urges and flaws?

The book of Psalms contains a beautiful passage by King David that provides guidance. Psalm 34:13 reads beautifully in Hebrew: *Mi HaIsh HeChafeitz Chayim, Oheiv Yamim LiRot Tov?* "Who is the man who desires life, loves days to see good?"

King David answers his question in the next two verses. For our purposes, we'd like to focus on one phrase in his answer: "Depart from bad and do good."

Note the order. We are being given advice to stop doing what is wrong followed by doing what is right. King David was never tempted by the lure of social media, by pings letting him know that someone wanted to be in touch, by the appeal of finding out how many likes his words scored. He did not have 10 windows open on his computer seducing him to switch from one to another. We face those temptations each day. We know that we should focus on the person in front of us, that our to-do list needs attention, and that we must tackle our less pleasant, but necessary, tasks. But there are other, delightful and effortless choices calling our name.

We can make doing the right thing easier by first "departing from the bad." We can leave our cell phones in another room so that our hands don't reach for them almost subconsciously. Close all the windows on your computer when you are working on one job. Yes, it will take time to reopen them, but the time you save by not pursuing the fictitious and slowing-down activity of multitasking will more than compensate.

Make no mistake: this is hard. Ignoring the wrong path and doing the right thing is a choice that needs to be made over and over. It is a choice made in the moment. This is why Alcoholics Anonymous tells addicts to take it "one day at a time." However, each time you refuse to do the wrong thing and each time you choose to do the right thing, you strengthen your ability to continue to do so.

We face this dilemma constantly in the business world, where we are regularly challenged to do the right thing even when it is not always pleasant. It is hard to find the strength to make another sales call after you've made seven sales calls without closing on a single sale. This can destroy our confidence and ability to act. We may wish the phone would disappear. We may look for any reason not to have to make another call. We hope the person we are calling won't pick up. "Let them be out of the office," we pray. If we are really discouraged, maybe we quit work for the day. Maybe we shirk our responsibilities while on the clock. Selling is a great profession, but it is hard, as all salespeople know. But no one is paying us to do something that is easy! The hard part isn't making any single sales call. We know how to do our job and maybe we're even good at it. The hard part is showing up every day without fail, always smiling, always doing our best. This requires that we make ourselves into a strong person who can endure the tribulations of life and the workplace. Such is the life of the successful business professional. We must find a way to always be our best if we want to succeed in business or in any other endeavor for that matter.

This book is meant to give you the knowledge you need to make money just as generations of our people, Jewish people, have always done. However, if all we gave you was the knowledge and we failed to provide guidance on how to turn from the path of wrong and become a strong enough person to walk the path of good, then we would have given you nothing at all—because knowledge alone is simply not enough. You need to act upon that knowledge, and you need the character and strength to do so.

Your two goals as a business professional are (1) to learn to resist doing things that are easy and often enjoyable and (2) to become better at doing hard things that you are not accustomed to doing. This is the ancient Jewish wisdom borne out in the book of Psalms. This requires you to retrain yourself because people are not instinctively wired this way; we have to make an effort to do the right thing and think the right way. You must be proactive in business and in all areas of your life.

What is your morale like? Do you hear that word *morale*? What does it remind you of?

We'll tell you: moral. We can hear the stark similarity in the way the words *morale* and *moral* sound and recognize that they are related etymologically. Our morale is and has always been related to our sense of moral conviction and moral worthiness. This is why people so often declare that they are "a good person." We understand the need. We all want to believe that we are good people. We are not animals. We're human beings. Animals have no need to believe they're good. Animals are instinctive creatures; it is very simple to be an animal. Being human means having a desperate desire to know that your actions are good and moral. The occasional sociopath notwithstanding, the majority of us want to know that we are doing good and need to keep a monitor on our morale and how moral we are being. This requires us to avoid those things that make us feel distant from God and to do those things that make us feel closer to Him.

You may not be a religious person. That is fine. This book and advice is accessible to people of every background. Your religious affiliation is not important here. We personally come from a place that draws upon ancient Jewish wisdom, and so we speak and think in terms of morality bringing us closer to God and immoral behavior making us feel more distant from Him. But even if you are someone without a personal relationship with God, you are still able to relate to wanting to be a good, moral person. You probably have aspects of your life and self that make you feel good and virtuous, and at other times, you probably feel as though you have let yourself down. Surely you relate to this?

The important thing is not the language and terms you use or your philosophical positioning; the important thing is recognizing where you stand morally. Why do we say this? Because success in business and life depends upon your ability to withstand temptation. You must resist all temptation that may steer you wrong: the temptation to sin; the temptation to overeat; the temptation to sit another hour watching mindless television; the temptation to relax at the coffee shop instead of squeezing in one more sales call. You must resist all temptations that prevent you from realizing your goals and becoming your better self.

This is a two-way street: the ability to withstand temptation is closely linked to your sense of your own moral self-worth. Resisting temptation makes you feel better about yourself, and feeling better about yourself makes temptation easier to resist. Resisting temptation is easier when you truly think of yourself as a worthy, deserving person who is above bad behavior. It is hard to tell yourself that you cannot scroll through TikTok or see if there has been another "breaking news" story (which now occur regularly every second). But it is much easier to tell yourself that you are not the kind of person who misses out on a sales call or wastes all day. "Who do you think I am?" you say to yourself, indignantly. "No way would I do those things. Not me!" This is you positioning yourself morally, building up your character, making temptations easier to resist and good choices more appealing.

But beware: the reverse is also true. Succumbing to temptation and experiencing failure beget more temptation and failure. If you overeat, you may feel less like going to the gym because you feel like you already have blown it. The alcoholic who takes that first drink is more likely to keep drinking until he passes out. If you waste half a day at work playing on the internet, you are more likely to waste the second half because you already feel guilty anyway. You see yourself as a failure, and it becomes a self-fulfilling prophecy. You must break the cycle!

In Victor Hugo's *Les Misérables*, there's a marvelous scene in which a character teetering between a life of crime and a moral life steals some silver from a priest. Later, when the thief is caught, the priest spares the man and tells the policemen that the silver was not stolen but was a gift to the man. This act of mercy completely turns around the criminal's life. The priest, who is one of the most positive depictions of a religious figure in all of literature, understands that once the man is branded a thief, he will continue on that path. By not labeling the man as a thief and by proclaiming that he had stolen nothing, the priest helps build up the man's morality. The man will have a harder time stealing in the future. Victor Hugo understood what I am telling you: every time you stay firm to the moral course, every time you resist temptation, you will have an easier time resisting next time. Each time you surrender to spiritual gravity and act immorally, you will find it easier to continue to do so.

In Judges, chapter 14, we are told that Samson wants to marry a daughter of the Philistines. For a Jew to date a Philistine was simply unthinkable, and Samson knew this. Note that the Scripture here says,

"Samson went *down* to Timnah," where he met Delilah. He descended morally. Samson did so knowingly and so was complicit in his own downfall. This language of descent, no coincidence, is a consistent pattern in God's message to man. Spiritual gravity hastens our moral descent.

Delilah's primary loyalty is not to her husband, Samson, but to her Philistine former boyfriends. She asks Samson what the secret of his strength is, planning his undoing, but he lies, telling her that if she weaves seven locks of his hair into a loom, he will lose the strength God has given him. When he falls asleep, she does this, and then wakes him up, declaring that the Philistines are approaching and he must go fight them. Enraged, he smashes the loom, his strength still with him. Later, after much badgering, he tells her the truth: his strength comes from the fact that he has never shaven his head and to do so would be to turn his back on God. This time, before she wakes him to say that the Philistines are again approaching, she shaves his head while he is sleeping. When he goes out to fight them, not knowing that God has departed from him, he is captured.

In both verses where Delilah declares that the Philistines are there, Scripture tells us that "Samson awoke from his sleep." In the English translation, these verses look exactly alike, but in the Hebrew, they are quite different. The first time it is written, in Hebrew, there are five letters, including two *yuds*, the most spiritual letter in the Hebrew alphabet. In the second appearance, the same phrase is written, but with only four letters. The missing letter is that second *yud*, representative of God's spiritual strength. When both of these *yuds* are in place, Samson has not yet betrayed God by yielding to his wife's enticements. But the second time Samson wakes from his sleep, the word is missing a *yud*. We know that God is no longer with him and, furthermore, that his moral failure will result in a collapse of his morale. The missing letter signals that this is no simple awakening, but a shift in his reality. This is borne out again and again in the Bible: moral failure begets a failure of morale, which begets more moral failure.

The Bible is very clear on this. In Genesis chapter 38, Judah takes an unsuitable wife. They have three sons, two of whom sin, and God ends their lives. Shortly after, Judah is publicly humiliated for enjoying a one-night-stand. Let's put it this way: early events in chapter 38 do not show us Judah's best day. This misfortune is evident from a subtle word at the beginning of the chapter. The first verse says, "And Judah descended from his brothers. . . ." Judah *descended*. He fell from a higher moral condition. The Bible is speaking spiritually, not topologically; he is heading in a negative direction.

Unlike Samson, however, Judah takes painful steps to correct his missteps. Later in the chapter (verse 26) he confesses his role and exonerates his daughter-in-law whom he had earlier mistaken for a girl of casual liaisons. She goes on to give birth to Judah's son who will be an ancestor of King David.

How do we develop the strength that we need to maintain our morale and moral center? There are many ways and techniques. One is to allow yourself to celebrate small victories. Do not think victories are insignificant simply because they are small. As you have seen, good acts lead to more good acts and greater rewards. Every small victory lays the seeds for the next slightly bigger victory. And the reverse is also true. Small moral defeats and failures lead to more of the same. Don't focus too much on the individual points along the path but on the path itself. Make sure you are on the moral path.

Use small competitions and victories as motivating rewards. Build them into your day as little self-challenges. If you make a sale at work, count the days until your next sale. Then try to close your next sale in less time. Or try to close a slightly larger sale. It doesn't matter if the sale is only 1% larger. The important thing is not that little victory—it's the string of victories that you will accrue, each one a little bigger than the one before. You grow as you go. That's the big secret.

Another technique is to write your goals down on paper. I don't mean your overarching life goals; those are too big and far off to revel in. Write down small actionable tasks that you can complete in short order. List them on paper. Then, achieve them. Having them written out both focuses you on the tasks at hand and it also helps you to avoid procrastination. It's helpful to set a specific deadline when possible. Remember, small actionable tasks only. If you have larger projects, break them up into smaller pieces. Nobody carries out a large project in one fell swoop; break it down into steps and put them on a timetable. You will feel like a different person when you do these things. Make specific and achievable goals, step by step, and you will have motivators and daily reminders to continue to do so.

A final helpful technique is to impose external accountability on yourself. Remember, even if you are working for an hourly or weekly or monthly salary, you are in business. See yourself as the business professional you are. You may want to approach several people to be on the "board of directors" of your small self-company. Name your business if you like: *Me, Inc.* Me, Inc. needs a board of directors like any other business, someone to hold the company (you) accountable. For this position consider your spouse or children, a coworker, a friend, people whom you trust and respect and who want you to be successful. Consider these people as members of "your own *personal* board of directors."

Regularly give one or more of these people your list of tasks and ask them to hold you accountable. Create a timeline and share it with them so that if you fail to follow through, you will not let down only yourself, but them, too. This will motivate you because we all want to please and serve others.

Offer this same service to other people. Maybe you can fulfill this role for a coworker as they do for you. This is a tremendous kindness we human beings can do for one another.

We realize that cultivating your moral character is neither easy nor does it come naturally. Being a human being is hard, and being a human on the road to success is harder. But the prize is worth the toil. Making choices about your behavior is what it means to really *be* human. Animals act on instinct. In nature, we never see a lazy wolf or a lion who overeats. Only human beings have these faults and virtues. Only we humans must hone our discipline and persistence through education and training. Very little of what we must do to be successful comes naturally. But we do have the capacity for change and improvement because we humans are touched by the finger of God. Even if you are not religious, avoid thinking of yourself in animalistic terms. Try not to yield to "instinct." Doing only what you feel like doing is an animalistic way of being, and resisting temptation is a profoundly human quality. We see this repeatedly in the Bible.

Another story from Scripture illustrates this point: In Judges, chapter 7, God appoints Gideon to fight the Midianites, a mighty and terrifying army. Gideon raises an army of 32,000 men, but God tells him that he does not need so many. Instead, he needs fewer of the right sort of men—a tight, fast-moving, hard-hitting small group of people.

God emphasizes quality over quantity. Gideon reduces the force to 10,000, but God declares it still to be too large.

Gideon takes his 10,000 men down to the river after a long day's march to drink from the stream. The men are terribly thirsty, and they rush to the water. Gideon watches them like a hawk. He wanted to observe which men knelt down on their knees, as if in worship, and then lowered their heads to drink from river using only their tongues, not their hands. Those were rejected. The others, who didn't kneel, but crouched and raised the water to their mouths with cupped hands made up the final army. Gideon sent home all the men who knelt and put their heads down to the water, drinking from the stream just as animals do. He is then left with only 300 men with which to battle the Midianites. These men raised water to their heads instead of lowering their heads to the water, and these are the men who reserved the act of kneeling for worship alone. These 300 chosen men go on to a triumphant victory in battle because they are quality men with God on their side.

These men are blessed and chosen because they acted like men, not like animals, both at the stream and in all aspects of their lives. They are men who make their own choices about how they will behave, and who hold themselves (and their fellow man) accountable for their choices and their behavior. Remember this when you are choosing business partners—you want to surround yourself with men and women such as these, those that resist temptation and animal urges and move through the world like human beings. Choose partners who take responsibility for their actions.

Once when I [RDL]was a little boy, my mother served chicken soup, which I slurped directly from the bowl on the table. My mother demanded to know what I was doing. I told her I was drinking my chicken soup. "You're eating like an animal!" she told me. Stubborn, sassy, and stupid, I responded shamefully, "Well, so what if I'm eating like an animal? Maybe I am one." I don't want to tell you exactly what happened, but I will just confide to you that for the next few hours, I carried four finger marks on my cheek. I never drank soup that way again.

Why would my Jewish mother react so strongly? Because she understood ancient Jewish wisdom and knew that we must behave like humans. We must not act like animals, for animals have no moral compass. What distinguishes us from animals is our spirituality. And where is our spirituality? Our head is its reservoir, that container for our spiritual strength. Lowering your head down to the river, or to your chicken soup, is akin to saying, "I am an animal." This is why civilized people use cutlery: so that we may raise our food rather than lowering our spiritual being to a material level.

The lesson of Gideon is that victory requires us to act as humans, not animals. The military is an excellent analogy for business because, as in business, no one can pull off victory alone. There are no Rambos in real life. We must depend on our comrades and our partners to overcome our enemies. In Scripture, the historic enemies of the Israelites from so long ago are also depictions of the enemies that are found inside each of us that obstruct our triumph and block our success. Ancient Jewish wisdom shows us how the various enemies of the Israelites each represent a different aspect of spiritual gravity that pulls us down and prevents us from achieving what we know in our heads we need to do. In the case of Gideon, we are shown how to overcome our animal urges and how we must band together and trust in our friends, family, and business partners.

Nobody succeeds all on their own, not on the battlefield and not in the boardroom. What allows us to succeed, in life and in making money, are our connections to one another and the morale we get from following our moral conviction. It is the discipline and character we cultivate that makes it possible to work well together. Have you ever had a coworker who was an immoral person? We don't need to tell you that they were terrible to work with! Surround yourself with the right people. Then surround yourself with more right people. This is not a simple task. Remember Gideon, who had to first gather 32,000 men to find a mere 300 with whom he could work.

Remember the accountability principle we discussed earlier? Surrounding ourselves with people of moral character makes it easier to hold ourselves accountable and be moral ourselves. And together we become a rising wave. Teach these principles to your friends, partner, and your children.

Deuteronomy 11:19 says, "And you shall teach these to your children," meaning God's precepts and rules. Do not fail to pass these principles and their meanings on to other people in your life as well. The Hebrew text offers an expanded understanding of what you are asked to do. Many passages in Scripture that instruct us to teach things to our children read: "and you shall teach them to your children," or use similar words. What many people fail to realize is revealed by Deuteronomy 11:19. The word "them" is spelled differently from its usual way. There is a letter missing, which changes this four-letter word to a three-letter word and also provides a second meaning to the word. It can now also mean "you" so that an alternative reading of that verse is: "And you shall teach them to yourself and to your children."

In other words, there is an obligation placed on each one of us to master these principles. Build your own character and moral center and then you will be ready to pass them along and share them with others. But do not forget: your actions and character must start with you.

Secret #12

Your Authentic Identity Requires Other People

A common trope in popular literature proclaims that man needs to escape into isolation in order to find himself. We see this popularized by Henry David Thoreau, who lived alone in a cabin by a pond, and Jack Kerouac, who popularized the "being alone on the road" narrative. Perhaps you yourself have romanticized the notion of seeking a guru on a remote Himalayan mountain peak or disappearing to a desert island. As crime and violence are on the rise in cities around the world, many of us feel the yearning for a homestead in a remote area, separate from all but our immediate family.

This is understandably seductive but misguided. It might be a needed emergency tactic, but it isn't sustainable in the long run. The truth is this: You can only find yourself when you are among others. Isolation doesn't work. People go crazy in isolation. In such a state, what you find is not your identity at all but a distorted perception because you lose perspective on yourself without others around. Our identity hinges upon connections to other people.

After a Jewish marriage ceremony, the bride and groom do not bid farewell to their assembled wedding guests and depart for a honeymoon where the two of them can be alone for a week. On the contrary. A Jewish wedding is followed by a full week of festivities during which the new couple attend a different party given in their honor every night. These celebrations are thrown by friends and family, keeping the new husband and wife surrounded by their community as the foundations of their marriage are being laid.

At the opposite end of the emotional spectrum, a similar seven-day period follows the death of a close relative such as a parent. A period known as shiva is observed by Jews, as the community comes to sit with them to share in their grief. In such a painful and trying time, the presence of others best helps one to navigate from a world that included the departed to a new reality, reshaping an identity with that person no longer in one's physical orbit.

Most of us need occasional periods of solitude. This is especially true for the introverted. However, it is important to avoid viewing the alone time as the "real-you." Sadly, there is no shortage of stories that start with the words, "I left my husband and kids to find myself" or "I quit my job and said goodbye to my family to discover who I really am." Life is full of paradoxes, and this is another one. You might think that by removing yourself from all other people and their influences the real you is free to emerge. What more often emerges is psychological disintegration. Who the real you is can only be developed and observed in the interactions you experience with other people.

How many of us, as teenagers, swore that we would be better parents than our own parents? We would never do with our children as they had done with us. When pregnant for the first time or holding a newborn miracle in our hands, we promise that we will shower this baby with love and warmth. Somehow, a few years down the road, most of us lose our temper and misuse our words with the now willful, disobedient, and taxing toddler that baby has become. By the time our children are teenagers, we hear our own parents' words coming out of our mouths, and what is more, we understand why they insisted on not allowing us to do whatever we wanted to do.

Of course, we should aim to be the best parents we can be. We should work on managing our tempers and our words. The point here is that it is easy to spout great theories and declare that we believe in certain ideas in isolation. When theory hits reality in the real world with other people involved, to our dismay we discover that living up to those ideals is not easy. Sometimes, our ideals (I'll never tell my child no!) are wrong. They don't work in the real world. Only when we test our ideals among other people can we see the difficulties and flaws in living up to them.

Our friend, Princeton Professor Robert P. George, regularly challenges his students. He asks them to imagine themselves as growing up as the children of slave owners in early 1800s in the United States. He then asks them to raise their hands if, upon inheriting the plantation from their parents, they would have freed all their slaves. Every hand goes up. Professor George then asks a follow-up question. Raise your hand if you can tell me of a time since you are in college, when you publicly opposed the commonly accepted way of thinking. Almost no hands go up. The students' image of themselves as independent and courageous individuals falters when it must exit their imagination and be tested in front of their peers.

How many of us have great business ideas? We know that this product will make us rich. As many a new entrepreneur has discovered, our imaginary customers do not always materialize. There are many steps between a business idea and business success. We need to stop focusing on what we think and instead discover the strength of our idea through the eyes of other people.

This idea of our identity existing in relationship to others appears early in Genesis. Consider the Adam. (We are deliberately writing "the Adam" because that is an accurate translation of the Hebrew. This may refer to both the future Adam and the future Eve.) He finds himself alone in the Garden of Eden. Never has a human being been so alone on the earth and never again will he be. In the book of Genesis, chapter 2, verse 18, God says, "It is not good for man to be alone." This isn't just a statement about Adam's matrimonial prospects. What He is telling us is that if you were the last person on earth, life would be miserable. Living alone is an absolute misery.

After making this declaration that it is not good for man to be alone, we expect God to make a mate for Adam. To our surprise, instead of doing so, He brings all the animals that He has created, all the beasts of the field and all the birds of the sky to Adam. Rather than introducing them to Adam by name, He gives Adam the task of naming each one. This is the first service man provides.

God wanted Adam to recognize that none of his existential loneliness can be resolved by any of the many creatures he encounters. There is a relationship between mankind and animals, but it is not equal. By giving Adam the responsibility of naming the animals, God is placing Adam above those creatures. The names reflect how man sees the animals, not how animals see themselves. In Hebrew, each animal's name reflects this.

Naming is a prerequisite for a relationship. Upon meeting a stranger, we extend our hands and, rather than saying, "I'm a plumber" or "I'm a pediatrician" we say, "I am Tom" or "I am Brittany." Even in our contemporary world, it is hard to form a relationship if no names have been exchanged. Thus, in order for the animal world and the human world to enjoy an interface, a naming protocol must occur. Only after it is clear that man and animals have a relationship, but not one that is ultimately satisfying, does God bring the woman to Adam. Upon seeing this bewitching creature, Adam understands that each of them, man and woman, get their identities in relationship to each other. Adam names this new being Isha. At the same time, he recognizes that his own identity is revealed only through her presence in his life. In the verse where he gives the woman a name, he gives himself one as well. Up until now he has been called Adam. He now has a new identity—he is an Ish. Reciprocal in a way that Adam's relationship with animals is not, here he and Eve both acquire new identities by virtue of their bond with one another. (Why did Adam name Eve rather than Eve name Adam? Perhaps they should have sat down over a cup of tea and jointly come up with names? We answer that question in our book, *The Holistic You*.)

In our work in the marital counseling field, we have observed that early challenges during the first year or two of marriage are often due to the new husband and wife not understanding the extent to which the person they married is not the same person that they dated or to whom they were engaged. Bonding with others impacts us at a deep soul level.

The lesson here is that by connecting with other people, by making commitments with other people, by establishing obligations between ourselves and others, we discover and hone our own identity. Alone we cannot know who we are. We cannot know who we will eventually become as we set out in life because it is our connections and relationships with others that mold us. As you set out in life and business, making connections to people who will steer the course of your life and character, choose these people carefully. When it comes to meeting new people, cast your net wide. Meet a wide variety of people so you will find those who allow you to grow as you want.

This is one of the greatest secrets of business that the Bible gives us. It is through human connection that we find ourselves and grow. Choose your colleagues and business partners based upon how you want to be and whom you want to be.

Know How Business Works; Understand Specialization and Cooperation

Thinking here is a widespread belief among the general population that business is unfair. Maybe you have met people who believe this. These misguided souls believe that business is inherently unfair simply because they see some people who do better in business than others. They assume that anyone who has more must be greedy. Business is bad, these naysayers of the free market suppose, because it rewards greed. If you are reading this book, we hope that you do not hold similar views. But many do. Ask people in your various circles about this, and you may be shocked at how many buy into this misguided notion. In fact, you may subconsciously believe this as well, even though you wish you didn't. This belief comes from a misunderstanding of what business really is.

Many books have been written that examine why some nations enjoy more successful economies than others. To name a few: *The Wealth and Poverty of Nations*, by scholar David Landes; *Why Nations Fail*, by James A. Robinson; *Civilization: The West and the Rest*, by Niall Ferguson; and *Guns, Germs, and Steel*, by Jared Diamond. We recommend all these books for insight into this topic: that differences in economic performance are chiefly dependent upon spiritual rather than physical characteristics. This is as true for individuals as it is for nations. The most significant factors in our success are things we have the power to change.

These books show us why some countries perform better than others do. When separate nations are bound by the obligations of economic alliances, as in the European Union, this can lead to the less efficient state leaching off the stronger state. For instance, in some years, 80 million Germans finance the siestas, supermarkets, railways, and retirements of 120 million Greeks, Spaniards, Portuguese, and Italians. Germany is by far the largest contributor to the budget of the European Economic Community. In most years, Germany exports twice the total of Greece, Portugal, Spain, and Italy all put together. Germany's BMW routinely sells close to $100 billion in cars while in some recent years, Italy's Fiat wasn't able to achieve 40% of its already anemic sales targets. Greece doesn't even manufacture bicycles, let alone cars. Germany literally pays for Greece and Spain to take it easy.

But why does Germany's economy function better than Spain's? Why do Scandinavian countries work better than Venezuela? Why does Singapore work better than Suriname? Why does most of North America work better than most of South America? What causes these differences? Climate, geography, and natural resources have an effect, but the wealth and poverty gap observed between countries is predominately the result of differences in culture. As all interested readers can easily determine for themselves, culture is the defining difference. Other factors, while real, are insignificant by comparison.

Culture is influenced by the language with which people of that culture communicate. Culture and language color each other. French is the language of romance, whereas Russian lends itself to brooding epics about the darkest side of human nature; these differences result in a noticeably different aesthetic in the art originating from these countries. Language helps define mood and political atmosphere as well. The differences found within languages give us insight into the priorities of that culture. Different languages allow for different ideas to be communicated, and this has an impact on the lives and mindsets of the speakers of that language.

As God's language, Hebrew has a very privileged position—it gives us insight into God's culture. By studying Hebrew, we can intuit what God deems important and proper and right.

Let's look at an important concept regarding money—the idea of earning it versus winning it. English clearly allows for delineation between "winning a sum of money" and "earning a sum of money." This allows English speakers to discuss the difference between earning and winning—indeed, it allows for a distinction to be made at all. Now consider Spanish. In Spanish, there is a phrase, *ganar dinero*. *Dinero* means "money" and *ganar* means "winning or earning money." French is similar. Their phrase is *gagner argent*. There are no distinctions between winning and earning. Whether I go to a casino and win money or spend the day laying carpets and earn a paycheck, the language allows for no distinction to be drawn. In effect, they are the same to the speaker and listener.

Hebrew doesn't even have a word for "winning money." Why not? When you earn money in a consensual way, both you and the person who pays you the money are winners. You each have what you value. Gambling, whether in a casino, at races, or in a government sanctioned lottery, is entirely different. There are winners and losers, and everyone gambling wants to be the winner. By definition, this means that they hope that other people will lose. Getting money in that fashion is ungodly. When a customer walks out of a store with his purchase in hand after having handed over his money to the proprietor, he is happy. When a gambler walks out of a casino emptyhanded after having paid his money to the roulette croupier, he is far less happy. To recap: French and Spanish make no distinction between winning and earning; English uses separate words for both; Hebrew has a word only for earning.

Which of these languages positions the speakers best to earn money? Obviously, those who absorb Hebraic culture have an edge. The language reveals a concept that sets one up to facilitate earning money.

When we earn money, everyone benefits: the one who earns the money and the one who makes a purchase so that he may receive a service or product. When you hire a tax accountant, he gains a paycheck, and you gain a correctly completed tax return without hours of stress and frustration. God smiles on the transaction because both the accountant and the customer are better off from doing business together. It is beautiful. Two human beings have come together. They collaborated. They created something. The accountant walked away with his wage; the person paying him can spend his time doing something else while being helped by professional knowledge that he doesn't possess.

Winning money does not create happiness for all involved. When you win money, you are taking it from someone *without earning it*. If you and I play poker and we both put $100 into the pot and I walk away with $200 and you have nothing left, have I earned money or simply taken your money? Was anything created? Was a good or service brought into creation? Are all participants equally happy? The answers are no, no, no, and definitely not. I won; you lost. That is how winning money works, and that is why winning money is such a bad idea. A language or a culture that combines the two words, *earning* and *winning*, implies that they are the same thing. They are not. Not even close. Obviously, people who play, shall we say, poker, for low stakes, for the pleasure of enjoying a congenial game with friends, are not the focus of this discussion. However, playing games of chance with anyone for whom losing will cause a real hardship or who will be downcast because of that loss is a different matter.

This is just one example of how language affects culture. You may draw your own conclusions about how this effect influences societies. Just note that in England, where they have a word for winning and earning, people have thrived. The industrial revolution was launched in England, not in France or Spain. Why? Partially because it was driven by the potential of earning money, and cultures that draw a distinction between the two words are better positioned to appreciate the power of money. If you integrate this truth into your everyday life, it can help you.

As we can see, even the language that forms Jewish culture encourages making money by serving God's other children. The Torah, the Five Books of Moses, contain far more laws about money than laws about kosher food, the dietary laws, about ritual, or about anything else. Why would the Torah have more rules about money than anything else? Because ancient Jewish wisdom recognizes that earning money is essential to life. Each and every one of us must eat and put a roof over our heads and care for our families, which means we must earn a living.

Whether we go it alone or collaborate with other people, we must earn a living. We discover pretty quickly that going it alone is a terrible way. Engaging in business with other people is thrilling, exciting, and effective. God wants us to collaborate, and so he makes it more effective to do so. He has put collaboration at the center of the moneymaking process by giving us the principles of business. If we want to succeed in business, we must understand these principles. This is what it means to understand business. You fail to do so to your own detriment. Now that we have gotten further in this book, let's review this important point discussed in Secret #1. Trying to go it alone in business is like swimming against the current. In the eighteenth-century Western world, Englishman Adam Smith identified the concept of specialization. Smith observed that specialization provided advantages over independent living. In villages where everyone does everything for themselves, people must sew their own clothing; look after their own cows for milk and after their own chickens for eggs; grow their own carrots and potatoes. Everybody takes care of all of their own needs. As you can imagine, this is exhausting and allows no time for pursuing extra work or leisure—it is a harsh life. And it is lonely. In such a village, the people don't need to ever get together because they are independent, and everyone is self-sufficient. But they are also tired and always working, terribly inefficient, and isolated from their fellow man.

This apparently was not part of God's plan for human economic interaction. As we saw in the last chapter, God doesn't want man to be alone. It doesn't work well.

Imagine two farmers working independently on neighboring farms. They never see each other because each has everything they need on their own farm. One day, they bump into each other and visit each other's farm. One farmer notices that the other has better cows that provide the most creamy-looking milk. He asks to try some and notices that it is richer than the milk from his cows. But he also notices the other farmer's rough, scraggly clothes. He asks about them and realizes that this farmer has inferior wool and little knowledge of sewing and weaving.

Pretty soon the wheels start turning in their heads. They realize that one is better at raising cows and producing dairy products, and the other better at raising sheep and making wool and clothes. They decide to exchange wool for dairy products. And—boom!—commerce is born! This goes on for a while, but then they realize that the farmer making wool doesn't need his cows anymore and the one making milk and cheese doesn't need his sheep. So they exchange those too! They no longer have to tend to these animals, and they have more time to focus on what they are good at. And—boom!—specialization is born!

This is an oversimplification, of course, and in modern culture we are far more specialized so that only a small percentage of the population needs to farm *at all*. But in economic terms, this model illustrates how specialization works. The farmer who is no longer raising sheep still has wool. He also now has more cows and time to produce extra dairy to trade for even more products, allowing him to further specialize and reinvest further time and energy in his burgeoning dairy business. The same for the other farmer—his wool business is taking off!

Furthermore, every time these farmers get together to trade, they talk to each other and exchange ideas. One day, in conversation, they realize a third farmer down the road has the best potatoes around. Together, they come up with the idea of cutting this new farmer in on their trades. Again, they are now all able to further specialize. The more people they trade with, the more they exchange products and ideas and the more everyone prospers. The whole process is viral.

Adam Smith observed and described this process of specialization in 1776 and realized that even in the limited experimental arena in which he was able to observe, geysers of economic productivity were let loose. More countries throughout the Western world recognized and implemented this knowledge on a grander scale than had ever been done before, but it was already a part of ancient Jewish wisdom.

As we noted in the beginning of this book, we see this idea as early as the book of Genesis, when we look at the end of the life of our patriarch, Jacob. Before Jacob died, he gave individualized blessings to his 12 sons, noting their particular traits and attributes. Jacob basically told his children: "You're all the children of Israel. You must all be unified. But each and every one of you is going to fulfill a different function. Some will be in business. Some will provide scholarly research and spiritual functions. Some will provide shipping and transport."

Each son, and eventually each tribe that they fathered, would provide their own specialty, and in this way, their individual needs and the needs of their fledging nation would be supplied collectively. None of them were meant to be independent. Each of them needed the other 11. They were thus tied to one another, combined if you will, the children of Israel were launched, and down the road the economic power of the Jewish people experienced exponential growth—thanks to specialization, trade, and collaboration. When you make yourself interdependent with other people in this way, as Jacob told his offspring to be, there's no stopping you. Each of you can do something, but together all of you can do everything.

This is what business looks like. These are the principles on which ethical capitalism functions. To bring us full circle, we ask, "What is unfair about this?" Everyone contributes, and everyone reaps rewards. Everyone contributes differently, driven by their own desires, hard work, and ability, and thus they reap different rewards based on their talents and effort.

The answer, of course, is that there is nothing unfair about it at all. People who feel differently are reacting emotionally rather than analyzing how business professionals make their money. However, these same people usually understand how NFL football players make their money. You very seldom hear politicians preaching the politics of envy against football players. You never hear them saying, "That football player got a 60-million-dollar contract! That's not fair. He's got to pay his fair share!" You don't hear politicians speaking like that about football players. But you do hear this type of language used about business professionals. You hear complaints that the chief executive officer (CEO) of a company makes a hundred times more than the janitor, but never do you hear that a football player makes a hundred times what the groundskeeper makes, though they do make that much more, if not even more. It's the same with movie stars and pop stars. Have you ever heard a politician say that these movie stars making $20 million for three weeks of working on a movie don't deserve it? No. But when we find out a CEO has made that much, politicians demand to know why. They demand to know how much he paid in taxes—and they are never appeased with the amount; they always want him taxed more.

Everywhere you look, business professionals are demonized for making lots of money while football players and celebrities get a free pass. Perhaps this is because the general populace understands why a football player gets paid so much. He can throw a ball farther than anyone else, or he runs very fast, or he is good at scoring goals. These are simple activities, and we can observe them. We see the thing that makes him distinctive, which also earns him his money. We all recognize that we cannot do what he does, and so we admit that he deserves his lavish compensation. Hollywood actors are the same: they are especially beautiful or charismatic, and we can see that they are a rarity, and so we believe that they are worth the millions of dollars they make. And make no mistake, they are! These people have rare talents and skills, which they have fairly leveraged for handsome pay. There's nothing wrong with that.

But what about the highly compensated business executive? Does he not earn his keep, too? Top CEOs also make a lot of money, often more than actors and football players. The richest people in the world are almost all business professionals, not entertainers. Now consider the CEO's case. The average person looks at a business executive and wonders what is so special about him that he can command a salary of millions of dollars. They think, "What does he do? He sits in the corner office on the top floor, talks to people on the phone, and that's it. I can do that! Anyone can do that!" This isn't usually true, but it is what people feel.

This is one reason business professionals are so easy to demonize: because many people do not understand what a talented and proven CEO brings to the table. Many fail to grasp the importance of the reputation that he brings. He brings competence and leadership. He brings understanding, administrative ability, expertise, and savvy. He brings connections with other people. People often do not easily understand how much this is worth. They do not see the tremendous value that a capable and experienced CEO brings to a company.

In 1991 and 1992, one of the great brokerage houses of America, Salomon Brothers, was in regulatory and financial trouble and starting to fail. The highly paid executives who'd performed poorly and run the company into the ground were fired, and the company needed a replacement. Whom did they get? They brought aboard Warren Buffett, whose Berkshire Hathaway already owned about 12% of Salomon, to become the head of the brokerage house. They wanted him to save the house. How much was he worth to them? There was almost no limit! He could've asked for anything he wanted because he was going to save a whole company.

So how did Warren Buffett do this? How did he, specifically, save the whole company? He did so through the magic of human connection, through the magic of reputation, through the magic of understanding and knowledge. The global business community realized that Warren Buffett was going to be in charge, a man with a remarkable track record, and so they continued to extend credit to the company. And the company was thus saved by the confidence that creditors, the government, and the markets placed in this one man. The world had faith in him. That's right. It's all about faith and reputation and a solid track record of doing good business, but many people find that hard to understand.

They just don't get it. Football players they get. Movie stars they get. He can really swing a bat! She has a face like no other! But when a business professional makes an equivalent sum of money, people don't get it. They just see a man in a suit in an office, a man that maybe looks nondescript like everyone else, and people don't bother to understand what he does or brings to the table. But they could if they tried, if they did a little independent research, if they bothered at all. If you are going to be taken seriously in the business world, you must take the business world seriously. Give your due diligence to understanding business or you will have no place in it.

There is another reason why people are suspicious of business and those who run companies, that does need to be mentioned. This reason, however, is sadly justified. Just as there are immoral poor people, there are also immoral business titans. The latter, however, possess the power to cause far more damage. One avenue pursued by companies that become very large and accumulate vast cash reserves is what the nineteenth-century British economist David Ricardo called "rent-seeking." This means that they collude with imperfect political leaders to manipulate regulatory agencies to give preference to their own businesses while hobbling or sometimes destroying their competitors.

The corruption of parts of the pharmaceutical industry became blatantly evident with the advent of COVID-19 in 2020. Collusion between government agencies, medical bodies, and drug manufacturers contributed to the opioid crisis that started sweeping parts of America in the mid-1990s with the prevalence of the drug OxyContin, promoted by Purdue Pharma and approved by the Food and Drug Administration. We see the government favoring and supporting industries such as electric cars while weighing down other industries with senseless regulation. Collusion between government and tech companies is damaging democracy around the world. These cases and many others involve collusion between business professionals, bureaucrats, and politicians that greatly enriches the players while bringing pain instead of benefits to everyone else.

Don't let the immoral and corrupt behavior of these oligarchs and manipulative individuals stop you from aiming to achieve business success, any more than you should allow knowledge of someone who beats his wife to stop you from getting married. Strengthen your own character so that when you are blessed with wealth you do not succumb to evil—and then get on the road to creating that wealth. You do want a place in the business world. Or you should. Business is a spiritual endeavor, and it brings us closer to one another and closer to God. Business is one of God's plans to keep us connected with each other and moving toward that vision of greater unity that is God himself.

Consider again our farmers from earlier: the wool farmer, the potato farmer, and the dairy farmer. These were isolated individuals forced to take care of themselves independently. But now they are part of a community, a co-op. Specialization has brought them together. And now it keeps them together. They now need each other. If one gets sick, the others will definitely be there praying for his rapid recovery because they are dependent upon him. Before, if one got sick, nobody cared because, economically speaking, it didn't matter. It wouldn't have mattered on a personal level even because without business to bring them together, they did not even know each other. But now they are all bound together into this invisible network of human connectivity that compels them to love each other. It is a fact that people who trade don't usually fight. Trade reduces the incidence of wars.

You can see God's hand guiding us toward business by how he has structured the world and mankind. He created man with almost limitless yearnings. We yearn for the infinite. We have infinite desires. But he also placed man into a world with apparently limited resources. There's only so much real estate, so many fish in the sea, so much oil in the ground, and so on. Most importantly, there is only so much time in the workday. It is only by following God's rules of ongoing and constant cooperation that we can create enough for everyone. Going it alone condemns us to a constant struggle for survival. Clearly, God has set up the world in mysterious and counterintuitive ways, but we can intuit his motivations here through ancient Jewish wisdom. Limited time and resources require us to be generous and giving to one another, to cooperate.

There have been other attempts to solve the problem of extracting a living from the world. They do not work. Isolation and independence do not work well. Communism coerces us to work together in unnatural ways. God finds these systems evil and has arranged for them to ultimately fail—the game is stacked against them by Him. There has never once in the history of the world been a communist nation that has been successful, and there never will be. It is only the voluntary cooperation between people that ethical free market capitalism encourages that finds favor with God, which is why it is the only economic system that works.

The wise and moral person accepts these truisms and truly understands business and economics as God intended them to look and be. Others struggle to understand how business works, how it works now, and how it has always worked. To swim against the current is futile and will find you in disfavor with God and ultimately unsuccessful at making money, no matter your endeavor.

Secret #14

Every One of Us Is a Business Professional

As we have said previously, you must begin to see yourself as in business now. Not later. You do not need an employer or the stock exchange or the IRS or anyone else to grant you legitimacy. It is a frame of mind you may simply adopt. If you trade your time, your skills, services, or products for financial gain, you are in business. You are a business professional. Regardless of what you do to serve humanity, you should strive always to be a business professional, not an amateur. It doesn't matter whether you are an executive or in retail. If your innate talent is that of a rodeo clown, by all means go out and be the most professional rodeo clown that ever existed. But do not be an amateur rodeo clown.

So what is a professional? How do you become one?

First and foremost, a professional is someone who does the work that he must do when he must do it. Do your work and do it on time. Wise King Solomon said in Proverbs 22:29, "If you see a man who is quick to do his work (prompt to do his work, not when he feels like but when it needs to be done) you are looking at a man who's going to stand with kings; . . . ." Promptness to do your work, doing what you must do, not what you want to do, is the mark of the true professional.

The professional busies himself with business, his true work.

Just because one is not idle does not mean one is actually working. It is actually quite easy to keep busy, but you must be sure you are busying yourself with the task for which you are actually being paid. This is easier to see in our day than it was in earlier times. How many of us have fallen into the trap of thinking we would start work as soon as we "just checked email," or "just took a quick glance to see who texted me," only to discover we were starting our day an hour late? We are faced with potential distractions in a way that earlier generations never were.

However, one can delay getting to work even when we think we are working. There was once a man who worked for me [RDL] as a sales professional, who used to produce the most beautiful graphs and charts. His job was to seek out new customers. Several times a week I would ask him, "When are you going to get started on those sales calls?" He had yet to do one. He told me he just had to finish a chart of all the potential customers in the region. The next day he gave me a chart with colors and tables and references. It was beautiful. I didn't even know how he had made it. I asked him, "Are you now ready to make sales calls?" He shook his head no. "I've just got to do a graph that'll show me which are the most potentially profitable customers," he said, nodding his head and clearly excited about his "work." He soon brought me a new graphic detailing where to find the best customers.

The thing about this man is that he was always busy. Whenever I went by his office, he was working. I never saw him around the water cooler. I never saw him hanging out in the break room. He was working and working and working—always. But guess what? I fired him. He wasn't doing what he *must* do. He was doing what he *wanted* to do. He just loved playing with Microsoft Excel and making graphs and charts. But he wasn't producing any value at all because he wasn't doing what needed to be done when it had to be done. He wasn't doing what we had hired him to do. This is not the mark of a professional. Resist the temptation to do only what you want, and do what you must do, and you will find the favor of your employer, your fellow man, and God.

We know a number of ex-government employees who quit their jobs because they weren't allowed to behave as professionals. When they diligently attended to their jobs, it annoyed their coworkers. "You will make us look bad. Take more breaks." Often, there was not enough work to justify the number of employees. However, unlike a business that needs to show a bottom line, government agencies do not go out of business because of mismanagement. Eventually, these workers realized that although the job was well paying, with great benefits, it was leading them to despise both themselves and their fellow citizens. They saw themselves as taking money rather than earning it and began to feel contempt for those whose taxes paid them. The opposite of a professional attitude.

The Latin root of *amateur* is from the Latin word *amor*, which means "to love." That's what an amateur is: someone who does only what he loves doing. A professional learns to love what he must do. He takes his professional life seriously. There is a time for play and a time for socializing and a time for hobbies and a time for family—but guess what? The time for all of those things is not when you are working on your business. When you are on the work clock, you need to be working. A professional takes his work seriously all of the time, full time.

A professional doesn't look for work that he loves; he makes himself love his work. Reporters on radio and TV are always asking people about their work and how they feel about it—maybe you have seen or heard one of these little segments. They interview people in all kinds of professions—doctors, policemen, firemen, businessmen, whoever. Inevitably the interviewer asks, "If you had to do it all over again, what would you choose to be?" You can tell that the interviewer expects them to say something grander, like a politician or an artist or actor or something. They expect the interviewees to say they would have picked a profession with more prestige and pay. Overwhelmingly, most people say they would do the same thing all over again.

Did all of these people luck out and just happen to find their one true calling? No. What are the chances? The fact is they were professional about their careers. And when you're a professional, you invest in your career; you set and accomplish your business goals; and, in the process, you end up loving it. As a professional, you do not find work you love—you find a way to love your work. You may not start off loving it, but by investing in your work, you begin to love it. Just as investing in people leads you love them, this is also true for work. Investment in your work leads to commitment, which leads to love for your work.

It's no accident that at the beginning of Genesis, chapter 2, verse 15, God put Adam into the Garden of Eden and said *"Le-Ovdah,"* which is Hebrew for "to work it." This may come as a surprise. After all, everything came easily in the Garden of Eden. What work was there to do? Adam didn't *have* to work. God had him work the garden anyway. God wanted him to do extra things: to make the garden look beautiful, to keep things spruced up and looking nice. It was still going to produce no matter what, but Adam was still put there to work. Why? Because God wanted him to love the Garden of Eden. God knew that only by working the garden would Adam come to appreciate it.

Follow Adam's lead and learn to love your work. Seek opportunities to sharpen your skills. This is a mark of the true professional— choosing to love what you do to serve others simply because it is what you do to serve others. There's nothing professional about sitting at your job eight or ten hours a day and hating every minute of it. This negativity will reflect poorly in your performance every time. There's no faking it. You must readjust your attitude. Invest in your work. Commit to it. Love will follow, just as it did for Adam. Love will follow and so will money, because God rewards those who serve others, and serving others is what professional business professionals do naturally.

Develop Four Dimensions of Your Life Simultaneously

rom the previous chapter, you may get the wrong idea that we overvalue work and undervalue other aspects of life, such as family, friends, faith, fitness, and even free time. This couldn't be further from the truth. We have a wonderful family whom we love and enjoy spending time with. We cultivate as many friendships as we can, as we have suggested earlier in this book that you do. We are boaters; boating is one of our greatest passions and joys in life. But this book is called *Business Secrets from the Bible*, not *Boating Secrets from the Bible* or *Family Secrets from the Bible*. The instructional focus here is on developing your professional life. We are talking about your work life here, not your personal life. At work, you work. Period. However, do understand that you cannot, in life, focus on only one aspect of yourself. You must develop all aspects simultaneously.

In Hebrew, there is a word that means ladder: *S-L-M*. In God's language, Hebrew, certain letters match with specific other letters. A word that starts with one of these letters reveals a secret of reality as soon as we replace that letter with its corresponding one. Such a word is: S-L-M, ladder. When we replace the S (the letter Samech) with an SH (the letter

Shin) we get the word *SH-L-M* meaning totality, completion, and peace. The idea is that a ladder, a route upward, leads to completion . . . completion of everything. You build your way to a complete life by climbing a ladder, moving upward in various fields to achieve totality. You cannot completely succeed in business unless you have met all of your needs, not just your professional ones.

We all probably know someone who has been deemed a workaholic. We're not crazy about that word because it is often used by lazy, idle people to shame productive people. Why do they do this? Because it is easier to tear down others than to work on improving yourself. Taking your work seriously and treating it with professional seriousness is noble. But, having said that, it is possible to lead an unbalanced life by focusing too much on work. You may know someone who throws himself into his career to such an extent that he ruins his marriage and neglects his children. We know a super-successful man who built a nationally known company and who wept at our dining room table. In between sobs, he explained that his son doesn't talk to him. He unhappily faced the fact that he didn't know what mattered to his son, what struggles his son battled, or what brought joy to his son.

Sadly, we've known several women who, almost from high school, were so single-mindedly focused on work that they postponed marriage and children until it was tragically too late. At any particular point in their career trajectory, they would have told you that they wanted children and were planning on getting married. Just not this year. Indoctrinated with the two mantras "Career comes first" and "You will be able to do family later," they constantly deferred the program of prioritizing marriage and family until it was indeed too late. Were you to ask these individuals a few decades down the road whether their careers were really worth it, they would almost all probe deep into their hearts and sadly acknowledge that they were not. This is true just as it is true that spending all of your time with your family and neglecting your work is also not worth it. If you neglect work, you cannot support your family. Being hungry and homeless is not a recipe for good living. But it is also true that if you neglect your family, then you may find yourself with nothing worth supporting. What is more, a work–life balance makes one more effective at both.

When people become despondent about not reaching a goal, often it is because they have adopted a one-dimensional view of their lives. They have a vision of where they should be, and they fall into a trap of focusing on only one dimension, the development of only one area, and can't see the forest for the trees. You need to consider the big picture and address the totality of your needs.

Abraham Maslow became famous as a psychologist in the 1960s for detailing the hierarchy of human needs. We don't know if he lifted them from ancient Jewish wisdom or whether he figured it out for himself, but, either way, he got the basic human needs right. However, while Maslow listed the four needs that ancient Jewish wisdom teaches, he didn't expand on why they are needed. It is important that you understand the four principles of ancient Jewish wisdom on which Maslow's four needs are based.

If you understand these principles, you will be able to develop all four areas simultaneously so that they are never out of proportion with one another. Your life will look and feel distorted if it is overdeveloped in one area and underdeveloped in another. Develop them simultaneously and you will cultivate a well-rounded fullness of life that will allow you to remain enthusiastic and excited about your present and future. If you fall behind in one or more areas, you could get despondent or gloomy, but if you develop them all simultaneously, you will feel good no matter what stage of development you are in. The key is to be able to identify what areas are lagging so you can focus on whichever specific area needs more attention, bringing your life back into balance and harmony.

In the beginning, God created the heavens and the earth. This is how the Bible begins. The Bible is the only sacred text among all the religions of the world that begins with that fundamental statement. Ancient Jewish wisdom notes that, if the story of creation were merely a historic account, the opening of the Bible would have read: "In the beginning, God created everything." Or perhaps: "In the beginning, God created the entire universe." However, because the volume is a comprehensive matrix of the totality of all existence and is intended chiefly as a guidebook to human existence, both on an individual and a social level, it begins with these words: ". . . God created the heavens and the earth."

Ancient Jewish wisdom tells us that there is a striking duality to our existence. Our lives are complicated by the fact that everything needs to be examined through two eyes: the eye of heaven, namely the spiritual, and the eye of the earth, namely the physical.

Physical includes everything tangible and visible in the world. It describes anything that can be measured in a laboratory. Height and weight are physical. Skin color is physical as is eye color or hair color. All of these things are physical measures.

Spiritual does not necessarily mean religious, holy, or sanctified. It doesn't even mean virtuous. Spiritual, in ancient Jewish wisdom, means very specifically those things that cannot be measured by means of conventional scientific instruments. Spiritual includes love and loyalty. It includes selfishness and spite. It includes determination. It includes hope and ambition, and it includes, yes, money.

Allow us to start off with an example to help explain the difference between the spiritual and that which is physical. Imagine a woman eager to discover more about the baby she is carrying in her womb. The pregnant mother might ask the doctor, "Is my child going to be male or female?" That is purely a physical distinction and easy to determine. She might ask if her baby is going to have a tendency toward being overweight or being large or slender. She might ask if her baby has a proclivity to any childhood diseases. All of these things are easily determined, or might soon be able to be determined, because they are physical, and the answers lie within the embryo's genetic structure, which is easily examined.

Since the doctor has been successful in revealing so much about her future child, she might continue and ask, "Please tell me if my child is going to be an honest human being. Is my child going to be a person with integrity? Is my child going to be a loyal friend, whom people will love? Is my child going to be a person of optimism or pessimism? Is my child going to be capable of resourcefulness and determination?" At this point, the doctor shrugs her shoulders helplessly and explains to her patient that the mother-to-be is now inquiring about spiritual characteristics. No tests exist. These depend on unmeasurable inborn characteristics as well as the surrounding environment and manner in which the child is raised.

When you get down to the question of that child's future financial success in the world, it should be clear that the physical characteristics about which the mother inquired are not as important as the spiritual ones. When that child one day seeks a job, for the majority of professions, the job will be awarded on the basis of the child's personality, integrity, skills, communication ability, resourcefulness, optimism, and acquired knowledge and skills. Even something like being a star football player or a prima ballerina demands spiritual qualities of perseverance and diligence in addition to certain physical qualities. It is those spiritual qualities that will determine if the child can make full use of his or her physical gifts. If the child should be raised with an awareness and understanding of only the physical world, that child is greatly handicapped in our hopes for his or her future success.

It is easy for us to recognize that we humans have physical needs. These are obvious. The point that is so easy to miss is that much of what brings us the fullness and joy of life is spiritual rather than physical. We have spiritual needs that are no less vital to our success.

Completion in life comes from understanding that we are not merely bodies; we are also souls, and just as the body has its needs, the soul has its needs as well. A well-nourished soul confers enormous advantages in life, and wise parents teach a child the things that his or her soul needs. Sometimes it falls to us as adults to make up for deficiencies in our upbringing, and thus later in life teach ourselves those things that enable our bodies and souls to cooperate effectively.

In the same way that we comprise both body and soul, having both physical and spiritual needs, the world in which we live supplies both our physical requirements and also our spiritual ones. It supplies our physical needs in the form of tangible items such as water and shelter. It supplies our spiritual needs in less tangible forms. We are going to explore these needs and these requirements by looking at ancient Jewish wisdom's depiction of them as falling into four separate areas.

The first consists of those physical things we need which the earth supplies for us in physical form. We're also going to look at the spiritual requirements we have and which the world supplies in physical form. Yes, there are things that the world supplies physically yet which fulfill our spiritual needs.

Then there are those things that the world supplies spiritually that nonetheless fill a physical need in ourselves. Finally there are
those things that the world makes available to us in a spiritual form,
without which we will not perish, but which add enormously to our
well-being.

Physical needs are straightforward. In the physical sense, we are
similar to animals, such as chimpanzees. We both have to eat and
breathe and drink to live. If an animal can recognize and understand
a need, it is almost assuredly physical, because animals are not spiritual
creatures as humans are. The other way to tell if a need is physical and
not spiritual is that when deprived of a physical need, you will die in
short order. We cannot live without oxygen, water, and food, for example. However, being deprived of a spiritual need will not necessarily
result in quick biological death, though it may indeed contribute to
death down the road. It will certainly greatly diminish both life effectiveness and joy.

And so, I am a human being who has physical needs *and* spiritual
needs. And I live in a world that supplies physical needs *and* I live in
a world that also supplies spiritual needs. The tricky thing to understand here is that physical needs can be supplied spiritually and spiritual
needs can be met through what the world supplies physically.

Take a look at this chart for clarification:

	World Delivers Physically	World Delivers Spiritually
Physical Needs	Food, Shelter, Water, Air, etc.	Esteem from Peers, Friends, Connections, etc.
Spiritual Needs	Savings, Discretionary Income, Financial Security, etc.	Faith, Spirituality, Understanding, Wisdom, etc.

We see four quadrants of needs. Let's examine them in detail.

In the upper-left corner, we have physical needs that the world supplies physically. If I don't get this thing, I am going to die rather quickly.
The world supplies this thing that even a chimpanzee can recognize.
When a chimpanzee sees me eating food, he gets excited. Chimpanzees
understand the physical; we share these needs with animals. This corner

includes food, shelter, water, and other physical items that meet my physical needs.

In the lower-left corner of the chart are spiritual needs that are met by something physical. If I am deprived of these needs, I will not necessarily die. These are physical things that the world supplies, but my personal need for them is spiritual. This includes things like financial security, investments, savings, and also physical luxuries that are not necessities, such as an occasional dinner out, a nice car, or a vacation home. Unlike air, which is a need all physical creatures share, these items vary from person to person. One individual thrives when fresh flowers are on the dining room table while another rejoices in savoring a unique coffee blend. These are physical things that I want and may think I need, but I will not die as an immediate consequence of being without them. Nonetheless, while I may not die without substantial retirement savings, financial security is important to my sense of well-being as well as to reducing unhealthy stress that will negatively impact my physical health. People deprived of physical touch from others get sick more often and have shorter life-expectancies. Nonetheless, one can survive without these things for quite a long time as the experiences of prisoners of war attest.

In the upper-right corner are physical needs that the world supplies spiritually. What are these? Like the needs in the lower-left quadrant I can live without them for a long time, but the lack of them may very well contribute to an early death. My chimpanzee will not comprehend this need or recognize it being filled because he does not operate on a spiritual level. You are probably wondering what intangible thing that could possibly be?

Let's answer with a story that my father told me. In the early twentieth century, there was a famous English professor of philosophy and ethics in England named Professor Joad. Back in those days, the London Underground (the subway system in London) worked on the honor system. You could just get on a train, and when it was time to get off, you told the conductor how many stops you had traveled. There wasn't a fixed fee throughout the system; the fare was based on how many miles and how many stations you had traveled. Professor Joad, for reasons of his own, got off the subway and lied about where he got on. As a professional good at spotting people who lied about fares, the conductor suspected that Joad was lying. By asking a series of questions, he ferreted out Professor Joad's lie. The conductor, and everyone else, could not understand *why* he had lied and cheated the system. Had his lie not been detected, Professor Joad would have saved himself eight pennies. Eight mere pennies! And he was a well-paid university professor and also a BBC radio celebrity.

Given his high profile, the London Transport decided to use him as an example and threw the book at him. The next day, the *Evening Standard* carried this outraged headline: "Famous Professor Joad Caught Cheating London Transport Out of Eight Pennies." Joad was fired from his university position, and he later lost his radio show. The university couldn't keep a professor of ethics and philosophy who would cheat the transit system. After this, he couldn't get another job because his name was all over the papers, outing him as an immoral thief. The public humiliation destroyed his health, and he started drinking heavily. He became bereft of close connection with family and friends and five years later died at the age of 61.

We recount this sad story to illustrate that we actually *can* die as a result of not having the esteem of our friends and associates. The care, concern, and respect we receive from our fellow man drives us to take care of ourselves, and while they are spiritual in nature, our need for them can be physical. Without the care and concern of others, we have no reason to take care of our bodies, maintain our hygiene, eat properly, exercise, or to resist abusing our bodies with alcohol and drugs if we feel so inclined. We take care of ourselves partially because we crave the respect from and connection with other people. If everybody else removed themselves from our lives, we would have less to live for, and we might very well stop meeting our own physical needs. We do have a real physical need for these spiritual things. Recently, as people live lonelier lives, there have been a spurt of studies showing the physical effects of a spiritual lack. In 2023, the U.S. Surgeon General published a statement on the negative health effects of social isolation and lack of community. It was entitled, "Our Epidemic of Loneliness and Isolation." Similar advisories have been issued by leaders in countries around the world.

The final quadrant in the lower-right corner is reserved for spiritual needs that the world supplies spiritually. These are important needs:

although I do not need them to stay alive, the lack of these will leave me feeling that something missing in my life. That "something" may be a faith connection, a spiritual connection, wisdom, or a deeper understanding of the world and my place in it. The chimpanzee does not see the world giving me knowledge and giving me understanding. The chimpanzee doesn't see the world giving me faith and a spiritual connection. As a human, I do need these things. If I don't get them, will I die? No. Millions of people live without those things. They don't live completely fulfilling lives, but they do live.

When we fulfill these spiritual needs, we become happier and better people and are better suited to find joy and profit by serving our fellow man. We can do so in business and also through charity. That's a spiritual need as well—supplying charity to your fellow man. If you don't give charity, you won't die—plenty of people lead selfish lives, giving absolutely nothing to others, but it is a real need. You live a better and a more fulfilling life when you are a giver.

There you have it—your hierarchy of needs according to ancient Jewish wisdom. These four areas of your life must be attended to simultaneously. This matrix of physical and spiritual needs is important and integral to a successful personal and business life. You may think that you can ignore one quadrant, and for a while maybe you can, especially needs that won't cause your death if they are not fulfilled, but over time, spiritual gravity will drag you down. It will cause you to fail in your personal life and to fail in your professional life as well. To complicate things a bit further, each of these areas affects each other. It is almost impossible to draw impregnable lines between them.

For the purpose of growing your capacity to make money, you need to simultaneously focus on making sure that your basic physical needs are met, including the needs of those who depend on you. You also need to make sure that you earn more money than is needed for your basic needs so that your financial security is in place—insurance policies, savings, investments, retirement accounts. Furthermore, occasional discretionary spending is not necessarily frivolous. It is wonderful to be able to do or have a little extra. You also need to focus on relationships so that you may earn the esteem and favor of others. We need family. We need friends. These deserve our time and attention and will not only bolster our morale, but they will also increase our ability to be better business professionals. Finally, you also need faith and a spiritual connection. You need to have greater understanding. Each and every day, we should be asking, "What did I learn today? What do I understand about how the world really works better than I understood last week?" That is a spiritual need we have, because without it, we will not continue to grow. Ignore any of these needs at your own peril.

The final point and secret that the Bible gives us here is this: not only does fulfilling these needs bolster our ability to earn money, but earning a living bolsters our ability to better meet these needs. In this way, our personal and professional lives—when all needs are attended to—feed off of each other with perfect synergy, catapulting us toward success and the fulfillment of our true earning potential.

Serve Authentically

This principle of ancient Jewish wisdom underpins and supports the Bible's intersection with business. You must internalize the fact that, for honest and ethical people, wealth is the result of doing the right thing. Money is the *consequence* of doing the right things. Do not focus on the consequence itself; focus on what causes the effect, which is serving your fellow man. When you serve other human beings, money follows. You bring about an effect by activating the correct cause, not by focusing on the effect itself.

This is one reason not to envy others. Often in business, as in life, we will see those who have done better for themselves than we have, and we will think, "I want that." When we do this, we find ourselves growing bitter and cynical when we fail to make progress on our goals. This is ironic given that the reason we aren't getting anywhere is precisely because we are focusing on what we want rather than focusing on what we should be doing. Instead of focusing on imagined rewards, focus on serving God's other children, for they are your customers. Let this and only this preoccupy your mind when you are at work. Ask yourself, how do I supply the needs and the desires of as many other people as I possibly can? This is God's will and is therefore the foundation on which the economy is built. Do whatever you have to do to serve your fellow man. If you need to develop a new skill, do so. If you see an unmet need in the market, provide it. If there is an invention that has not been invented but would be useful, build it. Whatever you do, if it provides other people value, they will provide you with wealth.

But you may ask, "How do I know what it is that I should provide other people?" This is another way of asking, "What should I do with my life?" Very often people tell us that they don't know what field to enter. Young people, especially those entering or leaving college, often say they do not know what they want to do with their lives. They look to advice from others, and one place they are sure to get bad advice is from many of the commencement speakers at their graduation ceremony.

Invariably the commencement speaker will advise the graduates to "follow their passion." The speaker tells the newly minted baccalaureates that they should just follow their hearts and pursue the thing that they most love doing. Do what you love, they say. If you only do what you love, the speaker asserts, you will never have to work a day in your lives because every time you go to work, you will be doing what you love.

Well, these speakers are right about one thing: doing what you love is not work. Or, at the very least, it isn't what defines work. It's not even a characteristic of work.

Here is a tip for young college graduates: ignore that commencement speaker.

These advisors are feeding you a terrible and destructive lie. They are misleading you. What they are telling you is this: think not about what the world needs but about what you really like doing. Can you imagine anything more selfish?

Not only is it selfish, it is also impractical, and it does young people a disservice. Work is not about doing what you want to do; work is about serving others.

Maybe your passion is music. You really want to be a singer or a rap artist or play the bass guitar. You hear your commencement speaker telling you to follow your passion and do what you love. So you decide, "All right, I'll go for it; I'm going to focus on my music!" There's only one snag in your plan, which you only realize after you've quit your job, and that is that there aren't that many successful bands looking for singers. And very few rappers or bass guitarists make a living. You find that there are many people wanting to do just what you want to do, and most of them will not get very far.

Given your situation, should you follow your passion? In your leisure time, perhaps, but the idea that singing should be your professional focus, your career goal, is naïve and misguided. Maybe it will work out. Probably not. Almost certainly not. In this situation, you have a better chance of winning the lottery—at least there you have as good a shot as the next person.

What do you do then? How do you pick a career?

Consider Jeff Bezos, the founder of Amazon. Success didn't come quickly. For the company's first several years the conventional wisdom was that it was doomed. Founder Bezos could have said to himself, "This has all been a terrible mistake. I knew that I should have followed my passion." But he didn't. Instead, he persevered. What was his passion? It certainly was not creating an online book company that would struggle until it pivoted into a veritable online marketplace. His passions? In a 2016 interview with Charlie Rose, Bezos spoke of his several passions. They were, in order, becoming an astronaut, becoming an archeologist, and becoming a theoretical physicist. But Jeff Bezos did not follow his passions. Instead, he asked himself, what do people need? Even if they don't yet know they need it, what would improve their lives so dramatically that they'd flock to try his service? He decided that no bricks-and-mortar bookstore can possibly stock every book in publication, but the newly popularized online world could do exactly that. We all know the rest of the story.

Delight in serving other people. This is the best career advice you will ever get. You want to choose a career? Look around, discover what people need you to do, learn to do it, and then learn to love it. As we have already discussed, you learn to love your work, whatever it is, by committing to it and investing in it. Decide that whatever your career is, you are going to be a professional and commit 100% and *choose* to love what you do. That's the thing—you get to choose to love your work.

And that is the key. You can't always follow the professional path of your dreams, but you can choose how you are going to feel about the profession you do have and whether to conduct your business professionally or not. It's up to you.

The unfortunate fact is this: few of us get to do what we enjoy doing in our leisure time as professionals. I [RDL] really love boating. But I wasn't exactly waiting around for someone to pay me to go boating. And this is why just "following your passions" is not good advice for most of us. It works for some, but only a very few.

Obviously some people are blessed with certain talents and abilities. Naturally you should not overlook that. If God has blessed you with athletic ability, you may or may not incorporate that into your professional plan. Be realistic. If you played outstanding college football and have a chance of being drafted to a professional team, you might want to pursue this path. But do so knowing that it is easy to be sidelined by injury and that many others are competing with you. Few will succeed. On the other hand, many careers incorporate physical activities rather than sitting at a desk. Recognize your skills and proclivities, but don't aim for a pipe dream of doing only what you love.

For those of us who don't have rare and extraordinary talents, we should not be focusing on what we love because we will not necessarily be able to serve people that way. We must focus on what other people need. Build this conviction deep into your heart, no matter what your profession. Everyone can serve God's other children in less glamorous fields. When we fully commit to our careers, humble as they may or may not be, we will find success, wealth, happiness, and a love for what we do. All successful people really do the same thing, be they the rare successful athlete, entertainer, or a middle manager working his way up the company ranks: they serve God's children by providing products and services to others. We implore the middle manager not to envy the rap artist, but to take pride and joy in his own service to mankind.

You cannot fake this conviction. You must really make yourself feel it. You must actually commit yourself to your work. Why can't you fake it? Because people can tell! Exodus 23:7 states: "Keep yourself distant from any falsehood and do not slay the innocent and righteous. . . ." Ancient Jewish wisdom explains that when you indulge in falsehood of any kind, the innocent and righteous person you are slaying is you! A lack of conviction will show through in your work.

Imagine that you are an employer interviewing an applicant. The applicant comes in for the interview, and you ask them why they would like to work for your company. The applicant says, "I've heard you guys have great benefits!" Right off the bat you are probably not feeling so great about this candidate. Why would you hire them just to give them great benefits? You do give great benefits, but someone's desire for them is not the basis upon which you make a hire. So, you ask them to tell you a little about themselves and they say, "Well, you know what I really love is playing jazz music. Oh, by the way, I really need to get off work early every Friday because the jazz club where I play the trumpet is pretty far from here." You're not really feeling great now, and you ask them if they have any other questions before ushering them out the door. They say, "Well, actually I do. What is the pay? And how many days off do I get a year? I like to take a month off in the summer to tour with my band."

Do you hire them? Not unless you want an unprofessional employee who is not ready to commit themselves to their "day job" and invest themselves in your company. When you are interviewing a candidate for a position, do you really care what they find fulfilling or what they need from you to pursue their interests? Of course not! You care what they can do for you, not what you can do for them. You are paying them, not the other way around! When an employer hires someone and is going to take company money and hand it over, they need to know exactly what the applicant is going to add to the company's bottom line.

But all this applicant is talking about is how they are going to get what they want out of the relationship. An employer understands that a business relationship is a two-way street—it has to be or both parties won't stay in the relationship—but they want to know what you can do for them, not how they can benefit you. They want to know this at the interview, and they want to see it once you are on the job. Obviously, the job has to benefit you, but they know how they can benefit you: they hand you a paycheck, and if they are wise, they show appreciation and care that you find your work fulfilling. But what they want to know in an interview is how you are going to benefit them. They want to see you committed to serving them. Again, you cannot fake this. You must truly invest yourself in being of service.

Culturally, we tend to think of certain professions as "helping professions." We might include nurses, teachers, and social workers in this list. Without difficulty, we acknowledge that plumbers, locksmiths, and farmers do tasks that help us. We start running into trouble when we look at salespeople, middle-managers, and similar professions. What about gift shop owners and clerks? If we are to be authentic in wanting to serve God's other children, we need to understand how those professions are also true service or else we should avoid them.

First of all, we must acknowledge that entering a "helping profession" does not mean that one is doing good. Sadly, this has become evident in the past few years. I [SL] listened to a podcast with a first-grade teacher. She absorbed the lessons from her school of education and taught her young charges for many years according to the "science" and "studies" of whole language reading that she was told were the professional method for teaching reading. Only after she gave birth and her own child reached the age of reading, did she realize that she had been teaching illiteracy and condemning her students to a backward start in life. Well meaning? Absolutely. Doing harm? Absolutely.

Without delving too much into politics, many doctors and nurses today participate in procedures that cause harm. Social workers sometimes destroy families and lives. There is no automatic assumption that wanting to help people and choosing your livelihood by that criterion will mean that you actually do help others.

Every job needs to be analyzed through the lens of serving God's children and many professions need to be reevaluated on a regular basis. If you do not believe that the way you earn money is ethical, moral, and helps others, you will come across, to yourself and to others, as a charlatan. Let's look at a few examples of often derided professions. How about a life-insurance salesman? Certainly, someone focused on making a large commission can saddle a customer with an unnecessarily expensive policy, perhaps one that won't even meet his or her needs. But a proper life-insurance professional knows deep down that he is providing security for a fellow human being and their family. Of course, he is helping them.

Does selling knickknacks in a gift store truly help people? Not if you are selling shoddy rip-offs and just trying to pressure someone into buying. But if you are selling tangible reminders of a cherished vacation with friends or family then, indeed, you are providing value to a customer's life. You are also enabling artisans, truck drivers, and other members of the supply chain to support their families.

Don't allow the outside culture to dictate whether your job is valuable or not. Ask yourself if you are doing a good thing. If the answer is no, find another field. If it is yes, hold your head up high and continue to serve.

We see proof of how others can judge our authenticity throughout the Bible. Let's return to the story of Samson and Delilah in the book of Judges, chapter 16. Remember how Delilah repeatedly asked Samson to divulge the secret of his strength? Several times he lied to her, but she could tell he was lying. The third time, however, he told her the truth: that it was his hair that gave him his strength. Before she even confirms the truth by shaving off his hair, we see that she understands that this time he is indeed telling the truth. How did she know that this wasn't yet one more lie? How did she know he had been lying earlier?

Before we answer that question, let's look at a second case. Consider when Jacob's sons show him the bloodstained jacket, telling their father that it belongs to their brother, Joseph, and proves he is dead. They don't tell their father the truth, that they sold Joseph into slavery in Egypt. Later, in Genesis, chapter 45, the brothers come to Jacob and tell him that they have seen Joseph in Egypt, where their long-lost brother is now the ruler of the entire country of Egypt! Jacob rejects this report as a lie even though it is true. He does not accept that what he has believed up until now is the real lie.

Why did Jacob believe his sons' original lie and not the truth they told him later? How did Delilah know when Samson was and wasn't lying?

Is Delilah more spiritually sensitive than Jacob? No. The truth is that there is one big difference between these two stories: when Joseph's brothers sold him as a slave to be taken down to Egypt, they truly and completely believed he was a goner. There was no way a Jewish boy was going to survive as a slave in Egypt, or so they thought. They truly believed that if he wasn't dead yet, he was going to be dead shortly. When they misled Jacob, implying that Joseph was dead, they held a deep internal belief that this was so. In their own minds they were not telling a lie.

In the case of Delilah and Samson, Samson was telling a clear lie the first few times, and only the last time did he tell the truth. But Samson knew his lies to be lies, and Delilah, like most people, possessed enough human sensitivity to recognize the difference between the way Samson spoke when lying and the way he spoke when telling the truth. This is why the verse says, "Delilah *knew* he was telling the truth." She didn't even have to cut off his hair to prove it; she knew beforehand because she could read his true convictions. For good people who are not practiced at deception, that which is in our heart comes across to those around us; they can see it in our eyes, hear it in our voices, and observe it in our demeanor. This may sound obvious, but we often do not realize that we only come across as authentic when we are being authentic. When we speak with conviction, people believe what we say. This is a difficult thing to fake.

The lesson here is not just that we shouldn't lie. The lesson is that we must be authentic because lying, over the long term, deceives no one. If we build into ourselves a deep understanding and conviction that serving the needs of other human beings is the reason we profit, that the reason we earn money is because we are focused on serving the needs of other people, other people will see this. We must commit ourselves to these convictions. Then and only then will the money follow. The question you have to answer is not, "How will I make money?" It is, "How will I serve my fellow man?"

Secret #17

Enhance Your Potential by Imposing Boundaries and Structure

C hildren used to not manage their own lives. They were governed externally by their parents. Their perception of what was and wasn't allowed was dictated wholly by what their parents said. As a child, perhaps you could not play ball in the street. Maybe you had to be in bed by nine o'clock. You might have had to finish your greens, to do chores, attend school, and say "please" and "thank you." You didn't necessarily understand why you had to do these things, only that you did. In past generations, children's lives were defined by limits, demands, and requirements. They did not necessarily know the reasons for these external limits. As adults, parents understood the reason for imposing the rules. The rules were there to keep children safe; adults imposed them because they knew better. This isn't a book about child-raising, but we posit that much of the stress, anxiety, and increased mental disorders in children today is a result of them being asked to shoulder too many decisions on their own as parents abdicate responsibility for being the adults in the room.

Children are not the only ones who require explicit boundaries and responsibilities—adults do, too. This is because, paradoxically to a certain degree, the more confined and structured you are, the freer you are. By imposing structure upon your own life, you gain a better understanding of the rules that govern you. Many adults do not comprehend this because it is counterintuitive. You may ask, how can limitations provide freedom?

God gave Moses the Ten Commandments. Exodus 32:16 reads, "And the tablets were the work of God, and the writing was the writing of God engraved upon the tablets." The Torah uses the Hebrew word for engraved: *ChaRuT*. This word has two meanings. The first, as we have said, is "engraved," as if marked in stone. When you write something in stone, it is indelible—no eraser can remove it. When you engrave something, it cannot be changed.

The second meaning of *ChaRuT* is freedom, which seems to be exactly the opposite of the concept of engraving. It is always significant when a Hebrew word has two meanings. Those meanings need to be looked at together to see how they intersect. This is not true in English. In English, for example, a rose is a flower and is also a verb for standing up. What does this mean? Nothing. It's just the same word used twice. Life is too short to ruminate on such nonsense. But Hebrew is different because it is the Lord's language, and in the Lord's language, a word with two meanings binds those two things. We are meant to know then that the concepts of freedom and engravement are somehow related, even though they appear to be opposites.

Freedom is the opportunity to be creative, to be a creator. When we have total freedom, we have infinite possibility to do more than most of us believe we can. We have the *potential* to get anything done, but potential does not mean actualization. It is only once we restrict our freedom by filling up our workweek with tasks that we actually get anything accomplished. But following a specific path closes off other possibilities, which in turn further restricts our freedom. As we close off possibilities in this way, our lives, so to speak, become more set in stone—engraved. This is where the paradoxical effect comes from. The more we restrict our freedom by setting rules and limitations on ourselves, the freer we are to actually be productive. The idle person who leaves himself free to do what he likes when he likes has the *potential* to accomplish anything, but he accomplishes less than the person who rigorously restricts his freedom and focuses on what he wants to accomplish. It is the person who carves his life and time, his schedule, into granite who is genuinely free.

The people who put no limits on their own freedom, who do as they wish when they wish, are embracing childishness. Children want to stay up all night even though they will be tired the next day and get nothing done. Put another way, children free to stay up all night are not free to get anything done the next day. But children who have their schedules engraved in stone for them, who are restricted from staying up late, are free to enjoy the following day free of exhaustion.

As adults, we should place limits on our children, and by setting limits on their freedom to do as they wish, we free them from the consequences of bad choices. By setting limits on a child's bedtime, a parent gives the child the freedom to be awake and alert the next day. In doing so, parents do children another favor: they teach them the value of rules and structure in life. The child can only see that he wants to stay awake. The adult can see how that desire, if fulfilled, robs the child of the freedom to be productive the following day.

As adults, we do not have guardian protectors to watch over us. We must establish rules and boundaries for ourselves much as we do for our children. We'd rather leave our schedules open and uncommitted, our days free to do as we feel, but this would be doing ourselves a disservice. By limiting our freedom, by requiring ourselves to be organized and forcing ourselves to use time wisely, we are giving ourselves the freedom to be creative and productive.

This is why time management is so important. Commit to time management. Engrave your schedule in granite so that you might be free to thrive in business. Lock yourself into productive commitments as much as possible. Every day on your calendar should be full of productive work. Block off every day, except, of course, the Sabbath, as you want to give yourself one day off a week. Many people take off two days a week, Saturday and Sunday, but this is, in our opinion, excessive. God did not create the earth and then on the weekend rest—he rested only on the seventh day. Of course, many social, family, and health commitments must coexist with work; we are not suggesting working 24/6, but we are suggesting that even those should err on the side of structure rather than the side of lazily spending the day on a couch.

Buy yourself a calendar if you don't have one and start making commitments. You may give yourself one day with more flexibility and on which you do not work. Religious people will choose their Sabbath, but for everyone it should be the same day each week and completely inviolable. On the remaining six days, lock yourself into commitments as much as possible. This is how you will succeed in business—fail to do so, and your competitors will outpace you. We encourage you to keep a journal in which you record whether or not you completed your daily, weekly, and monthly goals. It is not enough to set goals; you must meet them. You have to hold yourself accountable.

There are two common reasons people do not reach their goals. One is that their scheduling is overly optimistic, and they need to set more reasonable goals. The other, which is far more common, is that people fail to focus on what needs doing. At the end of each day, take an honest inventory and ask yourself if you worked as hard as you could or if you goofed off or procrastinated. Be brutally honest with yourself. Did you not get everything done that you set out to do because it was too much, or did you simply fail to fully commit yourself to working diligently all day long? Take an inventory of what you did that day. If you failed to get through all of your sales calls, and yet found time to watch a funny animal video on YouTube, send emails or Instagrams to friends, and played a few games of Wordle on your phone, then the problem is not that you didn't have the time to finish your work—it's that you simply failed to do your work.

True freedom is not the opportunity to do as we please, but rather, it is the opportunity to lock ourselves into the things that need doing. True freedom is the ability to be creative, by which we mean, to create. Remember, making money through creating commerce and business is one of the most thrilling and creative things we can possibly do. We don't win money, we earn it—we make it. Business creates money, and it creates good in the world. That is creativity, indeed, one of the most creative actions that people can undertake. When two or more human beings serve one another by trading, they are literally creating money, bringing it into the world, and this is good. But to be able to earn money, we must set limits on ourselves and our freedom. Earning money requires focus and a plan.

Imagine placing a rifle cartridge into a vise and clamping it firmly in place on your workbench. (Children, do not try this at home, please.) Now imagine taking a nail and holding to the percussion cap on the back of the cartridge and hammering the nail into the cartridge. What happens? There's going to be a big bang, no question about it, and a flash of light. Where is the lead bullet from the cartridge going to go? How far will it travel? The answer may surprise you: about 2 feet or so. The brass casing will spring open like a banana peel and the bullet will plop forward and drop onto the floor at your feet. But how is this possible? When you fire that same round from your rifle, pulling the trigger causes that same bullet to travel hundreds of yards at the rate of more than 600 feet per second. So how is it that it now just plops to the floor? What is the difference?

When the round is inside your rifle, the explosion is confined on all sides but one, and all of the chemical energy stored up in the powder causes the bullet to burst out of the brass casing and fly down the barrel. All of the energy is focused down and out the barrel. All of this energy is applied to the rear end of the bullet, and the bullet goes flying out. But when the cartridge is held in a vise and not in the chamber of your rifle, being fired causes the casing to burst open, dispersing the energy in every direction. Nothing productive happens. The bullet goes nowhere. The difference is that the barrel of a gun confines, restricts, and focuses the energy all in one direction.

In the same manner, true power is achieved by confining our own selves. When we focus our energies in one direction rather than many, we can accomplish great things. Freedom is obtained from direction, not from the potential to move in any which way. Without a goal and narrowed focus, without placing limits on our potential, our energies are wasted, dissipated, and ineffective. In our work, we must make our goals explicit. If we have a destination, then we will, like the bullet that is restricted to one option, know where to go.

You have probably heard people—indecisive, noncommittal, unproductive people—say that they prefer to keep their options open. A man or woman who avoids marrying in order to keep his or her options open in case something better comes along will never marry. Ever. He or she is waiting for an opportunity that they would not seize even if it came—because there is always a better *hypothetical* option down the line. What good is keeping your options open if you aren't ever going to select one and act decisively?

This same individual will probably have a hard time investing money because the ability to be productive, whether through getting married and creating a family or investing money and creating a business, is only possible when we limit our options and freedom by choosing a direction and focus. You want to confine yourself by making purposeful choices and following them through to their logical conclusions. Freedom, potential, options—can be traps. They can rob us of the chance to be productive and creative. Narrow your freedom, limit your options, choose your path, and you will be free to pursue your goals to their ultimate end.

Sometimes we overcomplicate matters. Avoid this pitfall. We immobilize ourselves when we view our lives, circumstances, and choices all at once. It is a panorama too vast to consider or handle. The view is overwhelming. If you begin to feel this way, take a step back for contemplation and seek outside counsel. Both quiet deliberation without distraction and thoughtful discussion with a trusted and more experienced advisor can provide a simpler and more accurate perspective on the challenges you face.

For instance, consider the incredibly complicated problem of inflation and its potential to cripple the economy. I [RDL] sometimes pose the following question to economists: Given that the British Empire had far-flung outposts spread across the known world at a time when there were no computers for tabulation or sophisticated communications, how did they avoid the ills of inflation for more than a hundred years? How did they print the correct amount of money that would induce neither inflation nor deflation for hundreds of years? Doing this required them to keep tabs on countless vendors across several countries and relay that information back to the Mint in a timely fashion. Doing so in that day and age was, of course, impossible. And yet they did it. But how?

These professionals will inevitably overthink the question. They seek a solution that fits their preconceived notions of how the economy works. But nothing fits. The true answer eludes these highly learned professionals. However, when one considers inflation in its most basic terms, the devaluing of a currency, and one remembers the almost mythical power of a marketplace, the solution becomes more visible, almost obvious.

The answer is that the British Mint did not keep tabs on all the economic transactions at home and abroad. They used a different method to balance the printing of money. To understand the method, though, you must understand a little bit about how inflation works.

Inflation happens when the prices of goods and services rise. This happens when the government prints too much money. We are told this is a bad thing. But I ask you, what is too much? Who decides how much money is too much?

As I said, there was a period in history when the British Empire had virtually no inflation for nearly a hundred years. The price of a bushel of wheat, a pair of shoes, a haircut and shave, and everything else remained the same for a hundred years. For a hundred years, the prices for all goods and services remained the same respective to gold. Back in those days, pounds sterling were convertible legally and at any moment into gold. This may sound miraculous. No inflation! That's great, right?

This was no easy task to accomplish. The government had to print just the right amount of money to cover all new commerce. The mint had to print enough money to cover the total value of what every human being in the empire was doing for every other human being. This is because every single time a citizen sells a good or provides a service, value is created by the transaction, and therefore money worth the equivalent value of that transaction must be printed.

Remember, in those days, the British Empire included Great Britain, South Africa, and parts of Canada, Australia, Rhodesia, New Zealand, and India—this is a lot of people and transactions to account for. The Bank of England had to know exactly how many pounds sterling to print, which requires knowing about what everyone is doing and creating. Keeping up with this correctly is a massive and notoriously difficult undertaking; even today, with the assistance of computers, governments struggle to keep track of and predict commerce accurately.

So how did the British Empire manage it? They simply kept track of how many people came into the Bank of England to exchange their pound notes for gold. The bank understood this to mean that there were too many pound notes in circulation, which made them feel uneasy for fear of inflation. When people began asking for gold in exchange for pounds, they stopped printing any more money. Eventually, people would start coming into the bank with gold to purchase pounds. They needed the pounds to conduct business, which told the bank that the market in London, which was at the center of the whole empire, was feeling that more good deeds were being done, more economic transactions were being made, and more value was being created than there was printed money. When this happened, they would again print money until people started wanting their gold back. In this way, inflation was defeated by the collective wisdom and ingenuity of human beings.

And during the entire time that the Bank of England scrupulously printed no more money than citizens' creativity warranted, the Empire's economy thrived. Through this honest discipline, the Bank surrendered the power to print money for political purposes. The great Bank of England imposed limits upon itself and through those limits and restrictions, it achieved greatness for itself and empowered every British business professional to reach for greatness.

Whenever people, institutions, or societies work effectively, limits and restrictions are being practiced. It goes without saying that there needs to be a balance with freedom. However, whenever societies, institutions, or people substitute rights for responsibilities, license for freedom, and anarchy for structure, chaos and unhappiness result. This is so reliable an observation that you can greatly benefit by incorporating it into your life. Whether in your physical fitness, your family life, your friends and family, and even your faith life, building yourself a structure of rules and regulations will greatly enhance your life.

You Cannot Lead If
You Cannot Follow

For many reasons, shopping is becoming more of an online activity. Even when going in-person to the supermarket or to a restaurant, patrons are encouraged to check their groceries out themselves or to order their meal via a tablet. Technological advances combined with government policies that discourage hiring young and inexperienced people combine to make it difficult for people to take one of the best steps to success a person can have—their first job. A major lesson of that first job, ideally at a young age, is learning to follow orders whether that means showing up on time, wearing a decidedly not-with-it uniform, or keeping one's cool with a customer who is being unpleasant.

A major flaw with educational systems around the world is that they do not prepare students for the job market or the workplace. They fail to teach the single most important skill necessary for avoiding poverty: obtaining and retaining a job. Paradoxically, schools fail in this task by conveying two competing messages, both of which mitigate against earning money. The first is a disastrous focus on self-esteem, a misguided movement that has caused tremendous harm. We make sure that young people feel good about themselves no matter how poorly they are performing. We remind them that they are special and unique. (Which in God's eyes they surely are, but they need to live with other people.) We don't impart the quality that employers most want to see in job applicants: a willingness to be part of a team even at the expense of personal discomfort. Supervisors and bosses want to see demonstrated perseverance and commitment along with a can-do spirit. Holding down a job, any job, will do more for your résumé than almost all other extracurricular activities. Do you know what extracurricular activities tell an employer? That you can spend time doing what you feel like doing. That's not all that impressive. But if you can show an employer that you held down a job throughout high school and college, perhaps also while you completed an internship, you have proven that you know how to fit into a company. Many employers tell us that the unspoken message they get from too many job applicants is, "I will be looking for ways that you offend me, and I hope to sue you and get enough money never to have to work again." These employers are desperate to find workers who appreciate the opportunity of earning a living.

The conflicting message to the previous one that we have lately been giving students is that they should be sheep. We demand that they parrot ideas rather than teaching them to think. The fear of cancel culture means that not only have educational standards lowered appallingly, but maturity, along with the ability to tolerate and respect others, is lacking. Educational institutions are teaching how to tear down rather than how to build up. Employers can teach many skills on the job to a candidate who has good character and a good work ethic. Unfortunately, schooling today often destroys both of those traits.

Isn't this contradictory? Should employees be individuals, or should they follow orders? The answer is both. They should be able to follow policies, but anyone who hopes to move beyond the first level at work must also exhibit a mind that can spot problems and innovate when necessary.

Nordstrom's, one of the world's most successful retail stores, used to exemplify these ideas. All executive-track employees started out on the sales floor in the shoe department. The company wanted their executives to understand customer service. In a very tangible way, they showed them that they must be willing to go down on their knees in front of a customer. This wonderful training taught their highest level executives that the customer is the true boss. Every Nordstrom's vice president had experience serving customers firsthand; they knew that they needed to provide the same caring service to the elderly lady looking for sensible shoes, to the teenager looking to complement the perfect prom dress, to the lawyer looking to impress a jury, and to everyone else who patronized their store. The customer's satisfaction mattered, not their own. Not even the CEO. Not even the majority shareholders.

At the same time, Nordstrom empowered all salesclerks to act on their own authority in order to best serve customers. Robot-like adherence to a script was neither required nor wanted. That is why Nordstrom's executives and the Nordstrom brand have been so successful. Interestingly, Nordstrom delayed opening in certain locations because they could not find salespeople who both understood the concept of service and also had independence of mind and the ability to deal with situations as they arose.

Ancient Jewish wisdom shows us that the only route to wealth is in serving other human beings. People are not going to voluntarily part with their money and give it to you unless you have done something for them. Therefore, earning money is always an act of service. This is true of employees, and it is true of business owners, too, because everyone in business has customers to serve. A retailer must understand that the customer is his boss. So too must the store clerk.

You have probably had the experience of dealing with a salesperson who has a bad attitude. This person fails to realize the debt he or she owes to the customers they serve or should be serving. Instead of serving the customer, they view them as nuisances—irritating people preventing them from chatting with a coworker or checking the messages on their phone. Though this can be infuriating, we probably should pity such a person. They will never move up in business behaving this way. And neither will you if you adopt such a negative and entitled worldview.

Service to others never ends. No matter how high up you are in your company, you must still embrace service. True leadership includes letting the people around you see your ability to be subservient. The earliest lesson in the virtue of subservience should be the Fifth Commandment: honor your father and mother. We must do so for their sake, but also for our own children's sake—and our own as well. You are your children's role models. When parents teach their children that they must act in a respectful way toward them, they are providing an early lesson in how to be employable. In Torah Judaism, a belief in acquiescing to a higher authority is passed down almost from birth. Very young Jewish children, perhaps only two or three years old, understand that if a delectable-looking candy at the checkout aisle is not kosher, no amount of pleading will get their mother to buy it. They are taught at the same young age that they do not eat meat and milk together. The concept that there is a higher authority over them and also over their parents is built into the system from the very start. Knowledgeable Jews understand right away that they are not the ultimate boss—God is.

Arrogance is seen as one of the worst character traits according to ancient Jewish wisdom. Displaying arrogance insinuates that you are the most important entity in the whole world. You are not. God is more important than you are. And just like you, everyone else is created in the image of God. You are not more important than other people. Everyone else you meet is somebody whom you can serve. You should view this as an opportunity, an opportunity to serve, not as a burden.

One of the reasons that we, along with many employers, view job applicants from the military favorably is that people with a background of military service have absorbed an intuitive sense of the importance of hierarchy. Following the orders of my supervisor doesn't demean me. On the contrary, I become a valuable link in the chain that connects vision and execution. Likewise, issuing orders to those who report to us doesn't make us better than they. We understand the power and effectiveness of a chain of command. The concept of a hierarchal structure is one of the secrets of a corporation, part of what makes it possible for many people to participate in an enterprise that acquires a legal standing.

In addition to serving our customers, a gift we can give ourselves is finding mentors. Looking up to others and humbly learning from them is one of the best ways to learn and develop skills. Finding a way to be of value—to serve—someone who is more advanced than you is a wonderful way to begin a relationship. This concept of service used to be a natural part of life. Children obeyed parents and teachers. As they grew, they took responsibility for leading others. Today's culture often shatters that pathway. Inculcate an attitude of learning to serve others, and you will prosper.

Vision Is Necessary; Sharing That Vision Is Not Always Necessary

How many faces do I have? Well, the Hebrew word for face is pronounced "*Panim.*" The "im" sound at the end of the word signifies that the word is plural. For example, the Hebrew word for water is pronounced "*mayim.*" The word *water* is a mass noun, meaning it is always plural. You would never tell someone to "bring me a water." You would say, "Bring me a bottle of water," or "a glass of water" but never "a water." What this tells us is that the word *water* is not singular. Similarly, *face* in Hebrew is plural. If you were to tell someone, "Look at my face," in Hebrew, a grammatical analysis would show that you are saying, "Look at my faces." The Lord's language recognizes that everyone is multifaced. This may remind you of the English phrase "two-faced," which has negative connotations. That is not what we mean by multifaced in ancient Jewish wisdom. We all put on multiple faces, and there is nothing wrong with doing so—in fact, it is proper to do so.

When my children look at me, they should not see the same face as the manager of my bank does when I am applying for a loan. I do not have the same face when I am speaking to one of my employees as

I do when I'm praying to God. You do not show the same face to your superiors as you do to those you lead, and neither of those two faces will be the one that your spouse sees. This is quite proper and acceptable. You do have more than one face, and you should not feel dishonest about this fact, as it is the only way to move through the world. Our face is the portal to our soul and the window into our heart. We should not share the same things, the same parts of our inner lives, with all people in the same way. This mass revealing of ourselves has been one of the harms of social media. Many a college student has discovered that a potential future employer does not look at a drunken revel with the same amusement as his roommate did. *Discretion* is an old-fashioned word that modern people should happily adopt. Our public face must not expose all sides of us for all to see.

Instead of reacting emotionally to a situation, we ought to deliberately choose how to respond and thereby purposefully select the face we will show. We should not wear our heart on our sleeve, which is another way of saying, if you will, that we should not wear our heart on our face.

Long ago, I [RDL] studied the Torah with a wonderful student for many years, a young man named David who lost his job without warning. His company ran into difficulties that the owner had been trying to conceal. One morning David came in for work and was told by his boss that the company was closing, effective immediately. At that point, David's wife had just given birth to their second child. He came to me shaking with anxiety and asking what he should do next. He only had three months of savings. He didn't know how to tell his wife.

I told him he had two choices. Did he think he could follow the best one? He said he thought he could. I told him the best thing to do would be to not tell his wife that he had lost his job. She would be rightly nervous and worried, which is not healthy for a new mother. Her worrying would do nothing to help him find a new job. Only he could fix this situation, and so it should be his burden to carry alone. I told him that what he needed to do was get up every day as if he was going to work, put on his suit and tie, kiss his wife good-bye, and then head down to the library and conduct his job search from there. He was to look at every company within a commutable distance, not just those hiring, but any company that he might be an asset to. And then we would network with people at the synagogue to see who worked where, and we would find him a job. I promised to share with him ancient Jewish wisdom on how to properly interview for a job. He had three months to get it done before he would need to tell his wife, but he would have to be able to hold it together for the sake of his family.

When I asked him if he could do this, he asked what his other choice was. What was second best? I told him plan B was this: tell his wife now. He would worry her, but if he couldn't hold it together, and she was going to have to carry the burden anyway, it would be best if he was open with her from the beginning.

He told me he could handle it and handle it he did. Magnificently. He asked his former boss not to tell his family what had happened and, should they call him, to take messages for him as if the company was not defunct. He hit the library and then the streets looking for a job, and within one month of starting his search, he found a new job . . . with 20% higher pay! Only then did he go home and tell his wife they were going out to dinner to celebrate. They hired a babysitter and went out alone. Over dinner, he took her hand and said, "I hope you won't be angry, but I have been keeping a secret from you." And at this point he told her everything. Of course, he was happy about his new job. She was also proud and grateful that he had carried the weight alone, allowing her to focus on their toddler and newborn and gain her strength back. His wife appreciated what an incredibly tough time he'd had for the past four weeks. She could see in his face how much he had silently endured for his family, and their marriage was stronger than ever before.

So, you see, not everyone need see the same face. In the case of David, I saw the face of a shaken, frightened man. His wife saw the face of the husband she loved who had made sacrifices for his family and remained on top of everything. She saw a man who had carried the family's financial burdens alone so she could tend to their children without worrying. He was able to show one face to me, one face to his wife, and yet a third face to the company where he was interviewed— that of a competent business professional worthy of a job. You don't have to share everything with everybody. Not everyone must know about all parts of you—just the parts they need to know. There is no shame in compartmentalizing your life. Certain things you must keep to yourself and bear alone. This is part of true leadership. David was a husband who understood leadership.

We have known entrepreneurs who were one payroll away from disaster. Each week was a constant struggle with cash flow. Yet throughout the challenging period they had good reason to anticipate the breakthrough in sales revenue that eventually arrived that put their enterprises onto firm ground. Had their faces displayed their fear and turmoil, some key employees might have become nervous and left for more secure employment.

General Eisenhower, supreme commander of the D-Day invasion did not share the poignant letter he penned early in the morning on June 6, 1944, with the more than 100,000 young soldiers who were about to storm the beaches. It was a letter to be opened and publicized if the invasion failed. He knew that, in spite of extensive preparation that had been going on for years, the chances of calamity were high. He agonized over that but never shared his worries with those he led. Whether in the military, in marriage, or in business, that is leadership. About 50 years ago, Randy Newman popularized a song called, "It's Lonely at the Top." He was right.

The flipside of this is to be alert when someone reveals a different side of themselves than they are choosing to share with you. This can even be unintentional. Matt and Sandy had been seeing each other for a few months when Sandy came to see us one afternoon. She was concerned about this relationship. Though they had only been going out for a few months, she thought they were very compatible, were drawing closer to each other, and potentially had a serious future together. They shared common goals, beliefs, and values. However, the previous Sunday she and Matt had attended a barbeque hosted by his old college buddies. She had fun and thought everyone seemed nice, but one thing disturbed her: Matt had avoided giving any indication of a special relationship to his friends. He had introduced her as if she were a casual friend or some random neighbor. Sandy wanted to know if she was making a mountain out of a molehill or if this was a real cause for concern.

We opened the Bible and read to her from Genesis, chapter 24, verses 2 through 8, a passage that details instructions Abraham gave to his servant, Eliezer, when he sent Eliezer to a distant land to bring back a wife for his son. Later in the story, the Bible spends valuable ink detailing Eliezer's arrival at the home of Rebecca. Rather than summarize what Eliezer tells Rebecca's family—which we have already heard straight from Abraham's mouth when he instructed his servant—the Bible repeats the story in detail. In any normal book, a repeated story like this would just be summarized. The author would write something along the lines of, "Eliezer related to Rebecca's family everything that his master Abraham had told him." An author would do this so as not to bore the reader with pages of dialogue repeating what the reader just read a few verses earlier.

Why would the Bible give a detailed repetition? It is not because the Bible is sloppily written! Everything in Scripture is there for a reason. Ancient Jewish wisdom tells us that anytime a story in the Bible is repeated in this way, we must search for differences in the story. These changes are important. If a story is repeated twice in detail, you can bet that it will not be verbatim. There will be differences, and they will be of significance.

In this case, there is a major variation between what Abraham originally said and how Eliezer recounts his master's words. According to Genesis 24:3, Abraham said, "Don't take a wife for my son from the daughters of the Canaanites, *among whom* I dwell." When Eliezer repeats this to Rebecca's family, he says, "Don't take a wife for my son from the daughters of the Canaanites, *in whose land* I dwell." Abraham said "among whom I dwell" because the land had already been promised to him by God. His statement reveals his belief that the land is his and the Canaanites are in his land. Eliezer, a servant, misses this point and misquotes his master as having attributed ownership of the land to the Canaanites.

The difference is that Abraham was a leader. He fully believed with a clear, unshakeable vision that the land was promised to him, and therefore he already visualized that it was his land and spoke of it as such. Eliezer was a follower who could not see beyond the readily evident reality of the here and now. He thought of the land as the

Canaanites' even though God had promised the land to Abraham and their time there was limited. The story is repeated twice to highlight this fact. On the surface, the two statements are similar enough, but if you dig deeper, you can see that the minor differences in phrasing reflect a massive disparity between the two men. One was a visionary and a leader. The other was a follower.

Our advice to Sandy was that while she shouldn't necessarily terminate her relationship with Matt based on what had happened at the barbeque, she was wise to pay close attention to small details. Before allowing herself to get more emotionally involved, she needed to see more than simply the face Matt was showing her in private. This is something you must train yourself to do as well.

God gave us one mouth but two ears so that we might listen twice as carefully as we speak. We have two ears also because God knows we need to listen more often than we need to speak. People reveal their inner thoughts by the words they use, and you must be attuned to the words of others because their words betray their real thoughts and feelings. What was clear was this: Matt had either a different view of their relationship than Sandy held, or he had difficulty communicating how he felt about their relationship. Maybe he didn't know what to say, or perhaps they really were on different pages. Whatever the case, clearly some mismatch or discord was being communicated, and Sandy had picked up on it.

Exactly a month after the cryptocurrency exchange FTX that he founded declared bankruptcy, Sam Bankman Fried was arrested at his luxury premises in the Bahamas and charged with fraud, conspiracy, and money laundering. We know a prominent and successful cryptocurrency trader who, unlike many, suffered no exposure in the immense FTX meltdown. We asked him how he had escaped involvement while many of his contemporaries were quickly lured into investing in FTX or its hundreds of associated entities. His answer: "I listened very carefully to everything that Bankman Fried said. For every statement he made about his core business, he made at least seven about his social and political passions. He spoke about making money only to participate in a movement called Altruistic Giving. He spoke about his many philanthropic endeavors and his futuristic visions. I just decided that his heart was not in growing the business. To him the business was part of a vast narcissistic initiative. And I turned out to be right."

More than 50 years ago an astute investor named Fred Schwed wrote a book on the stock market entitled "Where Are the Customers' Yachts?" The title refers to a famous story about a visitor to New York who admired the yachts of the bankers and brokers. He asked where all the customers' yachts were. Of course, none of the customers could afford yachts, even though they followed the advice of their bankers and brokers. Companies that do not appear to be prioritizing the "customers' yachts" at least as much as their own are not suitable partners as our cryptocurrency expert friend correctly discerned. And reading the faces, and hearing their words, helps us distinguish between suitable partners and those from whom we need to distance ourselves. When things go wrong in our romantic relationships, family lives, or, indeed, in our business interactions, we often say that we should have seen it coming. We are perhaps being jocular, but in fact, yes, it is often likely that we could have seen it coming. Do not miss the premonitions and red flags. You must be listening for when people inadvertently reveal themselves in their words. People do this all the time. You do it. We do it. Everyone does. We all give hints to what we are really thinking and feeling by the words we use and the way we say them.

An astute listener can pick up on subtle revealing language that helps him to better serve others. It is possible for a good listener to understand someone else's needs better than the speaker does. For example, a customer buying a scarf for her sister-in-law may seem to be having trouble choosing between the blue or green scarf. An attentive salesperson may pick up that she is actually looking for reassurance that this is an item her fashionable relative will appreciate. Perhaps a less subjective gift would be more suitable. The trick is learning to listen well. Never confuse what you want to hear with what the other person is really saying. Read between the lines. Do not minimize the importance of what people say and how they say it. Learn to read people and you will be well served in business interactions and in other areas of your life as well.

At the same time, a strong leader understands that he himself gives vocal cues and must be careful not to reveal all of his faces. The great military writer John Keagan called this ability the Mask of Command. Commanding officers don't allow their followers and soldiers to hear about information that they don't need to know and may actually harm them. Very often, commanding officers know frightening information, and there is no good reason to demoralize people. The job of a leader is often to carry the burden of worry and concern alone to spare his followers worry over that which they, as followers, cannot change or influence even if they had all the discomforting facts.

The Most Important Organ of Leadership Is Your Mouth

This principle may seem counterintuitive or hyperbolic, but we assure you it is not. You might have thought the brain was the most important organ for leadership. The brain is obviously very important to everything we do, but the mouth is the organ with which we communicate with others.

As in all professions, some realtors make more than others. Some make a fortune, while others barely make a living. Selling homes seems to be a lucrative profession. And, overall, it is . . . but not for everyone. What's the difference between those real-estate professionals who earn well and those who are barely eking out a living? Is it that the poor ones went to bad colleges and the rich ones went to good ones? This has no bearing on the matter. You most likely cannot name the various companies your realtor worked for over the past few years. It is also unlikely that you know how well she did on her qualifying exams. You probably don't know much about your realtor's professional history at all other than that she is licensed!

So how did you pick her? If you're like most of us, you found your realtor by word of mouth, either from friends or from reading reviews.

Either way, you chose her because her other clients spoke well of her. She sold your neighbor's house or helped your cousin find his home. And why did these people like and recommend her? Probably for the same reason you do: because of the way she communicates with her clients. She probably has excellent skills at listening to your needs and your fears. Her words and general countenance make you feel comfortable. Her knowledge of financing and ability to envision changes in a home are important tools in her work, but the gift of speaking and communicating well makes all the difference when it comes to running a good practice that makes money and matches sellers and buyers so that both are happy.

For all business professionals, good communication skills are often what make the difference between earning a lot of money or just a little. Speech is God's great gift to us. It's a unique gift that God gave to humans. Animals can communicate with noises and their bodies, but not by forming words to express their thoughts. Human beings communicate ideas that allow for nuance, detail, abstraction, and specificity. We are not born as good communicators, though. We must learn how to communicate effectively.

This is one of the most important secrets we can reveal: the importance of learning to communicate effectively. It doesn't matter how you make your living. However you serve other people, you will do so better by speaking more effectively. It doesn't matter if you're a bus driver or a salesperson. Whether you are a waiter, plumber, bookkeeper, landscaper, veterinarian, or a lawyer—whatever you do for a living, you will perform better and make more money if you learn to use your mouth more effectively than you do now.

Some people claim that they are simply not that articulate. They throw up their hands and say they are not good with words and are terrified of public speaking. Maybe they hesitate, mumble, search for words, have trouble projecting, or can't maintain eye contact when speaking. They accept this as an unchangeable fact of life. Does any of this sound like you? Whatever your shortcoming may be, you can correct it. You can improve and learn to articulate fluently and effectively.

One of the very important insights of ancient Jewish wisdom is that human beings are capable of change. More specifically relating to our topic, our souls are enormously impacted by what our ears hear our own mouths say. If you want to improve your speaking, here is our recommendation: listen to yourself speak. Become familiar with your speech patterns and decide how you would like to improve. Then it is time to do some homework. Carve out three opportunities a week at a minimum, more if you have the time and inclination, to read aloud to yourself for half an hour. Don't read just anything you have lying around; select a good book. You could, of course, read *the* good book, the Bible. But there are many other books with good vocabularies and grammar, well-written books out there to select. Don't just grab a tabloid magazine off the checkout stand at the supermarket and think that this will do. Pick a good piece of literature or an important book with good ideas—anything intelligent and well written. Start with something that is well written but at a reading level with which you are comfortable. If you are very uncomfortable with reading aloud, or you are not proficient in the language in which you conduct business, there are excellent books written for children that you might choose for a start. You can find recommendations on the internet. Classical homeschooling websites have excellent suggested reading lists. What you want is a book with decent vocabulary, great style, and good prose. As soon as you are comfortable with one level, move to a book with more advanced vocabulary and a more challenging style. Famous speeches from orators such as Abraham Lincoln, Winston Churchill, and Martin Luther King, Jr. are wonderful works to use for reading practice.

Reading aloud is an excellent way to train yourself to speak better. When your ears hear your mouth shaping those words, your tongue wrapping itself around the correct pronunciation and delivery, and your whole mouth articulating fluently, you will become more comfortable speaking. You won't have to pause to seek words because, when reading, the words are right there in front of you. Even many people who stutter are fine when they are reading aloud from a text. No matter what your difficulty is, you will improve, and it is going to sound and feel terrific to hear your lips and tongue shaping fluent words. The goal is to enunciate clearly and deliver the text naturally and powerfully. By regularly upgrading your reading material, you will acquire a stronger vocabulary and a more varied way of structuring sentences. All it takes is half an hour three times a week, and in no time, you will begin to see—and hear—improvements. People will compliment you on your improved speaking, and you will be able to smile and chalk one up for ancient Jewish wisdom.

Once you are comfortable reading aloud to yourself, you need to acclimate yourself to speaking in front of others. Start by sharing an interesting paragraph or two that you are reading with a friend. Then discuss it together. You may want to try spending some of your three weekly sessions of reading aloud by reading to someone else. The process is more enjoyable this way; moreover, it will allow you to practice speaking in front of others while you improve your skills. This will be less scary if you start with someone who loves and respects you. Your spouse may love to be read to—we regularly share interesting things we read with each other! Or maybe you have a child you can read to for part of your hours. There are many great children's books.

As you get more experience and practiced at reading aloud, you will begin to develop as a speaker. Now is the time to take a courageous leap. Jump at any opportunity to speak in public. Public speaking can be frightening, but you can overcome this stage fright with practice. The better you get at speaking in general, the easier it will be to speak in front of others. Initially, you may be speaking at a small family gathering, perhaps proposing a toast at an event, but the better you get and the more opportunities to speak publicly that you seize upon, the more often opportunities will come your way. People will recognize your developing talent and start coming to you when they need a speaker. Don't miss an opportunity to speak in public: speaking publicly is valuable training—eventually you may even find yourself getting paid for your efforts!

If you don't have family events you can easily attend and speak at, there are other options. There are organizations, like Toastmasters, that offer opportunities to fine-tune speaking skills while working alongside others who also recognize the importance of being able to use language well. You can even approach your friends about forming a club where you get together every few weeks to practice giving speeches in front of each other. Do not be afraid to ask—every participant will benefit, not just you.

Here are two tips on public speaking. The first tip is this: do not have notes in your hand or on your podium. In fact, leave your notes at home. You may think this sounds crazy and terrifying, but it is the only way to deliver a good speech. You do not want to practice *reading* a speech (that's what your three weekly sessions are for). You want to practice *giving* a speech. Reading your speech from notes will bore your audience because you will not make as much eye contact, and you will fail to fully reveal the window into your soul. If you read straight from notes, people will wonder why they came at all—you could have just given them your notes to read during their morning commute! A speech is not just the words but also your personal delivery of them. It is a performance, an interaction. When you look into people's eyes and speak from your heart, they will connect with you. This is the essence of being a good public speaker. Speakers draw energy from their audiences.

The second tip is a small practical matter that can pay big dividends. When people begin speaking in public, they often do not know what to do with their hands. Sometimes, they let their hands dangle, which is awkward and unnatural looking. Other people lock their elbows down and allow only their forearms to wave around. This can look as though you are doing a half-windmill motion—not good. Some people clutch the podium, which makes them look scared and timid, which, in turn, makes them feel scared and timid, which turns into a vicious cycle. Other people shove their hands into their pockets while they speak, which can come off as aloof, unconcerned, or unprepared.

What you want to do is this: move naturally. Gesture naturally. Let your arms reflect the words that are coming out of your mouth. But don't overdo it; you want to appear natural and comfortable. Watch videos of great orators and notice how they move—natural and unencumbered, but expressive. Their hands seem to mimic the meaning and emotion of what their mouths are saying. Study videos of famous speakers giving famous speeches and pay attention to the details. Watch the same speech a few times. One time focus on their body language; another time focus on how they modulate their voice rather than speaking in a monotone. Each time you watch the same speech, you will learn something new. Keep in mind, though, that giving a presentation on your company's performance in the previous financial quarter to your coworkers in the boardroom is different from delivering the State of the Union address. Make sure your countenance and delivery are appropriate to the venue and audience.

So, practice reading aloud and jump at opportunities to speak in front of others, and you will see improvements in no time. No matter what business you are in, if you are interacting with other people, learning to speak more fluently is priceless. You may find that it is worth $10,000 to you in your very first year—maybe tens of thousands of dollars, maybe more. Follow this advice, put in the work, and it will pay real dividends because your mouth, your ability to speak, is one of your greatest tools when it comes to making more money.

Recognizing What You Can't Do

Virginia Oliver, may she live and be healthy, sets out in her lobster boat every day from June to September in order to tend her two hundred traps. She tackles the not-always-friendly waters of Rockland, Maine, together with her 78-year-old son, Max. When we last checked in preparation for this book, Virginia was 101 and still lobstering.

Did her granddaughter ever say, "Granny, you can't take the boat out today, it's blowing 25 knots"? Did a healthcare advisor ever say, "Virginia, you can't lobster today; it's raining, and you could fall and break a leg on the slippery deck of that old boat"? Actually, we have no idea. But what we do know is that Virginia never listened to anyone who told her, "You can't."

We greatly admire Virginia. She teaches us something both useful and important. Many things are important but not useful. The Nagorno-Karabakh conflict between Armenia and Azerbaijan is certainly important in geopolitical terms, but for most people, knowing about it can hardly be called useful. On the other hand, knowing how to rip a long-tenured bandage off your arm without a yelp of pain as you tear out dozens of hair follicles is certainly useful but is not really important.

What we saw Virginia living is really a critical aspect of how we're created. Most animals on this amazingly varied planet prefer to avoid confrontation even when the rewards of victory would be substantial. Fight is preferable to flight only when escape is impossible. However, humans will face great risk for possible high reward or even sometimes nothing more than the reward of achievement.

We've known top rate sales professionals who accept commission-only positions. They confidently confront the risk of zero income in exchange for almost limitless upside potential. There are mountain-eers like Ed Viesturs, who has climbed all 14 world peaks of more than 25,000 feet, and climbers like Alex Honnold who climbed the cliff face of El Capitan in California's Yosemite Park alone and without ropes. No animals voluntarily place themselves at serious risk of bodily harm or death for little or no tangible reward. Humans are quite unique.

Having been touched by the Divine, we humans find the allure of the unlimited to be all but irresistible. We obviously lack God's omniscience and His omnipotence, but we sure seem to yearn for it. Even animals that store away food, as squirrels do, only store away the finite amounts needed to see them through the winter. Only humans possess a desire for wealth beyond the needs of a normal lifetime.

Many individuals expend immeasurable energy on the quest for power. Being able to exert control over others is for many, highly seductive. One need only observe with deserved dismay the extent to which government bureaucrats relish wielding power over citizen supplicants. The draconian remedies pursued by governments during the 2020 COVID-19 epidemic, and which probably did more harm than the disease, revealed the frightening extent to which bureaucrats were intoxicated by the ability to exert enormous power over their fellow citizens. Again, it is all but impossible to find similar behavior among animals.

Whether it is unlimited power, money, or any of the other human appetites for which we yearn in limitless quantity, that yearning is a reflection of our Divine origins. Many people, in particular children who have not yet been bludgeoned by the vicissitudes of life, find the words "you can't" to be an almost irresistible trigger to give it a shot. Whether it is the child pushing at his parentally set limits or the athlete stirred to higher effort and achievement by a friend saying,

"You couldn't do that," most of us humans find ourselves vexed by any external efforts to impose limits upon ourselves.

There is obviously both a positive side to this as well as a negative aspect. Finding ourselves stimulated to greater effort and achievement by the gnawing irritant inside of ourselves that whispers, "Go on, you can do it. There's nothing you can't do" is clearly at the heart of unimaginable feats like Usain Bolt winning the 100 meters at the 2012 London Olympics in a blistering nine and a half seconds or a teenaged Khatia Buniatishvili playing Rachmaninov's demanding second piano concerto in international competition. Although Usain retired from athletics in 2017, he still remains the only runner to have taken titles in three consecutive Olympic Games. Khatia is now in her mid-30s and is still seen as one of the finest Rachmaninov interpreters in the world.

The negative side of this allure of the infinite from which we humans suffer is the terrible danger of someone with the physical build of a refrigerator and a complete lack of natural talent being told that he could achieve the artistic heights of ballet dancing. He would sadly waste his life or a big part of it in a quite futile attempt to overcome the whispered, "You can't," when that is exactly the voice he should have attended. And this is why the book that you now hold in your hands is not only important but also useful. Not everybody will be capable of running a lobster boat into their 90s and beyond. That heavily built young man was never going to become the next Baryshnikov of the Bolshoi Ballet, but he might well have achieved excellence in another field had he not wasted his years dreaming of dancing.

This is admittedly difficult for a person of spirit to confront. We live in a time when educational institutions that are meant to help students learn how the world really works, instead indoctrinate their young charges to believe that men can become women and women can become men. That any part of your destiny is fixed or even limited in any way is anathema to the progressive person.

Bookshelves groan beneath the burden of the countless books speaking lyrically of hope and optimism. Believe in it and you'll be able to do it, they urge. And there are times when most of us urgently need this kind of encouragement. Yes, there are many occasions on which we need to be reminded that many of our obstacles are mental and can be overcome by changing our thinking. Anyone can find a book along these lines that will match his mood. But in this book we want to emphasize that we humans all do have certain limits and that learning what they are liberates us to reach for the sky in other areas. We have to learn to manage the exquisite tension between our souls that beckon us to the infinite and our bodies which, like all things physical, have limitations.

In May 1954, British medical student, Roger Bannister, became the first human being to run a mile in under 4 minutes. Some doctors had confidently predicted that even the effort would kill an athlete. After Bannister breasted the tape in 3:59 on that blustery day in Oxford, England, he fell exhausted to the grass and commentators assumed he had died. They were wrong. Not only did he go on to break his own record a few months later, but he enjoyed a long career as a successful doctor.

There was really nothing magical about a 4-minute mile that should have alarmed some doctors into mistakenly assuming that it was impossible any more than some experts earlier assumed that a 5-minute mile was impossible. But I assuredly inform you that no human being will ever run a 1-minute mile just as I assert that no Olympic high jumper will ever jump unassisted over a two-story house. The reason is because objective measures having to do with things like human metabolism and gravity reliably set those limits.

In other words, many challenges can be overcome by ignoring naysayers and refusing to hear the words "you can't." But wise people abandon those other challenges that truly can't be done. One can hardly overestimate the importance of being able to know the difference. This is one of those areas in which an outsider probably knows better than we do ourselves. We may be gnawed by internal doubt and a background of many failures. A wise and knowledgeable guide would be just the person to reassure us and encourage us to go ahead and succeed in what he or she knows to be eminently doable by you. Conversely, and just as importantly, that same trusted advisor can save you heartache, time, and embarrassment by steering you away from a goal that you cannot possibly win. Knowing what you really can't do allows you to fling all your energies and resources into what you can do. This is a critical take-away from this book. Read it, understand it, apply it, resculpt your life logistics, and prepare for success.

Secret #22

As Painful as Change Can Be, It Often Contains the Seeds of Growth

Avoiding change leads to stagnation. If you don't embrace change, you cannot grow. Some change is inevitable. No matter what you do, you are going to get older. One day you are going to die. And between now and then, many things are going to happen to you and around you. The important question is whether you proactively deal with change or passively endure it.

While change is automatic, growth is not. We know vibrant, exciting people who are still growing well into their 10th decade on earth, and we know stagnant individuals who are in their 20s. Growth involves effort, and pretty much by definition, it involves a willingness to change.

We cannot control change that is thrust upon us. Perhaps a natural event such as an earthquake or a tsunami forces us to build anew. The 9/11 terrorist attack on the World Trade Center in New York City upended many a business plan. In early 2020, tens of thousands of business plans were nullified by unprecedented governmental edict. In dozens of countries around the world, people's hopes and dreams were shattered. Many submitted and fell into a state of surrender. However, many others seized the opportunities that even abrupt and heavy-handed change presented. Vast numbers of people discovered that immoral government policies and political shockwaves could destroy what they had spent years building. In our private lives, dozens of things happen that did not go according to our hopes and plans. In instances like that, we can only control our own reactions to events. You cannot stand in place. Resisting change does not prevent it; such passivity simply prevents you from taking the reins.

Sometimes, our families are the source of great and sad changes in our lives. During his presidency (1969–1974), Richard Nixon appointed Walter Annenberg to the position of U.S. Ambassador to the Court of St. James in London. Prior to this, Annenberg was best known as the creator and publisher of *TV Guide*, which at its height was by far the biggest selling magazine in America. His prosperity also arose from other highly successful commercial enterprises. When Queen Elizabeth II of England visited President Ronald Reagan in California, she also accepted the hospitality of Walter Annenberg at his palatial Palm Springs estate. Annenberg took Queen Elizabeth out on a golf cart tour of his extensive property. Of this, he later told the press that he just wanted to show her majesty "how the average American lives."

Hold it, you might be saying. Walter Annenberg was no average American! He was incredibly rich! Well, yes, but in what used to be a paradigm for America, his family's story was not one of great ancestral wealth being passed down but rather one where hard work led to riches. His grandfather, a Jewish immigrant from Prussia, lived with his family of 11 children in a small apartment in Chicago. The most enterprising of the children, Moses, helped to feed the family by catching fish in Lake Michigan. Moses went on to start his own family and amassed wealth in a variety of publishing businesses. By the mid-1930s, he owned the *Philadelphia Inquirer*, among other papers.

At this point, you might think that Moses' son, Walter, had it made. He did not have to fight his way out of poverty as his father did. Yet, a difficult change was coming. When Walter Annenberg was 32 years old, his father Moses was incarcerated for two years in federal prison for evading taxes. In a flash, Walter's life was in a shambles. He had not chosen for this great change to come to his life, yet here it was. Walter's reaction to this debacle was to take control of his father's businesses and assume responsibility for the $5 million of unpaid tax debt. Walter Annenberg once found a quotation in a prayer book that had belonged to his father. It read: "Cause my works on earth to reflect honor on my father's memory." Walter had the words engraved on a bronze plaque for his office. These words served as a beacon to him to rehabilitate the Annenberg name. He became a great philanthropist and numerous institutions that benefited from his generosity carry the Annenberg name. The sad past spurred Walter into a creative drive of entrepreneurial fury that he might never have discovered within himself had he not had to grapple with the changes brought about by his father's incarceration. We don't know, but we wonder whether Walter's mother, who was a religious Jew, shaped his thinking and ability to cope.

While this story is writ on a large scale, its base idea is not unusual. How many times have you known someone, maybe yourself, who was laid off or fired for reasons that you thought were unjust, only to bounce back twice as strong? Not infrequently, people not only find a new job after losing their old one, but they also often find a better, higher-paying job. Had they not had the misfortune of losing their old job, they might never have looked to change. We all can choose to see ourselves as victims of unfortunate, or even horrible, events in our own lives or in the lives of our families. That road leads to failure.

Better to absorb this lesson from the Bible. Understand your purpose and cling to your principles. Once you have that unshakeable foundation, recognize that change begets opportunity.

Consider 2 Samuel, chapter 20, in which an unimpressive individual named Sheba launches a rebellion against King David. The king sends his best general, Joab, to kill Sheba, who has been holed up in a city close to the Jordan River. Joab's forces storm the city walls and are about to pour into the city when a mysterious old lady appears and demands to speak with Joab. She reprimands him for attacking the entire city without first giving them the opportunity to hand over Sheba peacefully. General Joab agrees with the woman's words and quickly apologizes. They strike a deal to hand over Sheba. The elderly woman returns to the city, and soon thereafter, Sheba's head is delivered to Joab, and the city is saved.

What made a powerful general apologize to an old lady and change his battle plans? Ancient Jewish wisdom explains that this venerable woman was a daughter of Asher, the granddaughter of the patriarch Jacob. And she had quoted to Joab this law from the Torah: "When you approach a city to make war against it, you shall call out for a peaceful surrender" (Deuteronomy 20:10). As a general in King David's army, Joab had to obey the word of God, the highest of all authorities, even when it came from the mouth of an elderly woman. Joab knew his purpose. He did not confuse his plan with his purpose. He was a wise leader who was able to recognize that his plan did not match the situation, and he willingly changed course, seizing upon the opportunity to take back Sheba's head without having to sack the entire city.

Being a general was Joab's way of serving God. We all serve God by fulfilling our destinies and serving our purpose in His plan. Joab recognized that his purpose was to serve God in this way, but he was flexible in how to carry out that plan. When called to account, he embraced change. Rather than arrogantly taking umbrage at an old woman who challenged him, Joab took the opportunity of being openly chastised to reassess the situation. He achieved his aim without wanton destruction, a better outcome than what originally would have happened.

By this point of our book, we hope you already feel increasingly comfortable about being in business, making money, and growing wealthy. You understand that the very act of receiving money as a consequence of serving people and providing them with their needs is usually inherently moral and dignified. However, this is not always the case. In addition to the instances that involve fraud or manipulating the force of government so that people are forced to buy from you, in many of the wealthiest countries in the world, and certainly in the United States, making money is sometimes pitted against living a principled and moral life. We may be called to temporarily work against our best financial outcomes if our purpose is pitted against our plans.

What do we mean? Here are a few examples with which we are familiar, but you can find more in the pages of any newspaper, on the campus of any college, and in numerous trade associations.

1. Cindy worked hard and painstakingly accumulated the money for tuition to achieve an advanced degree in nursing. The hospital where she now works for a good salary and with excellent benefits becomes a center for medical procedures that violate her ethics. She believes that these procedures harm patients rather than help them. In fact, by participating in these procedures in her role as nurse, she suspects that she would be damaging her own humanity. What does she do?

2. Tim is an up-and-coming member of a growing technology firm. He becomes aware that many of those who founded the firm and are in leadership positions do not allow their own children to use the products they produce and promote because they know how harmful they are to teenagers. By continuing on his career path, he expects to do well financially, but he worries that he will be harming members of his community and nation. What does he do?

3. A great deal of C.J.'s business comes from referrals. A sociopolitical movement takes deep roots in his city, and local businesses scurry to pronounce their involvement and support of this movement. C.J. is sure that this movement will cause great harm and injury to his area as well as diverting dollars from important causes into the pockets of a few charlatans. Yet, if he doesn't put a poster in his store window, pronounce his support on social media, and pretend to approve of this group, he will be ostracized by his peers. What does he do?

Perhaps these examples resonate with you; you are fortunate if they do not. Maybe your test will come when a higher-up asks you to falsify a document or when you have the opportunity to get a kickback for a referral. Life has a way of testing all of us. We are not answering the three questions that we just asked because we cannot. Questions of this sort are usually very specific and personal. We are simply acknowledging that these unanticipated and unwelcome situations that might necessitate drastic change do arise. Keeping your eye on the goal allows you best to make that decision.

The lesson is that change, while it is often scary and stressful, can carry the seeds of growth and good fortune. This is as true in business as it is in our personal lives or on the battlefield. We must remain true to our purpose but accept that change will happen and adjust our plans, behavior, and business tactics so that we may not lose sight of our purpose. Embrace change, and you may find fortune where you thought there was only misery.

Because Change Is a Constant Reality, Life Is More Accurately Depicted by a Video Than a Photograph

Imagine we show you two photographs. One picture shows a couple who look extremely happy together. The man and woman are holding hands and smiling at each other on a sunny day. The second photograph is of another couple. This second couple also looks happy. The man has his arm around the woman's shoulders. She has her arm around his waist. Same sunny day. Same big smiles. We have two pictures. A different man and different woman in each one, but everyone looks happy. You might think these photographs are more or less the same. They certainly appear that way.

What you can't tell from looking at the pictures is that the first photograph is of a married couple who are dedicated to each other and their family. They are looking forward to living out their lives in love, harmony, and tranquility. Regarding the second couple, what if we told you they were also married, but not to each other? Here we have two married people stealing an afternoon of illegitimate bliss in a local hotel while their unsuspecting spouses are home tending to the adulterers' kids and houses. Two different situations here, but you would never know that from looking at the photographs.

Now imagine that, rather than looking at a still photograph, we were watching a multi-hour video of the same two couples. You would see one couple meet, get married, have children, eventually spend the wonderful moment depicted in the video together and then go home to their kids, thank and pay the babysitter, and lie down in bed to read side by side. If the video were long enough, we could watch them grow old and live happily ever after. But we would watch the other couple, the adulterers, perhaps encountering one another on a social media platform online. We might see a long sequence of bad judgments resulting in the hotel tryst. We would probably see them emerge warily from the hotel. We would see them go home and kiss their betrayed spouses with the same lips they kissed their lovers. You would see them struggle to lie to their spouses and children. You might see them crying in the shower or drinking a little too much, and in time, you could witness the cheating individuals facing divorce. You might even see them remarry each other only to cheat on each other and divorce again. These original photographs still show two smiling, delighted couples; only by viewing a video can we see how their lives drastically diverge from that deceptively similar-looking moment. The key thing to realize here is that the photograph is misleading about both the particular moment when the picture was taken and the long haul both before and after the picture was snapped.

A photograph cannot capture reality as well as a video because a photograph is merely a snapshot of one moment in time with no context. A video captures the truth for all to see because a viewer can see the past leading up to the present as well as the consequence of the actions that follow the moment the snapshot is taken. A video captures the passage of time, which places fleeting moments into context. Life is far more like a video than a photograph, because we live in a world where time passes. We live in a world where change is continual and ceaseless.

When examining and assessing your finances, business, or the course of your career, do not use a snapshot. Examine your personal and business matters as if you are watching a video. In other words, don't focus just on the here and now. Consider where you have been, where you are headed, look for trends, and track your direction. Do not think for a moment that you can stand still in life. Life involves change, and change means that a snapshot cannot provide you with the truth about anything. The truth is only visible when you consider the passage of time.

I [RDL] once did consulting work for a struggling factory near San Diego. This kind of consulting requires that you get to know a business from the bottom up. To get a feel for the workplace before I began my formal training sessions, I spoke to a variety of employees, including a number of assembly line factory workers. One of the people I interviewed, Miguel Rodriguez, had recently immigrated to California from Mexico with his wife, two children, and mother in-law. He was very happy to have found work at the factory even though the job paid minimum wage. It's hard for me to imagine supporting such a large family on minimum wage, but with a little ingenuity, Miguel and his wife were able to get by. He worked overtime when he could, which paid time and a half, and his mother-in-law watched the children during the day so that his wife could also hold down a job. She, too, made only minimum wage, but on a dual income and with free childcare, they were able to manage. You might have thought that Miguel would be stressed and bitter about his situation. He was not. On the contrary, he was happy, hopeful, and grateful for the opportunity to have found a job—any job—in the United States. "We do real well," he said, genuinely. "We are as happy as could be to be here."

Miguel was a pleasure to speak with, a real inspiration, and I looked forward to talking to him again when I returned to the factory a year later for an annual review. I arrived early just so I could steal a few minutes to speak with him before going about my duties. I went to the human resources office to look up my old friend. This was a big factory with hundreds of workers, but the HR director knew him by name. His good attitude made him very popular around the factory. Now, I had suspected that with his good attitude and outlook, Miguel was going places. But I didn't know how far! Miguel was now in charge of maintaining all the forklift trucks.

How did he get the promotion? How did Miguel advance from being an assembly line worker in an unskilled position to heading a group of maintenance workers? The story went like this: One day, the company that the factory owner contracted with to maintain the forklifts raised their prices. It was more than the factory's management wished to pay. When Miguel saw a forklift sitting on the side out of commission, he offered to try to fix it. He told the boss that everyone in Mexico was an amateur mechanic because you had to learn how to make cars run forever. The boss gave Miguel a chance, and he succeeded! When I saw him a year later, Miguel was making four or five times the minimum wage because his boss valued his work. Miguel was delighted with his new salary, his boss was delighted to pay that salary knowing the Miguel was saving the company more than they were paying him, and both were looking forward to an ongoing relationship. With his new wage, Miguel's wife no longer had to work, a fact that had Miguel beaming with pride.

Let me ask you this: If I had looked at Miguel Rodriguez's life as a snapshot when I first met him, what would I have seen? Both he and his wife were working long hours, and his mother-in-law was also working hard, looking after the children, whom the parents barely ever saw. All that work and they were still just scraping by. That would be a pretty hard life to lead. I probably would have taken pity on him. But life isn't a snapshot. Life is like a video. Miguel was able to remain unfailingly cheerful and positive because he knew that he wasn't stuck making minimum wage forever. The "video" of his life up to that point showed him moving from poverty in Mexico to a minimum-wage job in the United States. He knew that more change was possible if he continued to seize upon the opportunities presented to him. And he was right. A mere 12 months later, he was earning substantially more. He no longer had to put in overtime to pay his bills. His wife was staying home with the kids. His mother-in-law was free to pursue her own needs.

This is what life looks like when you see it as a video, not a snapshot. Don't despair about your current situation. Change it! If you put in the work and seize upon opportunity, you can see great change. Remain cheerful. Stay positive and, like Miguel, seek and seize opportunity when it presents itself. Your life doesn't have to stay the same. In fact, it won't! It never does. As we have seen, change is inevitable, so there is no benefit to letting your fear immobilize you.

We have also seen that change is scary, even when it is a change for the better. A major promotion can be almost as scary as losing your job. No doubt Miguel had anxiety over the future at each change point of his life. What if he got to the United States and couldn't find a job? What if he couldn't keep the forklifts running—would he get fired and then not have the security of his old job? You bet he worried about these things, but he didn't let it paralyze him. Change is inevitable because God placed us in a world of time. Every ticking second, every minute, every day heralds the arrival of the new. Our ability to live safely and comfortably depends upon cultivating an easy adaptability to new circumstances. Change is scary because we are most comfortable when we live under stable and predictable conditions, but everything is ephemeral. Changes in health, in financial and social circumstances, in the well-being of your family—all these things are as scary as they are inevitable.

Change is best managed by acquiring courage. To guide us through change, the Tanakh, the collected Hebrew Scriptures, gives us a repeated message to be strong and of good courage, *chazak v'ematz* in Hebrew. Every time these two Hebrew words appear in Scripture, a major change in someone's life circumstances is about to happen. At the end of Moses' life, when he recounts God's appointing Joshua to be his successor, Moses says to Joshua, "Be strong and of good courage" (Deuteronomy 31:7 and 31:23). This phrase appears a few more times in Joshua's life and again when King David hands over the kingship to his son, Solomon (1 Chronicles 28:20). We can break this phrase down into its composite parts. *Chazak* refers to strength. The word first appears in Genesis 41:57 in reference to the famine that had overtaken Egypt. Scripture notes that "the famine was strong in all the land." Events can be so strong that they are overpowering; such was that ancient period of famine. Not surprisingly, when times like that occur, we need to match the strength of the circumstances with *chazak*, strength of our own. In Hebrew, *V'ematz* means "and be courageous." Putting the two words together is not a pretty piece of poetry. God's book is teaching us an eternal human lesson. Having strength isn't enough; one also needs to have the fortitude and courage to use it. For example, Winston Churchill claimed that World War II need never

have taken place. When Hitler invaded the Rhineland in the spring of
1936, violating the terms of the agreement that ended World War I,
Britain and the Allies could have confronted Hitler there and then and
precipitated his fall from power. Instead, they hesitated. They possessed
the military capacity. They had the *chazak*. What they lacked was the
courage and the willpower, the *ematz,* to do anything. Instead, they
chose the path of appeasement and much suffering followed. Scripture
teaches that we must first have *chazak,* strength, and then we need to
also gather the courage to do whatever needs doing. Gaining strength
is a matter of strategy. Gaining courage is more complicated.

Here are three pathways to developing courage. First, analyze each
challenge that you face separately so that you are not overwhelmed
by fear. Problems often come in groups, and tackling them all at once
can leave us feeling overwhelmed. If you are trying to start a business,
your needs seem to be endless. You might need zoning approval for a
store, suppliers for inventory, a loan from the bank, and dozens of other
requirements to get off the ground. Separate them into small and discrete steps. You can do them simultaneously, if need be, but separate
them in your mind. Use your journal. Use pen and paper. Use one of
the many good organizing apps out there. Analyze each one by itself,
organize the steps you need to take, and when you are tackling one
problem, force your mind not to stray to all the others that are awaiting
your attention.

The second way to cultivate courage is to realize that cowardice is
contagious. Cowardice is our natural default condition. Cowardice is
the result of spiritual gravity sucking us down. Armies treat panicked
soldiers severely because once the first soldier on a battlefield turns and
flees, the whole unit might soon break. When a fire or other emergency breaks out in a crowded area, injuries and death often result
more from the panicked response of the crowd than from the original problem. Over the past decades as news headlines shriek about
catastrophe awaiting us, anxiety and fear have spread throughout
populations. Terror and fear are contagious. They spread. When we see
our comrades running in fear, we too begin to feel fear, whether it is
warranted or not.

But did you know that the opposite is also true? Cowardice is contagious, but courage is equally contagious. On a practical level, this

means you should find people with courage and surround yourself with them. They will bolster your own courage and spiritual fortitude.

And finally, a third way to cultivate courage is to proactively seek strength in ancient Jewish wisdom. When you feel yourself faltering before fear, let the magic of the Lord's language wash over you. Repeat the phrase *chazak v'ematz* in your head and aloud. Let it be your mantra—a meditation. Be strong and of good courage. Be strong and of good courage. Be strong and of good courage. Repeat this to yourself over and over again. Be strong and of good courage. Develop the muscles you need and the willpower to employ them.

Scary, inevitable change is constant. But courage becomes constant with exercise and regular use. Courage will always be the best way to handle fear and cope with change.

The More That Things Change, the More We Must Depend Upon Those Things That Never Change

This is perhaps the principle I [RDL] repeat more than any other on my podcast. While some things change extensively, and perpetually, there are also timeless truths that remain constant, like these biblical secrets, for instance. They comprise ancient Jewish wisdom and are unfaltering. We may depend on them in the face of change.

And change we will face. Change is ubiquitous. It seems to be accelerating in the modern world. These days we see change that is more rapid and profound than we have ever seen before in recent history. Who could have predicted how many governments around the world would hobble businesses and micro-control their citizens citing COVID-19 as the reason? Likewise, few pundits predicted the extent to which internet platforms such as YouTube, Vimeo, TikTok, and many others would draw eyeballs away, not only from the living room television set, but also from everything happening around them. Even as late as 2007, when Steve Jobs, to great fanfare, announced the first Apple iPhone, who anticipated just how many functions would migrate to that small handheld device? The realtor who that same year drove from one appointment to another with a notebook of contacts and phone numbers, a thick Thomas Guide street map of the city, another book of listings, and yet another with details of local schools and shops did not predict that in a few short years all that paraphernalia would be replaced by a small smartphone. The progress of technological and social change, for good and bad, has been going on since Adam and Eve left the Garden of Eden. You can pretty much date a photograph just by examining the buildings, cars, and clothes people wear and the gadgets that they use.

Technology, science, and medicine change. Progress in these areas brings great opportunity as well as great danger. Even when change is for the good, it brings great disruption, which is why it is also scary. All change, good and bad, creates uncertainty. Fortunately, we may take comfort in the knowledge that there are some things that are unchanging, and we may draw energy and insight from these timeless truths. We can use those things that never change to help us capably cope the many things that do change.

As the internet has matured to become a prominent feature of daily life, investors, pundits, and professionals became increasingly excited about new business opportunities unleashed. New websites and dot-com startups emerged daily. Some were business to business; some were business to consumer. Not all online entrepreneurs realized that website traffic, eyeballs, and reviews did not equal revenue. The markets were often bullish about trendy technologies like solar and wind power, autonomous vehicles, and cryptocurrency, but they often failed to realize that the driving force behind these websites and trends was not dollars, but delusion. Investors, politicians, and media were getting excited by the number of eyeballs and the hype, not by the cash they were bringing in. Disregard for financial realities was often flagrant. They ignored a crucial unchangeable truth: a business is something to which customers are willing to hand over their money in exchange for the goods or services it provides. Regardless of how flashy the prospectus is, if it doesn't have customers, it is not a business. Building vast numbers of battery-driven cars might look good in the world of public relations and at the parties in Davos, Switzerland, but if those e-cars back up on huge lots of unsold inventory, you do not have a business.

What never changed was the fact that earning money (in a free capital market) proves you're delivering value to other people and is fundamental to running a business. It turns out that profit is a priority for everyone wanting to be in business, even those whose businesses are largely online! This was a major problem for industries, and the stock market as a whole, because people invested vast sums of money in all kinds of websites that, while they were good at attracting eyeballs, had not found a way to monetize their presence. People were coming online and leaving without paying for anything. A lot of people lost a lot of money when the market realized this. The stock market bubble burst, and many websites and their owners went out of business. The equity that stockholders held in these companies vanished practically overnight.

These are examples of the failure to cope with change that results from not remembering that which never changes. One thing that never changes—and business owners should always remember this—is that a business cannot last without making a profit. A business can float by on loans and investment capital while getting established, but it must eventually turn a profit.

The creation of wealth is also a necessary part of the foundation of societies. The creation of wealth is a desirable thing for both society and individuals. Ancient Jewish wisdom recognizes this tenet, which is enshrined in the Lord's language. The Hebrew word for wealth is spelled O—SH—R, pronounced *osher.*

One thing that is unique to the Lord's language is that certain important words that mean one thing will mean the opposite when read backward. For instance, the Hebrew word for rubbish is R—P—SH. Reading that backward, we have SH—P—R, which means "super." The word meaning rubbish spelled backwards gives us the word meaning super or valuable because something that is rubbish is the opposite of that which is super. A word having the opposite meaning when read backward is a common occurrence in ancient Hebrew and is meant to draw attention to the polarizing connection of opposites.

What is the opposite of *osher*? You might think *poor,* but you would be wrong. The opposite of a wealthy *person* is a poor *person,* but *osher* refers to wealth as a concept. *Osher* is the principle of wealth. What is the opposite of the principle of wealth? Spelled backward, *osher* reads R—SH—O, which gives us the word *R-SH-O*, which means *evil.* The opposite of wealth is evil. In this way, ancient Hebrew tells us that it is God's will to create a healthy, vibrant, successful society, which requires the concept of wealth. Earlier we learned that wealth is God's reward for serving other people. If wealth is not being created, then evil is being done, which means that people are making mistakes in their behavior. When people make good choices, when they serve one another, wealth is created, so it isn't surprising that the absence of wealth, *on a societal level,* means an absence of good in the structure of that society.

This understanding has a profound impact on how we should do business. You probably already felt that wealth is a good thing. Almost everyone wants to be wealthy! You may not have realized that we need to look at the ability for individuals to ethically earn wealth on a societal level. When a government legislates in opposition to individuals accumulating wealth in upright ways, for example, by redistributing money or stacking the game so that only the elite or their supporters can be financially successful, what is happening is evil. In other words, God's natural ideal default condition would be people in society creating wealth. Poverty and destitution are the results of society making mistakes and disobeying God's plan. Societies that are not prospering are engaging in behavior and practices they should not be doing. God designed a system that rewards correct human interaction. We want to stress that we are not by any means suggesting that any single impecunious individual is evil. In no way should those individuals enduring financial stress automatically see themselves as lacking in virtue. Similarly, we don't accept that any wealthy individual is, by definition, good. The formulation we are discussing applies chiefly to a society or an economy. If an economy is struggling and wealth is not being created, the reason is not, as the old-time Soviets would suggest, the weather. It is nearly always the consequence of corruption and following a destructive economic model.

A common myth bandied about in famous literature and popular culture is that poverty is virtuous. This is fallacious. Never associate poverty with virtue. The truth is actually the reverse. If a society appears not to be blessed economically, we must take a hard look at the society and question whether it is truly behaving as it should. Sometimes individuals are complicit in their own poverty, but other times people can be doing all they can, but they live in a hopeless, degenerate nation or neighborhood that precludes wealth. A person who is suffering financially is neither automatically virtuous nor automatically vice ridden.

However, something is very wrong when the wealthy and successful are unthinkingly portrayed as evil. It wasn't until about 1934, due to a book by Matthew Josephson, that men like Andrew Carnegie began to be referred to as "robber barons." Until then those titans of commerce and industry were seen as worthy of admiration and emulation. Of course, to this very day, the envious do-nothings who malevolently defame those nineteenth-century wealth creators as robber barons never actually treat them as unique individuals, identifying just whom each is supposed to have robbed or how they robbed them. Ignored is the great philanthropy that many of them practiced such as Andrew Carnegie, who donated a library to each of hundreds of small towns across America, Were all these super-rich men upright and noble? No. Neither were they all inhumane and malevolent.

And so, you can see that ancient Jewish wisdom shows us that the concept of wealth is and always will be a foundation of society. It is something that will never change, even as the instruments of business evolve to accommodate and make use of technology. But this is only one of many things that will never change. There are others.

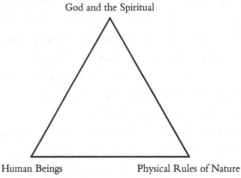

God and the Spiritual

Human Beings   Physical Rules of Nature

There are three spheres of reality that are what they are. There is no more point in shaking a defiant fist at these three areas than there is in trying to stop the incoming tide. These three unchangeables are (1) God, (2) human nature, and (3) rules of true science, such as the laws of physics and chemistry.

That is not to say that individual humans never change or that the environment never changes—clearly, they do—but that the principles governing human behavior and the way the world works are unchanging. Thus, those two things, along with God and the spiritual world, are the things that never change. Understand them because they are tools to help you cope with the maelstrom of change in the world. They are your pillars; see them through the principles of ancient Jewish wisdom as best you can. The reality of these things does not change over time, though our personal knowledge of them is something we must develop. This is, in fact, the way in which personal growth (change) happens—by understanding the unchangeable principles that govern your life. For example, the rules of buoyancy—what floats and what sinks—have not changed over history. However, as we better understand the rules, we can craft more advanced ships, whether they use oars, coal, steam, or nuclear power.

While we learn more about science and develop more technology as time goes by, our collective knowledge of God, and human nature, often becomes less, or goes through cycles, as we move further away from the revelation at Mt. Sinai. We get seduced by the idea of *progress* without evaluating what we mean by that word. For example, consider your knowledge and contrast it against that of your grandparents. You almost certainly know more science and technology than your grandparents did, but it is completely possible that you know less than your grandparents about marriage and raising children. It is possible that, in general, families of years ago had a better understanding of two people committing to each other and to their children. We may comfort ourselves by saying, "Well, times are different! Things are more complicated today!" But this is exactly the point. As we learn more about science and technology, we find it increasingly incumbent upon ourselves to develop our knowledge of what does not change so that we may not be confused or led astray. Perhaps everyone and everything is telling you that you must focus exclusively on your own happiness and what is best for you in the moment without regard to the bigger picture. Marriage is optional and if entered into, not meant to last, while children get in the way of happiness. There is no excuse for not recognizing the fallacy of those arguments. The knowledge is there, to be had now just as it was at any point in history. But it is up to you to seek it out and master that knowledge.

The areas of knowledge that change over time do so because human beings can accumulate more knowledge of these areas as time goes on. Technology, medicine, and science fall into this realm. We know more about medicine today than our grandparents ever did. We know more about electronics. We know more about computers. We know more about nuclear power and other sources of energy. We know all kinds of things our grandparents did not know, and so it is very easy for us to start thinking we are smarter than our grandparents simply because we know so much more about these new and expanding areas of knowledge. But the only reason we know more about these things is because there is now more to know. We can learn from those scientists and thinkers who came before us and build upon their achievements. That is because these fields expand and change. There is always more to learn about technology as new types of computers, machines, and tools are invented.

But let us remember that there are the areas of knowledge that do not change—knowledge of God, human nature, and the physical rules of earth. Everything to know about these things has been accessible forever. They are unchanging. So while our personal knowledge of these areas may expand as we pursue studies into the spiritual side of life, there is not necessarily more to know, just more for you or me to know. But the principles that underpin these areas are the same now and forever.

Let's return to the example of childrearing. It is never good to spoil your children. It does not matter whether you live in Beverly Hills, and you spoil your children with gadgets derived from twenty-first-century technology, or if you lived in Montana in the 1800s and you spoiled your children with ponies and rock candy. Both then and now, spoiling a child is a bad idea. Give a child too many things they do not earn, and you will spoil them. Period. You can spoil a child in any generation, in any century, anywhere on earth. There is no technological information that changes our understanding of how to raise a child because raising a child is an issue of morals. It is a spiritual matter and is thus governed by the Biblical principles of ancient Jewish wisdom, which do not change. Whether it is the twenty-fifth century or the ninth century, those principles always apply.

Understanding that all spiritual matters are governed by the principles of ancient Jewish wisdom, you should see that the existence of smartphones, automobiles, and personal computers does not affect the principles by which children and parents should interact. Nor do the trappings of the modern world change the way siblings should relate to one another. The process by which two people enter courtship, marry, and build a life together is similarly unchanged. Technology has no fundamental impact on any of these or other such spiritual matters. The biblical secrets of ancient Jewish wisdom will always apply in these areas the same as they have before and do now.

That is not to say, however, that modern technology does not appear to complicate these matters. That children have access to all kinds of questionable material on the internet is something that parents must consider in our current day and age. There are now websites on which married people can meet other married people for extramarital relations. But there are positive changes as well. Cell phones allow us to stay in better contact with our children and business associates. In the world of commercial interaction, we see radical change brought about by technology. We now have smartphones, internet conferences, online investment trading, online job application systems, e-commerce, and many other changes to the way that business is conducted. But all of this technology does not fundamentally impact the way we *should* or *should not* behave in life or business; these technological advances merely impact the *how* and *can* of that behavior. The means by which I do right or wrong—whether with a wooden club, a modern rifle, a homemade computer virus, or my bare hands—is ultimately immaterial. What matters is whether I have done right or wrong, not *how* I have done right or wrong.

Thankfully, we have a toolset for coping effectively with the drama and the change that technology brings, and that toolset never breaks or rusts or gets outdated. It is the set of permanent principles of ancient

Jewish wisdom, and because this rests on the top of the unchanging triangle with God, it will never fail you. We may use those pillars of unchanging wisdom to help us cope with the areas of our life and modern world that are in constant flux. This is why we must rely on what does not change in order to cope with what does. We will always be able to face that which comes tomorrow by looking at the past for guidance. We look to ancient Jewish wisdom to make sense of the modern world.

Tomorrows are important—they are the future. If we view tomorrow as something bright, positive, and exciting, we can go to sleep tonight, in the present, with a completely different attitude than if we approach tomorrow with fear and trepidation.

Secret #25

Press Forward Even When the Road Ahead Is Not Clear

B y now you should understand that tomorrow will bring change, but with ancient Jewish wisdom as your guide, you will be able to face whatever comes. A verse in Deuteronomy, chapter 28, reads: "And it shall come to pass that, if you harken to the voice of the Lord, your God, to observe and perform all His commandments that I command you this day . . . then all these blessings will come upon you, if you harken to the voice of the Lord, your God." Scripture then lists the rewards we can reap—prosperity, children, success, a life without want, a life without fear. In a scary passage that follows, we are also given a warning of the bad things we will face if we do not follow God's commandments. God tells us that we will face these things if we fail to serve Him in joy and jubilation in exchange for all the good that He has done us. In the Torah, these promises are expressed in the second person plural meaning that they are made to the group or society practicing the underlying principles rather than to any particular individual in that society. Nonetheless, every one of us can derive a sense of confidence from this promise. This sense of excitement, happiness, positivity, and optimism is essential to facing the change that tomorrow brings in both business and life.

In Exodus, chapter 14, Moses leads the Jews out of Egypt and to safety after parting the Red Sea. This story teaches us a valuable lesson about facing the future. We want to draw your attention in particular to two verses: Exodus 14:15 reads: "And the Lord said to Moses, 'Why are you calling out to Me? Speak to the people of Israel and they should march forward.'" Exodus 14:16 reads: "And you, lift up your rod and stretch out your hand over the sea and divide it. . . ." The thing to note here is that God is demanding action. While prayer is important, it is not a replacement for action. Furthermore, Moses is instructed to raise his rod to divide the sea only after telling his people to march forth into the water. The Israelites needed to be in the water, some of them up to their necks, and to keep marching forward before the water split. God's message was very clear: walk first into the water, and the sea will split afterward. Had the Israelites waited around for the waters to part, they would have been waiting a long time—perhaps forever. They had to actively participate in bringing about their own miracle. To succeed at life and business, you too must face the future as the Israelites did at the Red Sea. Get moving now. Do not wait for the bridge to be built or the ferry service to start running. Start crossing, and the way through will present itself. For example, imagine that you realize that it is time to start making money. You need a job. Many make the mistake of wasting weeks and even months analyzing what the perfect job would be and limiting their search to only that sphere. That strategy can work in occasional vibrant economic cycles. Far more often, the best strategy is to immediately find a job—any job! Excel at what you are doing and keep your eyes open to accept more responsibility and deliver more value. It is easier to move into a better suited, new position from an existing one than from an extended period of not working.

Such a leap of faith requires us to view the future as if it has already come to pass. You must have faith that, somehow or another, you will cross that sea, that river, that obstacle, that challenge. As you navigate your professional life, you will be faced with all kinds of trials and tribulations for which there will appear to be no feasible solution.

Do you sit there, day after day, week after week, trying to figure out the perfect solution? No, you get moving. Problems—all problems—are solved not by just sitting and thinking, but by moving and doing. No one ever solved a problem by thinking about it forever. You eventually must get in motion, and you had better do so right away, because your top competitors will. You can think while you walk! Get out there and test a hypothesis. Use trial and error to find the way. Find a path by exploring. Remember, a path must be *cut* through the forest, not *found*. Act based on the knowledge that somehow you will overcome the challenge, even if you do not know how or when. It may be later today, or tomorrow, or next week, or next year when you solve the problem. You will take however long it requires you to do so. Dallying will get you there no faster. The solution presents itself enroute. This might seem like a counterintuitive way to approach problems, but it makes sense if you recognize the complexities of time.

God created four basic dimensions in the physical world for us. As human beings, we can measure these four physical properties. They are length, weight, temperature, and time. For our purposes, length encompasses all physical measurements. We may measure length alone. Or we may multiply length by width to get the area of a two-dimensional space. We can add height and calculate the volume of a three-dimensional space. Temperature is relatively easy to calculate, as is weight. They are both straightforward measurements that tell us how heavy and how hot or cold something is, respectively. The fourth measure, time, also seems straightforward (though, as we will see shortly, it is not). Time is measured in seconds, minutes, hours, days, years, centuries, and so on.

These measurements may also be combined with each other to give us other important information about the physical world. For instance, you can combine length with time to determine how fast something is moving. When you drive on the highway and see that the speed limit is 70 miles per hour, you are combining measurements of both length and time. Density is a combination of volume (length cubed) and weight. Lead sinks when put in water because it is denser—it has more weight per volume—than water. Wood floats because it has less weight per volume than water. Such measurements are very important to engineering planes, ships, cars, and other pieces of machinery.

These four measurements, used alone and in combination, can tell us everything we need to know about the physical world. We can use various instruments to take these measurements, but most people are pretty good at sensing three of these measurements intuitively to a certain degree of accuracy. With practice, most of us can eyeball a table and doorframe and know instantly whether a particular table will fit through easily, will need to be tilted to make the passage, or is unable to fit through at all. By reference and memory, we learn to intuit what something will weigh. You can probably guess how much a book or a brick weighs. You may not know how many ounces and pounds it is, but you can imagine how it will feel in your hands just by looking at it. Temperature is also relatively easy to judge. You may not be able to tell that it is exactly 78 degrees outside by feel, but you can tell that it is somewhere in the upper 70s based on past experience.

However, one measurement is less intuitive than the others—time. Time is far more difficult to intuitively judge because it is so subjective. The same span of time can feel different based on conditions and circumstance. When a child is waiting for an approaching summer vacation, his perception is that every day seems to drag. On the other hand, when he is already on vacation and having fun, time seems to speed up. Time doesn't actually speed up; it just appears to.

Similarly, years seem to pass differently as we age. A year seems like a very long time to a 10-year-old child. And why shouldn't it? A year represents a whole tenth of the child's experienced life! But by the time that same child turns 50, a year seems like not so much time anymore because a year, while it is the same objective length of time, only represents 2% of the adult's experienced life. A year represents a smaller fraction of our lives as we get older, and so our subjective experience of a year is that it feels shorter the older we are. The year does not change, but our perception of it does.

Time is harder to intuit than the other measurements is because time is far more complex. When Einstein began to study the speed of light, he described strange distortions of time and space. Light travels at 186,000 miles per second, a tremendous speed that, while seemingly quantifiable, leads to distortions of time and space. Without getting too technical, something moving that fast creates substantial distortions in time. Nothing other than light can travel at the speed of light, so that speed is approachable, but impossible to reach. The speed of light is more of a theoretical construct than an achievable speed, at least in terms of space travel. Einstein also tells us that it is impossible for two people to experience the same simultaneous moment of time and that the exact speed and location of an electron cannot be measured simultaneously, which is the foundation of quantum mechanics. These concepts are very difficult for humans to understand or visualize, just like the concept of infinity, because time is complex in a way that temperature, length, and weight are not.

Have you ever paused a video recording? You see a still picture of the landscape or scene that was showing at the moment you hit pause. Nothing moves, but you can view a still image frozen in time. Now try pausing an audio recording while listening to music or speech. What do you hear? Nothing. This seems obvious because it is a phenomenon to which you are so accustomed, but what accounts for this difference? Why can we pause an image but not a sound? We are so used to this phenomenon that it seems normal and so we don't afford it a thought, but when you stop to think about it, why does an image not vanish when we pause a video in the same way that sound disappears when we pause a recording? The image is there. You can look at it. It's not moving, it's not contiguous, and there is no movement through time, but the image is still there. So why can't I see or hear frozen speech or paused music when I hit pause? It is the strangeness of time that makes music and speech meaningless without the passage of time. This is why rhythm and beat are so important in music. If you remove the element of time, all other aspects of music become meaningless. There can be no notes or tune without beat, without time. Time and music are inextricable.

Words and conversation also cannot be divorced from time. You cannot pause a sentence in mid-speech without causing it to disappear. A 10-word sentence might take a few seconds to relate, but if I tried to stretch it over an hour, it would become meaningless. It would just be low rumbling sounds, impossible for the brain to decipher. Likewise, highly compressed speech is inaudible; it is too brief and high-pitched for the human brain to untangle. Time is inextricable from the delivery of speech and music. What this tells us is that, when we fail to properly appreciate and relate to time, we cannot fully understand language or communication. Learning to become an effective public speaker necessitates learning to gauge tempo, constantly adjusting how many words we say in a given period. Failing to do so contributes to a dull delivery. In effect, we cannot fully appreciate the entirety of existence and human experience without also experiencing time.

As humans, we enter the world and begin passing through the stages of life. We are born into the world as infants and over time we grow up. We become toddlers, then teenagers, and finally adults. The passage of time is so intertwined with our day-to-day existence that we don't notice it except at times of great transition. Often, we become blasé about our own existence. We get bored. We fail to appreciate time and its passage. This is one reason the Bible relates the experience of Adam in the Garden of Eden. Adam is brought into the world right at the beginning of Scripture. But, unlike us, he plops down into existence as a full-grown man. Adam experiences creation in all its glory in one fell swoop.

Try to put yourself in Adam's shoes. Imagine if you yourself had been just dropped into the world at the age of 25, suddenly brought into existence with the snap of His finger. With no earlier memories, you look around at creation for the first time. Everything is wild and unbelievable. You have a hard time understanding what anything is or means. This is what happened to Adam. Everything, even the most mundane, was blissful, wondrous, and amazing. God gives Adam a strawberry and the sensation is utterly indescribable—such a small thing to us, but to Adam the strawberry is *literally* like nothing he has ever experienced before.

Of course, that is not how we ourselves enter creation. We enter the world as infants and experience creation as a slow unfolding drama. When we first experience a strawberry, we have similar experiences against which to compare it, such as breast milk or baby food. By the time we hit 25, we have been desensitized by two and a half decades of taking things as they come. This causes us to miss out on much beauty and wonder that is right beneath our noses. We simply don't appreciate it for how amazing it is. By age 25, a strawberry is simply a strawberry—old hat. Right? To us, maybe, but not so for Adam! He had never known such a delight.

Adam also has never experienced fear. When Adam notices the shadows getting longer and the sun beginning to drop in the sky, he asks God what is going on. Soon it grows dark, and he is terrified— the beautiful world he just encountered has vanished. This is when Adam is brought to understand that he is not in a static world. This is a world constantly in movement and flux. And so, he comes to a *sudden* appreciation of time. He undergoes a rapid inoculation of change, with which he now must learn to cope. Adam must learn to understand and handle time and its effect upon the world.

And you, too, dear reader, must learn to do this as well. By doing so, you are going to learn from Adam. Moreover, we want you to become like Adam. We want you not only to be able to cope with time, but also to be able to fully appreciate it. When you fully appreciate time, everything can feel fresh and new, just like the first time you saw or experienced it. By appreciating time for what it is, by understanding how our view of it is distorted by our own circumstance, history, and perception, we can overcome our own innate limitations. We can overcome the distortions of time our human perspective imposes upon us.

This understanding is imperative to good business sense. We must be able to look upon things with fresh eyes, as if experiencing them for the first time, like Adam did, to see them as they truly are. So much of proper business interaction and accurate economic analysis is born from an ability to appreciate and understand change for what it is. And because change is a process, understanding change requires an unintuitive understanding of time and its passage.

In an age past, iron was crucial to the world's economy. Iron smelting was big business, and ironworks were everywhere in the developing world in both America and Europe. And then, in what seemed to be a sudden transformation, steel was invented. It was a revolutionary innovation. Combining iron with carbon, nickel, and various other elements allowed man to create steel, which was far superior to and more useful than iron. Steel revolutionized the manufacture of countless goods and tools. For example, cannons had always been made of iron, but because iron is brittle, the more times a cannon was fired, the more likely it was to fracture and explode, killing the operators rather than enemy combatants. Steel was far less brittle, and suddenly militaries had at their disposal cannons that could be safely fired indefinitely.

Overnight, thousands of iron factories went out of business. New technology had come to the world, through the metals industry, and most of the iron producers were finished. Steel was the future. Or at least it was for a little while. The first generation of steel plants soon went out of business as a new and better way of making steel was discovered. This is how it has always been: one cutting-edge technology and its purveyors usurping what came before, over and over again. In 1900, more than a quarter-million Americans were employed taking care of horses, shoeing horses, building harnesses, making buggy whips, and scooping manure off the streets of America's cities. But then 1908 rolled around and with it, the Ford Model T, the first consumer car developed by Henry Ford. By 1914, the Model T was rolling off production lines at a staggering pace, and almost overnight the entire horse-and-buggy industry vanished.

Hundreds of thousands of people were suddenly out of work. What a tragedy, yes? No! Some people saw the change coming. Some people didn't and waited until the last minute to figure out to whom they could still sell a wagon wheel or horse harness. These people abandoned the horse-and-buggy industry and started up businesses supplying car parts and petroleum products. Some learned to work on the new machines and opened the first mechanic shops. Some opened gas stations and travel centers. Others learned to pave and repair roads. But what these successful people had in common was what they *didn't* do: they didn't go to school to study horseshoeing—that was the past. The automobile was the future of business.

Of course, this process did not stop with the Model T, nor has it stopped yet, nor will it ever stop. Time will continue to march on, and the successful business professional understands this truth and is always looking ahead. Successful business professionals try out new paths *before* they become ubiquitous. This is how you adapt to the market, by getting in on the ground floor. The agile business professional is always looking to provide new services and the next product before the wider public even recognizes the need. If you wait—to turn to ancient Jewish wisdom and speak metaphorically—until the sea has parted, you are too late. Your competitors will have already swooped in. You must be able to go forth even when the road ahead is not clear or even visible. We do this by grasping time, understanding its mysterious ways, and taking control of our perception of it. We need not exist at the mercy of time. We can make it our ally.

In Hebrew, the Lord's language, the word for time is *ZeMaN*, which is linked to the word for *invitation*. This serves to remind us that the passage of time is an invitation to make the most of it, to manage it effectively, and to integrate our understanding of how the world works with a true and accurate perception of the reality of time.

Do Not Let Fear Conquer You—Press On

et us be clear that we are not telling you that pressing on when
the path is unknown is easy. We are simply telling you that doing
so is necessary to being successful in business and life, even when
it is scary. So how do we eliminate our fear?

The answer is that we do not.

Like Moses and the Israelites, you must step into the sea before it is
split, but do you think they were not scared to walk into the water up
to their necks? Of course, they were scared! But they did it anyway.

No one said that following these biblical secrets will be easy. But
no one promised you a calm life, either. Every person who has ever
lived has experienced fear. That does not mean we cannot, and should
not, overcome our fear. The dirty little secret of true heroes is that they
do not overcome fear by eliminating it. They overcome their fear by
learning to cope with it. Courage does not come from eliminating fear;
it comes from the ability to act and plow ahead in the face of fear.

Alex Honnold performed the "Moon Landing" of climbing in
2017, when he climbed the sheer rock face of El Capitan alone and
without ropes in under 4 hours. Honnold calls fear, "A climber's good

friend." He doesn't try to eliminate fear, he reads it, analyzes it, and answers it. Then he masters it and pushes through to his goal.

Consider the job of a firefighter. Do you think a firefighter ever overcomes the fear of stepping into a burning house? Not if he has any survival sense! Stepping into a burning house is and should be scary! A courageous firefighter understands the danger, but he does what must be done despite his fear. So do not feel small or weak because you experience fear—that is a sign that you appreciate grave situations. Courage is all about understanding the direness of a situation and forging ahead anyway.

Let us relate a story from the shipping industry. We love boating and spend a lot of time on and near the water and so we are accustomed to seeing huge ships piled high with freight containers. These container ships seem to be everywhere! But it wasn't always this way. Freight used to be loaded onto ships by longshoremen, a process that took forever. Not only that but docks also experienced a lot of inventory shrinkage due to pilferage of the cargo. It was a problem that caused greater loss of stock than piracy, until 1956, when a man named Malcolm McLean came up with a better way. He invented the standardized freight container, which can be loaded at a warehouse or factory, locked, put on a truck, and taken to a harbor. There, the container is lifted with a crane and put on the boat without ever needing to be opened. Nobody has to touch whatever is inside the locked container.

In no time at all, the overwhelming majority of the world's cargo was being shipped in McLean's containers.

How do you think the longshoremen felt about that? Not great! Loading a ship, which was a mainstay of their work, now took only a fraction of the time that it had before. A single crane operator could do the work previously done by hundreds of men. Literally 90% of dockworkers were suddenly in the same situation as all those people who were making buggy whips in 1913 when Henry Ford started up the world's first auto assembly line for his Model T. It was a new world, and it was a new era. The longshoremen were scared. And, as you can imagine, quite angry at Malcolm McLean, who invented the freight container, founded the Sea Land Company, kickstarted everything we now know to be the shipping industry, and put all these dockworkers out of business. It was a huge change. It was scary. But this incredible change also ushered in much opportunity. For example, a whole new kind of eighteen-wheeler truck came into being. A cab and an empty chassis with nothing but bolt-down holes for the 40-foot shipping containers that were to be loaded upon it shipside. These new trucks needed to be built, driven, repaired, and serviced.

Such changes are inevitable. We must learn to understand and cope with new circumstances because we cannot prevent them from happening. Remember what God showed Adam—this is not a static world. How do you face this fear? Simple: you just face it! Despite old folktales, no one's blood ever froze from fear. The fact is you are always going to experience unease and fear in the face of change. We feel more comfortable with a stable, static situation, but understand that such a situation is never permanent. Some of us are innately better at facing change than others, but we all have it in us to learn to stand our ground. Each one of us has the capacity for this self-improvement.

There is an important caveat here. Going on a new path requires us to leave the old one. Sometimes, that is the most difficult part. In Genesis, chapter 28, Jacob leaves home, running away from his brother Esau, and heading out to make his fortune and embark upon a new destiny. Genesis 28:10 reads: "and Jacob went out from Beersheba and went toward Haran." Why didn't it just say, "And Jacob went on a journey to Haran?" Why does it need to say, "And Jacob *left Beersheba* and went to Haran?" There are several references, such as Genesis 26:23, that leave no doubt that Jacob is in Beersheba. Why does the Bible not save a few words here? There is a principle in ancient Jewish wisdom that states that there is not a single unnecessary letter in the Torah. In this book every letter counts. Needless to say, every word and every sentence do, too. This tells us that the words "and Jacob left Beersheba" must not be redundant at all. What then do they tell us? What new information do they provide? These words indicate to us that, before you can embark on your new destiny, your old destiny must be left behind. You will never get to Haran if you are not willing to leave Beersheba.

Fear can make this leaving behind, this breaking away, very difficult. Fear causes us to clutch the familiar close to us. Fear causes us to hold on to that which we have rather than to go out and find what is waiting for us. But you must let go of the old to reach out as far as you can for the new. Imagine yourself crossing a suspension bridge over a canyon. You don't want to leave solid ground so you put one foot tentatively onto the bridge, which causes it to start rocking and shaking. And you say, "Well, I can't do this!" But once you put both feet on the bridge, it becomes steadier. Things get easier and the path becomes clear. But this requires you to first step away from solid ground.

This is how our minds, hearts, and souls work, too, not just our bodies. You must leave one psychological place before you can reach another. Our hearts want us to stay where we are. They want us to stick to that which we know, that with which we feel confident and comfortable. But you will never get ahead in business if you don't expand your outlook. Overcoming this feeling, this fear, is a tremendous obstacle to succeeding in business and life. We see this in Genesis 28:10, in which Jacob is on the threshold of the most incredible things that are waiting for him—marriage, wealth, family, a future—but first he must leave Beersheba. Only then can he truly go to Haran. This is not a purely physical departure. Nor is it purely symbolic. Jacob has to get Beersheba out of his head before he can really get to Haran. He must leave it totally behind. To parody a phrase that we're sure you have heard before: it's easier to get the man out of Beersheba than it is to get Beersheba out of the man. You must be able to leave one place before you make it to a new place. It's against our instincts, it goes against our nature, but it must be done.

A point we keep on making is that one of the enormous differences between people and animals is that a cow or a cat or a camel or a kangaroo will be exactly that in five years' time. Nothing's going to change for them. But a human being is different. We can change. We must change. The excitement of life comes about through change, and success in making money comes about through an ability to change and deal with change.

There is an old John Huston movie from 1951, *The African Queen*, starring Humphrey Bogart and Katharine Hepburn. Bogart's character is a drunkard who runs a steamboat, *The African Queen*, on the rivers of that continent. One day he wakes up drunk on the boat to find that a missionary, played by Hepburn, has tossed all his alcohol overboard. He scolds her for this and demands to be left alone. "It's my nature to be drunk," he tells her. The missionary looks at him and says, "Nature,

Mr. Allnut, is precisely what we were created to rise above." This is one of our favorite moments in all of cinema, and a true message that we need to assimilate into our being.

Nature, Mr. Allnut, is precisely what we were created to rise above.

It is our nature to be fearful. That is the default condition. Human beings default to fear, which leads us to inertia and complacency. Courage takes an enormous amount of spiritual effort. At the risk of seeming vulgar (though we point this out not to be vulgar, but to be candid), we will remind you that it is in our nature to relieve ourselves whenever we feel like it. Relieving yourself is perfectly natural. But as human beings in civilized society, we are expected to wait until we reach an appropriate room that has been designated for that function. By doing so, we overcome nature. The whole idea of civilizing a baby is to train a baby to overcome its nature. The nature of an infant human is to scream for people to do what he wants until he or she is blue in the face. That's what babies do. Which is why civilizing a baby, showing a baby how to become a spiritual being, involves teaching the baby to start overcoming its nature. This training is essential for every baby, every man, woman, and child. Our natural instincts are very often going to pull us in the wrong direction; we must resist them.

We must be able to move ahead in life with no preconceived notions of how our nature inhibits us—this is what it means to truly be open to the myriad possibilities of life.

Now, if we fear change, and if we know change is inevitable, then we obviously must learn to act despite that fear. From where can we gain strength and courage? You guessed it—in addition to lessons we've already learned, we can add another one from ancient Jewish wisdom.

Chapter 37 in Genesis deals with the life of Joseph. Joseph's brothers sold him into slavery out of jealousy because their father favored him above all his other sons. In the final verse of the chapter, the Yishmaelites took Joseph to Egypt and sold him to Potiphar, an official in the court of Pharaoh. It is not until the next chapter in Joseph's life that we find out that Joseph quickly rose through the ranks in Egypt. Only this is *not* the next chapter of the Bible. It is not until chapter 39 that we continue with Joseph's adventures in Egypt. In the meantime, chapter 38 in Genesis follows an entirely seemingly unrelated story about Judah, Joseph's older brother. The chapter is a massive interruption to the story of Joseph, which is just getting interesting when we abruptly move away from talking about him. Genesis chapter 38 is about Joseph's older brother Judah's life, his marriage, and his public embarrassment for not behaving correctly to his widowed daughter-in-law. From this embarrassment is born Scripture's second set of twins, the set that leads to the dynasty of King David.

Why would the Bible change focus like this? Throughout Scripture, Judah and Joseph are seen in juxtaposition to each other. The prophet Ezekiel in chapter 37:16–17, for example, speaks of taking two pieces of wood and writing the name Judah on one and the name Joseph on the other and then putting them together. We are given our first clue to the interaction between the two here where their two stories run parallel to each other.

We can look at chapter 38 in Genesis and see Judah as the orchestrator of his own misfortune while seeing Joseph as a victim of his brothers' reprehensible actions. While this isn't entirely true and a deeper dive than we have room for here would provide context, we can learn a great deal just from the basic fact that their two stories are intertwined. Too often, people fear making mistakes. They think if they make a single mistake, all will be lost, their lives will be ruined, that it will be the end of everything. Alternatively, they see themselves as victims of sorry circumstances above which they cannot rise. Thankfully, life doesn't work that way. We all sin from time to time, but we have the ability to change paths and repent. If we live an active and full life we will, by definition, make mistakes. Human beings are all fallible. The thing to accept is that, in life and in business, you are going to make missteps. You will do the wrong thing from time to time, and it will cause bad things to happen. Sometimes, events completely out of your control, such as an earthquake, war, the malice of a neighbor, or government corruption, will overturn all your efforts. But we cannot fear these mistakes, and we cannot fear their repercussions. We cannot throw up our hands in despair and proclaim, "I wasn't treated fairly; I give up." If we do, we will fail to act; we will fail to carve ourselves a path through life and out of our present circumstances. Judah and Joseph are the Biblical characters who represent the ability to make mistakes (or be the victim of circumstances) and yet to repent and face the future with optimism and hard work, ending up in positions of greatness and leadership.

In Ecclesiastes 7:20, King Solomon says: "There is no utterly righteous man on earth who achieves any good without sinning." Solomon is not saying that there are no righteous men. There are plenty. He is saying that there are no righteous men who achieve anything without sinning. You must interact with the world to achieve things and doing so means inevitable sinning and inevitable missteps because that is the plight of humanity. The only way to avoid doing anything wrong ever is to do nothing. Do not build a family. Don't start a business. Lock yourself away in a cave and escape the world. Make no friends; build no businesses. Then, I suppose, there is the likelihood that you will be able to die totally without sin, other than the sin of locking yourself in a cave, of course. If you cut yourself off from all other people, no one will treat you wrongly. But doing nothing or separating yourself from the world is also a sin. We might argue it is the worst kind because it means you are ignoring God's other children and focusing only on yourself.

If you're out there in the world living life passionately, committed to your life, passionately committed to your family and your community, passionately committed to your career and your business, you are going to make mistakes, and you are going to be mistreated. It's going to happen. You will make a mistake, suffer a setback, be treated badly, and then you will move on from there, wiser for the experience. There is no need to fear the path forward. Eliminate the fear that you have of making mistakes or being hurt and simply travel forward and be the best working professional, the best husband or wife, the best father or mother that you can be. Make this type of fear your friend. Now that you know it is an inevitable part of a busy life filled with passion and creativity, read these two verses from Proverbs: "Be not petrified of (even) sudden fear . . ." (Proverbs 3:25), and "Happy is the man who fears always . . ." (Proverbs 28:14). With these Proverbs, wise King Solomon is communicating this very principle. We cannot allow ourselves to be paralyzed by terror, yet we also must remember that ordinary fear is quite normal. Don't allow fear to paralyze you, and what is more important, know that you can find happiness in fear. It is evidence that you are not a vegetable. Were you not striving toward goals and if you had no dreams, you'd have little fear. The presence of fear can bring a small private smile to your face. You know what is going on, and you know how to allow it to lift you to new heights.

Secret #27

Become Strongly, Even Radically, Open to New Directions, Soft Sounds, and Faint Footsteps

I [RDL] often work late into the night after my family is fast asleep, and it's only me awake in the house. I sit at the kitchen table where all is quiet. I have a beautiful office to study and work in, but late at night I prefer the kitchen table because the presence of my family can be felt there. That kitchen table is the core of my family's existence. I feel surrounded and supported by the cocoon of their love, but I don't have to endure the noise they make bustling all around me as they would during the day. Sitting at the kitchen table at night, I get the best of both worlds.

An experience I have over and over is that I will be sitting there, deep in my work, when suddenly I notice the refrigerator cycle on. The compressor kicks on, and it clicks away and hums in the background. It isn't terribly loud, but it can be terribly distracting when it is so quiet in the house. However, I have never noticed the refrigerator running during the daytime. I know it runs during the day, but I don't hear it. You have probably had this experience as well. Why is it that we hear the refrigerator working only at night? Because the house is loud during the day, and the other noise around you, the hustle and bustle of life, blocks out the soft hum of the refrigerator. It is completely drowned out. It's not just that these noises are hard to hear over the commotion of the day—you just don't hear them. You don't notice them at all. But when everything around you is quiet, individual noises sound loud. You hear every little change, every motor turning on, every clink as a newly made ice cube drops. You can, in other words, detect the faint footsteps of approaching events. The more noise and bustle about, the less attuned we are to small changes in our environment. The silence can be a healthy thing to experience from time to time because it reminds us of how we perceive the world.

For this reason, we encourage you to block out a certain amount of time for yourself on a regular basis. Make an appointment with yourself. This need not take up an inordinate amount of time; once a week is fine for most people. And it doesn't have to be very long; 10 to 15 minutes is plenty of time. Fifteen minutes alone with no distractions (leave your cell phone and any other electronics in another room) will definitely feel like quite a long time. No one should be around at all—you shouldn't be able to see anyone or worry that they might interrupt you. You might turn down the light so it's not bright, as you don't want to be bombarded by too much visual stimuli. Finding a time and place that fits these requirements, where you can truly be alone, might be more difficult than you think. Plan for this just as you would for any other business meeting. Calendar it into your schedule even if it means driving to a nearby park or secluded area.

Once you find a quiet time and a place to be alone, just sit and make yourself into an open receptacle. Do nothing other than the unusual activity of spending time with yourself. It is a wonderful and rare experience for a busy person. So unaccustomed are most of us to doing this that you might need some training. You can practice any number of meditation techniques at a different time and then implement during this appointment. Stop your mind from thinking about the last movie you saw or the last book you read. If you have been arguing with somebody, block that from your mind. You want to put yourself into a 100% receptive mode. It's a little like resetting the odometer to zero.

So much of our lives are spent in projecting mode. We project ourselves at the world around us by suggesting, selling, persuading, bending, marketing, repairing, twisting, restoring, pushing, pulling, heating, cooling, joining, separating, and all the other verbs that describe how we constantly try to sculpt our worlds into reasonable facsimiles of our deepest desires. The Sabbath provides us with one day each week of rest from aggressive control of our environment. Twenty-five hours during which, not only do we not have to hurl ourselves at the world, but we're actually prohibited from doing so by the Jewish lifestyle system known as the Torah. It's a wonderful time for introspective creativity. Our minds and our souls reset.

During the 1970s, two good friends, Ben Cohen and Jerry Greenfield, opened a business together. Though we heartily disagree with their religious and political views, their experience nonetheless provides a lesson. They wrote out a comprehensive business plan, put everything into place, and then Ben and Jerry started their first bagel delivery company. Now let me ask you, have you ever bought any bagels from Ben & Jerry's? Probably not. The idea was not very profitable. They knew they needed to do something different. So they looked around. They decided to create a brand of ice cream, and their ice cream company went on to be one of the most successful ice cream companies ever. But the thing to take note of is that they didn't start out with that idea. They started out with the idea of delivering bagels, but when that didn't work, they allowed themselves to be receptive to a new idea. There is such a thing as intrinsic instinct, and Ben and Jerry listened to it. We don't always want to trust our instincts, especially our animal instincts, but we do want to trust our human intuition, and we do want to be receptive to the idea of changing course.

Ben & Jerry's Ice Cream isn't the only such story, either. One Mr. Toyoda in Japan spent the early years of the twentieth century trying to build a fabric weaving company because he saw that the standards of living were rising in Japan. People were going to want fine clothing, he thought. He tried to invent a new and better way to weave fabric, but none of his ideas worked. Then one day in 1937, he repurposed the machinery that had been devoted to building weaving looms and started building cars instead. The mighty Toyota Company was born from the ashes of a failed weaving business. And perhaps you have heard of Wrigley's gum? William Wrigley started his company trying to sell baking soda and soap, but he never turned a profit, and so he turned to making and selling chewing gum instead.

These men share one thing in common—they were open to responding to what was around them, and they listened to their intuition. Sometimes we hear a whisper in the air that guides us positively. This whisper we hear is not passive—it is a response to our own enthusiasm, passion, and commitment. We put in the effort, and we get back a divine message. Call it inspiration if you want. Call it an entrepreneurial muse. But it feels and sounds like a whisper in your soul. If you hear it, listen to it. You must be willing to change course when it tells you to.

This whisper is not restricted to business enterprises at all. Often spouses hear a similar whisper when they realize their relationship is faltering from lack of attention. They may realize they need to change directions, which, for a marriage, can be a very good thing when done properly. Sometimes a couple realizes they've fallen into a rut. The marriage may have lost its spontaneity. Perhaps the spouses have not nurtured their enthusiasm for each other. They can see it in each other's eyes, which no longer light up when they see one another at the end of a long day spent apart. That's never a good sign, and when this happens, a wise couple will sit down and say, "We need to reengineer our marriage. We must change directions completely. It is time for a reengineering of the way we interact." This can be a very exciting process. It can be scary, yes—change always is. It may be painful, too. But pain is a part of life. You must be open to experiencing both pain and fear to make big changes. Don't allow yourself to succumb to the very natural human instincts of complacency and inertia. If there are changes that need to be made, make them, no matter how scary or dramatic.

A surprising number of biblical leaders were shepherds, including Moses, who tended his father-in-law's flocks. It was while doing so that, as we read in Exodus chapter 3, he comes across a bush that is burning but not being consumed. Ancient Jewish wisdom tells us that many others saw this bush; only Moses turned aside to question its unusual appearance. Had that bush been in the middle of a busy street in Cairo, even Moses might have missed recognizing that it needed further examination. However, tending to sheep in the desert of Midian, Moses had left his old world and was open to new input. As such, he could receive the messages that the world was sending his way. The book of Numbers opens with the words: "And the Lord spoke to Moses in the desert of Sinai." Here, the Lord tells Moses to count the Israelites and deduce how each of them must position themselves around the tabernacle. This is before God decrees that they spend 40 years in the desert; the Israelites are anticipating arrival in the Promised Land in three days' time. Despite their belief that they will be in the Promised Land soon, much time and several chapters of the book of Numbers are devoted to counting and positioning everybody while they are in the middle of the desert. This seems nonsensical— why would they waste so much time in regimental geometry?

What you must realize is that the children of Israel are being vectored toward their destiny. A vector combines both direction and movement. A vector gives us the direction of a force. For example, telling us that the wind is blowing 10 mph from the northwest is a vector. This can also apply to people and their destinies. The Israelites are being told where and how fast to move toward the Promised Land. They are told what position to assume. We can literally see them physically vectored into their destiny.

But remember, they are in the middle of an arid, inhospitable desert; no place to spend time, if you ask us. Find a beach, we say! And yet God chooses to give the Israelites this important vectoring information in the desert. This wouldn't have been our first choice and probably not yours. Considering all the miracles God has just wrought in Egypt, surely He could have jumped the people right into the land of Israel? Why not give them the Torah once they are already in their new land? One reason that God chooses the desert to impart this information is because, in ancient Jewish wisdom, a desert isn't just a dry, hot place with lots of cactus, sand, and not much else. The desert is a symbol for total emptiness. Little grows or lives in a desert. When deserts appear in Scripture, their metaphorical significance is that of total emptiness. In order to go forth into a new destiny, the children of Israel must leave everything behind. They cannot envision a destiny filled with potential, opportunity, and unlimited possibility if they are still clutching to a vision from the past. By speaking to the

Israelites in the desert, a place where there is literally nothing else and no distractions, they are being shaken free of their past lives and thus free of any preconceived notions of the future. This, perhaps paradoxically, opens them up to accept their new future.

This is true for us as well. When contemplating your own future, you need not hop in the car and drive a thousand miles to Arizona or fly into Africa to venture into the Kalahari Desert. We are speaking metaphorically of the desert. Perhaps a cleared-off table in a quiet room at midnight is all of the emptiness you need to contemplate your life, conceive of new business plans, or envision a new entrepreneurial enterprise. Perhaps you need to find a place outdoors. But when you have a business plan in place and you are ready to start a new enterprise, or a new job, or even just a new routine at work, be prepared to leave your old ways behind for good. Get them out of your head so you can focus on your future. But you have to be able to sense the sometimes soft sound of approaching possibilities.

Secret #28

Use the Power of Words, Sentences, and Sound

The exodus of the Israelites from the slavery of Egypt and deliverance into the Promised Land is the Bible's most dramatic account of transformation from darkness to light, from oppression to happiness, from pessimism to promise. God takes the Israelites from Egypt into the desert, that place of metaphorical and literal emptiness. The desert is not just an empty place, though—that is only half of the story. Ancient Jewish wisdom has more to tell us about the desert as it appears in Scripture.

But first, let us decipher the etymological meaning of the holiday we call Passover, on which we celebrate the exodus from Egypt. The word *Passover* is a translation of the Hebrew word *Pesach*, but as is always the case with the Lord's language, much is lost in translation. *Pesach* does translate to *pass over*, as in the angel of death *passing over* the home of the Israelites. However, *Pesach* also means "talking mouth." *Pe* means "mouth." *Sach* means "talking." Put them together and you get "talking mouth." Mouths and talking feature in the Exodus. As the Israelites cross over the borders of Egypt they arrive and stop at a place called *Pi HaChirot*, which translates literally into "the mouth of freedom."

You may be asking what that has to do with deliverance. Quite a lot. We observe Passover by holding a formal meal called a seder, which is governed by a book known as a Haggadah. The word *Haggadah* is also Hebrew for "a telling," and/or "a recounting." One of the first rituals carried out at a seder involves somebody, often the youngest capable child present, asking four scripted questions. However, should a child not be at the table, ancient Hebrew knowledge demands that an adult ask the questions. Even if you are by yourself (incredibly, some people faced this situation just recently during COVID-19) you need to ask yourself the questions. You cannot skip them. They are crucial.

Ancient Jewish wisdom shows us time and again that asking questions is vitally important. Questions and answers are a medium for developing relationships. Children ask each other, "Do you want to play?" This is a means of connecting. Romantic relationships often begin with a question meant to engage conversation. Don't all business dealings start with some variation of the same question: "What can I do for you?" Questions beget conversation and communication, the foundations of human interaction and business. Questions are too irresistible to be ignored. The serpent even begins his tempting of Eve not by telling her to eat the forbidden fruit, but by asking her if God had forbidden them to eat of all the fruit of the garden. Eve leaps to God's defense, explaining that only one tree was off limits, and at that point the battle was already over. A question is an irresistible force. The essential part of Haggadah begins with four questions precisely to stimulate conversation, even if it is with oneself.

Here is the second meaning of the Hebrew word for desert, *midbar*. It doesn't just mean an empty, arid place, but also means "speaking." Do you see the convergence? The mouth of freedom. Talking mouth. Speaking. Everything about Passover and the Exodus, that ultimate transformation from slavery to redemption, revolves around talking, around using our mouths. The mouth is a vital tool that can take us from slavery to freedom. It is a vital tool that can move us from darkness into light. As noted previously in this book, the mouth is the most important organ for leadership—and now you see why. Speaking liberates us from the desert of our own solitude.

Much modern research has been devoted to improving the academic performance of students. In the United States, for many years the SAT was the most common test to objectively evaluate the academic performance of high school students. Because SAT scores played a central role in college admissions, researchers tried to isolate the most important factors in predicting high SAT scores. Can you guess what the number-one most important factor was? The quality of a student's teachers? No. A good school district? No. The one factor most positively correlated with high SAT scores was whether the student had family meals at home that involved conversation in which the child was encouraged to participate. This more strongly correlated to high test scores than a high IQ! Family meals were not enough. A family meal with everyone watching a movie or where each family member focused on their own electronics had little effect. But a family meal where there was interaction between children and parents made a substantial impact on a child's future academic success and, consequently, overall performance in life.

Knowing this, it would be sheer folly for a concerned parent to come to a family meal without a list of four or five conversation starters. If you have children, we encourage you to start doing this. It is best if these conversation starters come in the form of cleverly worded questions—not, "What did you do today?"—but something that tempts a child to speak up. These questions should be specifically designed to bring your children out of their shell, out of themselves, out of the metaphorical desert that keeps their thoughts inside themselves. In a sense, that's what a desert is: a place lacking in external stimulation, where nothing else is going on. Nothing but sheer emptiness.

Have you ever noticed how hard it is to endure silence in a conversation? It makes us feel awkward and uncomfortable. It is unsettling. And here is where internalization of this principle becomes directly and practically applicable to your business life. It is the sales professional's task to start the conversation rolling and open effective two-way communication. However, sales professionals are also taught that there is a certain point at which they should stop talking and just remain quiet. This puts immense pressure on the other person to start talking to avoid the discomfort of the silence of the desert. Silence draws out the person you are speaking to, and if that person is a customer, it is to your advantage. So whether you employ speech actively by asking questions, or whether you use the technique of silence to encourage the other person to speak, it is clear that the mouth is the paramount tool of human communication and connection. Speech enables us to bring about deliverance, to bring about hope and optimism, to bring about communication and commerce. And while phones and the internet have given us the amazing ability to speak from afar for the sake of expediency, and to "chat" without any audible sounds being expressed, there is no replacement for face-to-face conversation.

Have you ever called a company or "chatted" online with someone purporting to be there to help you, only to begin suspecting that you are interacting with a machine, not a person? Rather than feeling cared for, you feel annoyed and brushed off.

The airline industry exists to this day, despite becoming increasingly crowded, inefficient, and unpleasant, because of this need for humans to talk to each other face to face. It thrives on serving "business class" passengers. Holidays may be the busiest times of year for airlines, but their meat-and potatoes is the year-round business of ferrying business professionals across the globe to hold in-person meetings. People still must move from place to place to do business in this globalized marketplace. Sure, they could rely solely on video chat and phones, but they don't. Those are marvelous tools that have a place in the modern world, but when it comes to the final analysis and exchange in an important business transaction, two or more people benefit from sitting face to face. A valuable deal that brings profit and prosperity to both sides almost always takes place with people meeting in person, not on a Zoom call. During COVID-19, many corporate employees began working from home. "It's a new world," we were told. Yet, most companies found that the quality of work went down, and increasingly, companies are demanding that employees spend a certain number of days in the office. For a young employee, much was lost. Mentoring that used to happen around the coffee machine was lost when the paths of senior and junior employees stopped overlapping.

Speech is what it's all about, and we must understand its power. No matter how technology progresses, there will never be anything that totally usurps the place of direct communication. The higher level the transaction is, the truer this is. In a complex B2B system, my computer might execute a purchase at a certain strike price from the computer running your company's e-commerce platform. However, long before that could happen, you and I will have had to meet and establish a business relationship and then a contractual relationship governing the details of the transactions that our computers will have been programmed to perform. It may appear as if no human speech undergirds a certain transaction, but be assured that the owners of the two interacting platforms did meet and talk with one another.

For instance, an investment fund may have a standing order with a brokerage house to execute purchases of certain stocks at certain predetermined prices. The investment fund and the brokerage house will have discussed and settled details and terms, after which both companies will program their computer systems to effect the transactions according to the established formula. It might look as if no personal communication is involved in each trade, but of course each trade is really the consequence of detailed conversations and negotiations. Words, sentences, and questions—the building blocks of conversation—are the most powerful tools we have at our disposal to do God's work. Words and sentences are the building blocks of plans and ideas. Language allows us to give order to our lives and world by placing things into a narrative. We can use words to take control of time by inscribing our schedules in words. Whether you are writing a long-term business plan or simply filling up your day planner, you can employ written language to give order to your days and your greater life. Think of this process as plotting your own life against the passage of time. In doing so you avoid procrastination and allow yourself to focus on what needs doing. Like God did for the Israelites, you too can vector your own destiny by focusing your energy in a single, planned direction. The best way to stay on track is to put your goals and obligations into writing.

Your goal is to commit yourself to a planned course of action and sign off on it. You want a string of actions that build a narrative. One action should lead into specific following actions. These actions need not be grandiose projects. We aren't putting a man on the moon here. We are simply planning out our workdays. The biggest, most grandiose goals, which you should have, require many steps. And each step is made of many small actionable tasks. Whatever your long-term business plans are, you will have to take small steps to get there. That is the nature of large projects; they are made up of small parts. No one establishes a successful business in a day. You cannot cross "Establish successful business" off your to-do list. But you may research a few potential markets for your new enterprise over the course of a few days. Maybe you pick one and write a business plan the next day. Then the following week you look at one possible business location per day until you find the right storefront. Assemble a list of vendors another day, open the store on opening day, and market to 12 customers a day for the first month you are in business, and so on and so forth.

Oral communication is just as important as written language. No matter what specific business project you are working on, you will have to use the principle of the talking mouth, the principle of Passover. Every business transaction along the way will require communication. The whole system of monetary prosperity given to us by God is there to get us all communicating with each other. The economy is there to get us talking to one another as well as talking to ourselves.

Don Isaac Abarbanel, one of the great transmitters of ancient Jewish wisdom, was the minister of finance for the court of Ferdinand and Isabella, the king and queen of Spain in the fifteenth century. In 1492, the Jews were expelled from Spain with short notice. They were barred from taking any possessions with them. This included even someone of the high rank that Abarbanel held, who hit the road with nothing but what he could wear or carry on his back. When Passover came, he found himself alone and friendless in the city of Genoa, Italy, where he had escaped to as a refugee. Being alone, he held a Seder of one. Did he skip the questions? No! As we said, child or no child present, you do not skip the questions! If you are the only one at your Seder, then you ask them of yourself. But Abarbanel was an ambitious man, and he did not only ask four questions; he set himself the task of formulating one hundred questions about the timeless implications of the Exodus from Egypt and then he answered each one. All these questions and answers are collected in one of our favorite books. The great Abarbanel Haggadah comprises his thought-provoking questions about the exodus of the Israelites from Egypt, a hundred questions we had never thought of on our own. He did this with no one else around. It is a fantastic act and work that shows the power of the question to initiate conversation. Even in the desert of his loneliness, he was able to reach out by writing down his questions in a conversation with posterity. And before that, he carried on the conversation with himself.

Don't underestimate the power of this. When your own ears hear your own mouth say things, those words penetrate deep into your soul. Speaking aloud is very different from just thinking about something. This is why we told you earlier that the best way to practice public speaking is to do so out loud. Walking around and thinking is mere contemplation. Putting your thoughts into words, even if they are just for you, gives order to those thoughts. Oral language requires chronology and order and simply putting your thoughts into words will help you organize your thoughts. It is a way of "orally inscribing" your thoughts.

The importance of language to ordering your thoughts is why we encourage you to not just use words, but actual sentences, when writing out notes to yourself. And when you are thinking out loud, use full sentences. When planning out a speech, whether on paper or by talking it through, use full sentences. Don't just use bullet points; form sentences and paragraphs. Don't write just "Samantha—hiring" Instead, write "Talk to Samantha about hiring criteria for new department." Our minds are accustomed to connecting words into sentences and paragraphs and doing so imposes order upon our plans and thoughts. This does not take much effort and you will find that not only are your notes more useful, but your thoughts will be better composed because you took the time to write them out. When you start looking at your journal, planner, or calendar, everything will fall into place in a more organized fashion. You will see the meaning in your actions written out explicitly. The process of trying to recall your intent and reassemble the sentence in your mind slows you down and weakens your energy. Furthermore, it is simply redundant—it requires you to do the mental work twice. This may seem like a small thing, but it adds up over time with every action you do. So put down the entire sentence the first time.

If you do this regularly, you will find that your schedule and your calendar begin to make more intuitive sense and that you begin to become more productive and more focused. You will be more motivated when the way is clear and plotted. Looking at a sequence of sentences, rather than lists, motivates us to get into action because sentences and paragraphs have actions, instructions, and direction. Sentences seep into our souls and minds; individual words simply do not. Words, while powerful building blocks for sentences, lack narrative, and thus focus, when used individually. As God creates man, He breathes into his nostrils the breath of life (Genesis 2:7). In ancient Jewish wisdom, that breath of life means the ability to speak. Cherish your ability to speak and constantly work on improving it.

Feeling Right About Money Makes You Act Right

S ay you are traveling to New York City. You know that New York City, as is the case with so many cities, is increasingly dangerous as criminals, individuals with threatening mental illness, and illegal immigrants are being ignored by the institutions whose job it is to keep a city safe. The bad news? You have no choice but to make this trip if you want to keep your job. You are going. You are also a responsible person who believes in being prepared, so you decide to download a book on self-defense. It has detailed illustrations and chapters on every martial arts style. It tells you what to do when your assailant has a knife, what to do when he is carrying a gun, or if there is a group attack. It's a long book, a real compendium, 20-something chapters, but you go ahead and buy it because you don't want to be caught defenseless during your perambulations through New York City. You download the book onto your tablet and feel confident in your choice.

Sadly, the story takes a turn for the worse sooner than you had expected. On your trip, as you walk over drugged out bodies on the street, a man with a knife starts advancing toward you. What do you do in a situation like this? Ask your assailant to please wait one moment while you read up on the relevant chapters of your book about being attacked with a knife? Not likely. Chapter 17 of your new book may totally cover this situation, but that does you no good. It's too late. Had you known right away how to swivel around, or sweep him off his feet in the first place, that would be quite different. But you don't know how to do that. Your book may have been a great guide, but you should have started studying it before you needed it. The book is no help now.

What's more, the book would have been no help during a trip to New York City one week later, either. Quick defensive action must be instinctive, an impulse with no conscious thought involved. Thought slows you down and trips you up. Such quick reactionary movement is only possible when there is a unity of body and soul. And the only way to achieve such unity is through repetition. A week is not long enough to internalize something as complicated as martial arts. To act quickly, assuredly, and appropriately when you are attacked, you must internalize your knowledge of self-defense. Through repetition, you need to move the knowledge of martial arts out of your head and into your body and soul, but this takes repetitive practice.

What you want is for your heart and soul to tell your body to act without your mind getting in the way. Those 18 inches from the top of the head to the heart is what we are talking about here—you have to close that distance. In a situation like this, in any trying situation, you must be able to travel those 18 inches instantaneously and automatically. This is when you know that you have really internalized a discipline or a principle: when you can act properly and instantaneously without involving your mind. Your soul takes over and tells your body to move. You do not decide what to do in situations like this. You feel what to do. And through study, training, and repetition, you can teach yourself the *right* thing to do.

This is a very important principle in business. The lesson is that you cannot think your way out of some problems—you must feel your way through to the solution. As a business professional, we must know how to feel right about money, not just how to think right about it. Once we have thought through the correct attitude or action, we must move that thinking deeply into our soul. It is not enough to know intellectually how to handle and view money if our hearts don't feel that knowledge naturally. We cannot fake this.

Have you ever known someone who was visibly uncomfortable giving you the bill for their services? Aspiring first-time salespeople and small business owners sometimes face this dilemma. They have been so indoctrinated to feel bad and wrong about money that they will look down at their feet and mumble what you owe. They don't feel right about money, which is why they come across as unduly apologetic. They feel like accepting money for a job well done is equivalent to taking something away from you. Under this misguided notion, of course they feel bad and ashamed! But they shouldn't, and neither should you.

If you feel this way about money, you need to overcome these feelings. They are misguided, and they are holding you back in your professional life. They define you as someone who does not understand the business world. Neither of those things is good for your bottom line. What you need to do is the same thing you need to do to teach yourself self-defense. Learn the right way to feel about money, and practice those principles until they are integral to the way you feel. If you feel right about money, you don't need to give yourself a constant lecture; you will think correctly about what you are doing. Feeling right about a thing, in this case money, leads us to act right about it. This is as true for business as it is for all things. This is where business sense comes from. Good business sense is a practiced intuition.

Here is an analogy. I [RDL] have a beautiful car—a BMW with a 12-cylinder engine. I am of the firm conviction that every man should own a 12-cylinder vehicle at least once in life. One thing about my car is that it is congenitally unhappy when in operation under 70 mph. It just is. Now, it's also my strongly held belief that a happy car makes for a happy driver, and so I regularly take my BMW out on long winding roads in western Washington where the landscape is so breathtaking that it is hard to keep your eyes on the road. I take corners at 75 or 80 mph. The feeling is fantastic. The car grips the road as if it were on rails. Now, I'll say that I do not advise you to do this, but I will also go ahead and say that I enjoy it.

Now let's suppose that one day I am driving along and all of a sudden I see a police car on the side of the road. I'm going to tell you right now that this is all hypothetical! The officer has pulled over some other unfortunate motorist to issue them a ticket. What do I do at that point? Do I slow down? Of course not. My head has done the math. I don't know exactly how many police cars they have in the area to catch speeders, but I know it is a finite number. It's a rural area, so maybe there are three, or maybe five, I don't really know. But I do know that there is now one less squad car in the area, lying in wait with a radar gun. My odds of getting a ticket have just gone down. So I put the pedal to the metal. I'm on my way. I have thought this over very carefully and logically.

Around the next bend I pass an accident on the side of the road. Police cars and ambulances are everywhere. It's really very disturbing. How do I drive now? Slowly and carefully. But wait, aren't *all* of the police cars in the area now here and busy? Yes, but I don't care about that. I am very impacted by the disturbing scene. I *feel* like I should drive slower because I have seen the repercussions of reckless driving. And so you can see that how I *feel* about my bad behavior is a much more powerful motivator than what I think about it. I may know I should change my behavior, but I don't do so until I feel that I have to. It makes all the difference in the world. And the thing to realize is that this decision was basically automatic. My soul told my foot to lighten up on the gas—my mind had nothing to do with it.

This is why we have to develop the correct feelings about money in our hearts. Otherwise, we aren't going to act correctly around money. You cannot rely on on-the-spot thinking to do this for you. When a job offer or a business opportunity presents itself, you don't always have the luxury of limitless time for analysis. You must develop your intuition. You want to be able to feel the right course of action. You cannot think yourself into a place where you are comfortable with money, by which I mean you cannot trick yourself in the moment to believe money is good when deep down inside you are uncomfortable with money. You must accept this as true and internalize it now so that, in crucial moments, you will not have to convince yourself that making money is a good thing.

For a few decades now, scientists have been mapping out the human genome, which is quite fascinating. Scientists want to understand DNA better so that we can better understand ourselves. They have told us that humans share about 95% of our DNA with chimpanzees, which is meant to be taken as proof that humans are descended from chimpanzees. Regardless of where you stand on that issue, we want you to know that we also share 97% of our DNA with whales. As a matter of fact, depending on different ways of measuring and estimating, it could be said that any male human actually has a more common genetic relationship with whales than with human women. This stuff is complicated, and we implore you not to jump to simple conclusions based on half facts.

Clearly genetics are not the only thing that dictates who we are. One other important factor that scientists have identified is what is known as epigenetics. Every single gene has a little on/off switch, and some of them have a slider switch like a volume control or a dimmer switch that controls how strongly a gene manifests itself. Your epigenetics influence which of your genes are turned on and off. It is like nature's circuit breakers! So, while you may technically share much DNA with another of God's creatures, you do not share the same percentage of *functional* and *active* genes. What differentiates human DNA from animal DNA is not just genes, but also our epigenetics. This is a very new and exciting area of scientific discovery because it's not altogether clear exactly what makes these epigenetics work. Scientists don't know what causes genes to turn on and off.

During our research into all of this, we encountered the story of a researcher who isolated himself from other humans by retreating to a remote base camp in Antarctica for three months every year. One amazing thing he noticed was that, two or three days before he was preparing to return home, his beard growth would suddenly accelerate. He and his colleagues studied this bizarre phenomenon and concluded that it was due to a change in testosterone. Physical intimacy with a woman releases a flood of testosterone, a hormone that affects beard growth and other secondary sex characteristics in males. Testosterone really gets a beard growing!

But here's the surprising thing: not only does the aforementioned activity produce testosterone, but mere anticipation of sexual relations appears to be enough to raise testosterone and promote beard growth. What was happening was that the researcher, knowing he would soon return to his wife, was producing more testosterone as if he were with her already. This anticipation induced a switching on and off of certain genes, triggering the release of testosterone and accelerated beard growth. In other words, his body was reacting to something that was going on inside of him, inside his soul. This is truly remarkable! What it tells us is that how we feel affects our physiological state. Furthermore, since hormones also dictate feelings and behavior, what we think and feel further affects our states. This can create feedback loops. Have you ever noticed how when you force yourself to smile, you eventually start feeling happy and then you start smiling for real? This is the same effect. How we feel about a thing affects how our minds and bodies react to that thing! This is why it is imperative that we control our feelings. Taking control of our feelings means taking control of our thoughts and bodies, too.

Now, you have probably heard the phrase "crass commercialization" before. We very much dislike this phrase. It is one of many examples of people unfairly ascribing a negative connotation to anything to do with business. Negativity about wealth is quite common in modern society, and so, not surprisingly, we tend to feel and therefore think of money as a negative thing. Money is not a negative thing, though. Wealth, as we have discussed, is how God rewards us for doing good and serving his other children. But we live in a society where many political and social forces try to condition us to think of wealth as bad, as an evil, though you and we know, thanks to ancient Jewish wisdom, that evil is actually the opposite of wealth. But not everyone knows that, and when people allow themselves to internalize these negative associations with wealth, they cause themselves to perform poorly in business. If the point of business is to make wealth by serving your fellow man—you can't do very well at that if you're walking around thinking that wealth is a bad thing and loathing and lamenting every dollar in your pocket!

The bottom line is this: feeling right about money is one of the things that separates the best business professionals from the rest of the population.

All Olympic athletes are at the peak of human performance. No athlete even gets a shot at competing in the Olympics unless they're already at the very top of their sport. The differences in their abilities, physiques, and talent are negligible because their bodies are all so close to the absolute peak of physical conditioning. Top runners win races by milliseconds because all contestants are approaching the same peak of physical perfection. They are all at about the same age. They train perfectly. They do everything exactly right and by the book. Each competing athlete has a reasonable shot at taking home the gold. What then dictates who will come in first, second, and third? Any athletic trainer or veteran Olympian will tell you the answer: the winner takes home the gold largely because of his or her spirit, not his or her body. The winner is simply the one who can demand more of their perfect body than anyone else. At that level of competition, all the competitors have the right body. But the winner has the body plus the right spirit, the spirit that allows them to extract just a little bit more from his or her body.

This is also true in business. You can train and study until the cows come home. You can get an MBA. You can get an MBA from a top-ranked program. You can learn to do fancy business models and do an internship with a Fortune 500. These will hone your business skills and knowledge and they will increase your chances of success. But to really get into the upper echelons of your industry, you must also work on your spirit. You must develop the correct business spirit. Part of that means viewing money in the right way, not as a product of greed, but as a product of creation and subservience. You must understand money. So important is this, that having the right spirit without the fancy MBA, can yield better results than having the MBA without the spirit.

What is money? Physically, money is an economic marker of wealth that facilitates business transactions. But what is it in a spiritual sense?

One Hebrew word for money is also the same as the word for blood: D-M. As we have discussed previously, a word with two meanings in the Lord's language is never accidental. The two meanings always need to be merged in a way that provides us with a unified concept that tells us something about their connection. In the case of the Hebrew word D-M, what is the connection between blood and money?

Let's investigate. What similarities can we find? Note that we have banks for both—blood banks and financial banks. Not surprisingly, both carry nutrients. Blood carries nutrients throughout the body.

Money carries nutrients throughout the economy. Both are crucial to the functioning of their respective systems. Another similarity is that blood and money are both mass nouns. Nobody asks, "Can I have a money?" Nobody says, "I need a blood." There is no singular form because both blood and money are only useful in conjunction with more blood or more money. And finally, blood and money are both fungible, meaning they are both mutually interchangeable. If we borrow your car for the day and bring back a different one, you are probably going to be upset (or really happy if it is a more expensive one!). This is because cars are not fungible. Now on the other hand, if we borrow a 20-dollar bill from you, you don't care what form of cash we use to pay you back so long as you get $20 in return. We can deposit the $20 directly to one of your accounts with no one ever seeing a physical form of money. This is what it means to be fungible. In the same way, blood is fungible. If you get into an accident and need a blood transfusion, they don't have to track down the bag of blood you donated to the blood bank last month; any blood of the same blood type will do, no matter whom it came from. Money is like blood in that you can receive money from millions of people no matter who they are.

This points us to a profound connection between money and blood. Money is our economic lifeblood. Money is not just one part of your life; money is integrated into all aspects of your life. Money is essential to everything we do. We are not saying that money is the only thing of value in your life, not at all. But money is *always* of value in your life and therefore holds a valuable place. You may really like swimming, and so it is very important to you to swim a few times a week, but on the other days of the week, swimming is probably not a major part of your life or thoughts. Swimming is not a lifeblood, but money is because it is always important. You have probably never said: "Wednesday, I think I will swim, and Thursday, I will think about money." Tennis, stamp collecting, watching movies, reading books, or whatever your hobbies, are only important when engaging in them. But money is always important, even when it is not at the forefront of your mind. Just as with blood, money affects what you do every day of the week. It lubricates and fuels the economy and is also a primary measure of our professional and personal success.

In Genesis 2:12, God says, "The gold of that land is good." Which land does He speak of? Any land upon which there is regular economic interaction and transactions, because that is how gold is produced. Gold is a metaphor for money in Scripture. It was a currency of biblical times, but gold has always been the most monetized metal. There are few practical reasons why we don't use some other metal, such as platinum. The reason we use gold to store value is because God chose gold to be the symbol of wealth when He said: "The gold of that land is good." What He is saying there is that money is good.

You need to internalize that lesson: money is good. Do not be ashamed of owning or earning money. When you take money from a customer, you do so in exchange for serving them. You are doing them a favor for which you are being rewarded. There is nothing shameful or immoral about this—on the contrary, it is the most basic way in which you can and must serve your fellow man. Someone who has acquired much wealth, ethically, in a free and just society is someone who has done much good in the world. Once you internalize this lesson, once you really feel it, your whole relationship with the world, customers, and other business professionals will change for the better.

You Can Best Attract What You Best Understand

Now you have a fairly firm understanding of what money is and what its role in the economy is. This benefits us as business professionals because it is imperative that we understand that which we seek. This is true of all things, not just money.

I [RDL] should not offer fishing advice. During our family's boating in British Columbia, Canada, I have spent considerably more time fishing than catching. The breakthrough discovery in my frustrating quest for the elusive Chinook salmon was the miracle of fishing guides.

I had spent several weeks' earnings on fishing gear. It seemed so satisfyingly primitive to think of feeding my family by rowing away from our ship before dawn, to return in a few hours laden with my catch of beautiful, fresh salmon. Except it never worked out that way. It didn't matter that I had fine fishing rods, gleaming Penn reels, electronic fish finders, and colorful lures whose effectiveness had been solemnly testified to by the fishing store clerk. I even had a small library of books promising to persuade salmon to leap from the waters of the Georgia Strait onto my dinner plate. I caught nothing.

Then I discovered Bill, the fishing guide. He had simple rods, nothing fancy. But he knew salmon. Whenever Bill guided me, I returned with fish. It was satisfying. But more importantly, it taught me that knowledge of your quarry is more important than fancy equipment.

Similarly, a solid understanding of money will facilitate the accumulation of wealth. As business professionals, we must fully understand money. After reading this far, you understand that money is good and that it is your lifeblood. But can you define money?

Your instinctive response might be that money comprises those metal discs in your pocket and the green strips of paper in your wallet. Or maybe you think of money as that magnetic strip on the back of your credit card or sum in your bank account statement. Perhaps cryptocurrency is money. What happens if someone promises to pay you $100 next Friday? Is that IOU also money? Does the promise of an IOU constitute the same creation of money as if someone prints a hundred-dollar bill or buys $100 in Treasury bonds?

The answer is that all these things can be money.

Money is a token showing that you are someone who has served God's other children and so they should serve you in turn. This makes it useful as a means of facilitating transactions. When a roofer fixes a roof and receives a handful of $20 bills for his service—certificates of performance, if you will—he may take those with him to the local Surf and Turf restaurant to buy his family dinner. The restaurant owner is unlikely to want to serve him without these certificates because a man who has not earned money is a man who has not served others. People may not think of this in these terms explicitly, but they do so subconsciously. Earning money is your ticket to an elite club to which only those who understand the value of service belong. When you participate in the economy, you get to take part in this incredibly wonderful club of human beings who are happy to serve each other. Dollar bills, credit cards, electronic payments—these are simply tokens to keep track of who has served whom. The more you serve, the more tokens you collect, and the more people want to serve you. Money is a representation. It is proof of performance. It shows others that you care to serve other people.

The only stipulation is that these tokens must have been transferred in good faith for a service or product provided. Otherwise, you have served no one, and your wallet is not full of real money. Then it is full of ill-begotten gains. But that's not what we are talking about here: we are talking about money you have earned legitimately. If you have a dollar in your pocket or bank account that was not obtained by theft, extortion, fraud, unlawful coercion, or in any other immoral or unlawful way, then you earned that money by pleasing one of God's children. Any dollar given to you voluntarily, no matter the physical form, is a certificate of performance and validation of a job well done. Usually this will be from a customer, but even if it was from a family member giving you an allowance, you still earned that dollar. You may ask, "What of money received as charity?" Only individuals can give charity; governments can transfer money from one person to another, but that is not charity. If I choose to help my fellow human being, who for one reason or another is down and out, I have decided that the individual serves a purpose for me, perhaps the very purpose of allowing me the gift of being charitable. But it must be my free choice. That it was given to you voluntarily says that you are someone or did something that somebody else greatly valued. Maybe you sold them the latest gadget. Or perhaps you fixed their latest gadget for them. Or maybe you just got straight As in school and stayed out of trouble and collected an allowance from your parents. Whatever the case, we know you earned that dollar by pleasing someone or they would not have voluntarily given it to you. You provided a service to one of God's children.

Part of understanding money means understanding how it is created, the process by which money is brought into existence. To illustrate this point, we want to tell you the story of Grandpa Lapin. He is a real person, but the story we're going to tell here is a fictionalized version of his life, though the spirit of the story remains true. We are distilling the story of his career down to a hypothetical business day for dramatic and educational purposes.

Grandpa Lapin had a career as a peddler, which, once upon a time, was a very noble occupation. Peddling was the way that many Jews who immigrated to the United States made their living in the 1800s and early 1900s, practicing the trade they had learned in the Old World. Peddlers were basically mobile traders. They went from house to house and town to town and bartered and sold items for a profit.

Imagine that Grandpa Lapin knocks on the door of a house and asks the lady who comes to the door if she has any items she no longer needs. She says that she was about to put a wobbly old table out in the alley. It's worth nothing, but the city is going to charge her $5 to cart it away. Grandpa Lapin says he has a better idea. He offers to pay *her* $5 to take the table off her hands. She happily agrees!

Pause here to do some math. How much better off is the lady now that Grandpa Lapin came to her house? She does not have to pay $5 to the city and she is getting $5 in cash out of Grandpa's pocket. She is $10 better off because Grandpa Lapin knocked on her door. Keep that in mind.

Grandpa Lapin takes the wobbly old table. He stops at the hardware store and spends a dollar to get some screws and a brace for the leg and some new varnish. Once he is done fixing up and varnishing the table, he takes it to another house down the road and asks if anybody needs a table. As it turns out, the man who lives there has a son getting married next week, and he will need furniture to furnish the apartment he will live in with his new bride. The son says that he was going to go down to the furniture store to get a new kitchen table for $20. Grandpa Lapin says he has a perfectly good table out on the truck that he just fixed up until it looks as good as new. He says they could have it for just $10. The newlyweds look at the table and decide it makes a pretty good starter table. They buy it.

So how much better off are the newlyweds? They were going to pay $20 for a table but got a perfectly good one for only $10. So, they are $10 in the black. Add this to the $10 the lady who originally owned the table is up. Now the community is up $20 because of Grandpa Lapin's wheeling and dealing. But wait, don't forget that the till of the hardware store has another dollar, too, in sold hardware supplies. So far, the village has benefited $21. And this is before you factor in any money Grandpa Lapin spends on the hotel where he spends the night and for the food he eats. And he's going to knock on other doors today and make more deals. His presence echoes throughout the village economy!

Of course, let's not forget that there's an arbitrage, which is the profit made by buying and selling products. There's now extra money in Grandpa Lapin's pocket, too. He paid $5 for a table, spent $1 fixing it up, and sold it for $10 for a cool $4 worth of profit! Even after creating $21 of wealth for the community, Grandpa Lapin has also created $4 for himself—all out of thin air! Where does this money come from? This is not some rabbinic smoke-and-mirrors trickery. This is how the economy creates and distributes wealth. It is both mundane and miraculous, simple and perfect. This is the way God has designed the economy to work. Money is created when human beings serve one another. Economic transactions create money. We literally will money into being by serving one another.

Still skeptical? Think this doesn't apply to the complex modern economy? Think again.

One of the few internet companies to ever make money from day one was eBay, an online auction site. It turned a profit from the first day it went into business, unlike Amazon, which lost money for years before turning a (now very tidy) profit. Why was eBay so successful? Because it was basically thousands and thousands of Grandpa Lapins working simultaneously: thousands of peddlers and merchants making deals with each other and the general public. The vendors on eBay buy things that people don't need and sell them for a profit to people who do need them. The people who are selling these items to the vendors want the money more than the object. The people who are buying want the object more than money. And the vendors, the middlemen, the "peddlers," are also able to make a profit by brokering the deals. Even eBay and its shareholders are able to pocket a little bit of the money off each exchange as well.

The reason eBay is so successful is because it functions as a microcosm for the larger economy. When we do things for one another, we all benefit because we are doing exactly what God wants us to be doing. God never promised me I would be rich. But he did create a world where we could all be obsessively preoccupied with filling one another's desires and needs. He wants us to be totally focused on serving his other children. When we engage in this kind of economic activity, getting together to collaborate and serve one another as God planned for the entire schematic of human economic interaction, we are also carrying out His will of rewarding one another for doing His will. Being a good and loving God, he rewards us for doing this by bestowing on the participants the incredible blessing of bountiful prosperity.

You Must Know Your Money, Which You Must Be Able to Measure and Count

Losing weight is difficult enough; imagine trying to do it without a scale. How would you keep track of how much you lost? How would you even be sure you had lost, and not gained, weight? You need a system for keeping track of all of this. Most personal trainers and nutritionists recommend that you weigh yourself at the same time every day and record the measurement so that you can track your progress and assess your methods. No cheating, either. You have to write down the truth, even if it horrifies you! Especially if it horrifies you! The truth will help motivate you.

And then you work hard to lose weight every day. You cut back on junk food. You do cardio and lift weights. And if all goes well, you weigh a little bit less every day. Wonderful! But you would be lost without a way to keep track of your progress. Seeing that you have lost a pound is encouraging and so you keep at it. And a week later, you are down another pound. And by the end of the month, you have lost 4 pounds. And so on and so forth. The numbers are encouraging, whereas the gradual improvements are imperceptible on a day-to-day basis. The numbers provide substantiated proof that you are making progress.

Similar to losing weight, creating wealth takes considerable sustained effort. Saving money is another gradual process that requires the same kind of long-term commitment to see substantial results. You put away a little more each day. On a daily basis, it's not much, but it adds up. How do you know? By looking at your monthly and yearly statements and watching your savings grow over time.

Saving money is hard because people would rather spend than save. When you spend money, you get instant positive feedback. You put down $200, and you get a nice new, fashionable pair of shoes that feel comfortable and luxurious. You put the same $200 in the bank and you get—well, $200 in the bank. Of course, you also get security and the accumulation of capital with which you can later launch a business. However, as important as those are, you cannot hold them in your hand. The tangible items we buy tend to lure us more than the intangible future benefits we will get from saving money.

While the idea of $200 locked away in the bank isn't exciting, you can make it exciting by tracking your savings. Count exactly how much money is there. Watch your interest payments and add that in. With a bank account, these days, interest is infinitesimally small. However, once you have accumulated a basic nest egg, you might switch from a bank savings account to a mutual fund or even to investment in stocks and bonds. Once you reach that level, the dividend and interest payments start becoming significant and very satisfying. Track how your wealth grows over time. The actual counting, tabulating, and tracking gives us encouragement to keep saving because it keeps us involved with our money. You don't need to save it and forget it; save it and invest it. Put the money to work for you. And by working with your savings, you will increase your desire to save because you will no longer see savings as an abstract thing.

As humans, we love order and enumeration, which is why we love lists. Comedians constantly exploit this love of lists for the sake of humor. Books are structured as lists, even the one you hold in your hands now. Online media outlets are full of articles with titles like "The Top 10 Reasons to Do So-and-So," "The Top 100 Most Influential People in Business," and "The Top 10 Things You Must

Know about X and Y." We like things to be enumerated because it brings order and efficiency to information. What are you more drawn to read, an article called "A Marital Mistake Made by Men" or a piece called "The 10 Worst Mistakes that Husbands Make"? Clearly the latter—the list and title tell you that here are 10 things you need to know, and you can see that the author has taken the time to organize them for you.

In Hebrew, there are five words that all mean "counting." Each word has subtle nuances that distinguish it from the others, but they all mean some form of counting. That we need so many words for counting in the Lord's language tells us that the concept of counting is very important.

Let's discuss these Hebrew words for counting. *P-K-D* means counting in the most traditional sense of counting numbers—tabulation. But *P-K-D* also means "a powerful official." *N-S-A* translates to counting and is the word used in the book of Numbers (1:2) when God says to Moses, "Count the heads of the tribes." But *N-S-A* has another meaning, which is "prince" or "president." The word *S-P/F-R* means to count but can also refer to "a distinguished scholar or teacher." The fourth word for counting, *M-N-E,* also means "an important appointed official." The last Hebrew word for counting, *CH-SH-V* is also still used in modern Israeli Hebrew to refer to accountants. *CH-SH-V* also means "prominent person of importance" in ancient Hebrew.

Are you seeing a pattern here?

The Lord's language repeatedly reinforces the connection between counting and importance. You cannot separate the idea of counting from importance because counting something indicates its importance. Why would you take stock of something unless it was important? No one wastes time counting the individual grains of sand on a beach because no one cares how many grains of sand are on a beach. You may want to swim in the water or even relax on the sands, but you do not spend time thinking about the grains because they aren't important to your life.

But money, as we have established, is our lifeblood, and so we spend a great deal of time counting and taking stock of our finances. My weight is something I also take seriously, which is why I measure it regularly. My counting of pounds signifies the importance of my weight. Moreover, the importance of my weight is why I spend so much time counting pounds. Given that money, that certificate of service we discussed earlier, is even more important, you should spend even more time counting and keeping tabs on your money. And just as you would not try to lose weight without a scale, you should not try to count money without the right tools and know-how. This is why we urge you to take the time to learn how to read and interpret financial statements.

Maybe you are saying to yourself that you are not really a numbers person. Well, to that I say: choose to be. You can be any "type" of person you want. When I [RDL] was 16, I had enough pimples for 10 teenage boys. What did I do? Did I say, "Well, I guess Daniel Lapin is a pimply type of guy"? No, sir. I washed my face regularly. I spent a good chunk of my high school income and allowance on pharmaceuticals to rid myself of my accursed acne. You may not be a "numbers person" today, but that doesn't mean you can't be tomorrow. It's just a matter of learning simple math, good monitoring habits, and a little knowledge of financial statements and instruments. Although it may take you a little while to become familiar with accounting methods, the knowledge will pay great dividends to you as a business professional.

You will find it thrilling to become financially literate. Make it a point of pride. Know what a balance sheet is. Know what a cash flow statement is. Understand basic financial documents and those that are relevant to your profession and business. Everyone should be able to read and fully understand their bank statements, credit card statements, and investment account statements. These things are important and valuable, and you will feel better in your heart knowing that you are taking your money seriously. It really isn't as hard as you may think. Learning to read financial statements is a little more complicated than just knowing how to add and subtract, as there are other calculations and financial concepts, but this isn't rocket science and anyone can master these concepts and principles by putting in a modest amount of effort. There are great books, video tutorials, and websites that explain these things. Your own bank is also a valuable resource; your local banking associates will be happy to sit down and explain some of these things to you for free if you just ask. You can be an expert in basic finances in no time, and you will feel and be much more in control of your money and business affairs once you have committed yourself to understanding how to count your money properly.

Money Is Spiritual

We have referred to the spiritual nature of money several times in this book. You already know about the difference between the spiritual and physical elements of the world. We looked at the difference between physical and spiritual needs and the ways in which the world meets those needs spiritually or physically. We placed money squarely in the spiritual realm because money represents a token of participation in the economy. We learned that money is both God's way of rewarding us for serving his other children and of motivating us to do so. Now we want to delve deeper into what it means for you as a business professional to realize that money is spiritual. Let's look at what is at stake, what you have to gain and lose here. We are going to take all of these earlier concepts and biblical business secrets and meld them into a unified theory of money.

The first thing that we want to establish is that when we speak of money, we are talking about money as a concept—money as wealth. We are not speaking of physical dollar bills and coinage. A characteristic of physical objects is that they can only be in one place at a time. A dollar bill is this way. So are coins. So is this book in your hands. These things can only be in one place at a time because they are physical objects. But we are not talking about money here as a physical object; we are talking about the spiritual construct that legal tender is meant to represent. There is no spiritual underpinning to a pen or a book, but that is not true of legal tender. While this dollar bill can only be in one place at a time, the value that it represents flows through the economy as its lifeblood. The spiritual aspect of money—wealth—is infinite. Think back to Grandpa Lapin who rode into town to perform the magic of exchange and transaction. This enabled him to create $21 of value for the village, and $4 for himself. All this, out of thin air as it were.

The distinction between legal tender, which is physical, and the concept of money, which is spiritual, is not mere semantics or some kind of chicanery. This distinction matters. If you view money as only a physical object, then you must believe that it is finite. And if money is finite, then you can only accumulate more money by taking it away from someone else. No decent human being wants to do that.

In that system, money can be redistributed, but no new money, representing value, can be made. Governments can certainly print more money, but if it doesn't represent more creation of value, then it simply lowers the present value of each unit of money that is already in circulation. If you operate under the misguided belief that money is physical and thus finite, you can logically buy into closed-system economic theories in which earning wealth means taking it from others. If money were physical, socialism would make a lot of sense, and indeed, early socialist theorists believed that the world was like a pie that needed to be divided equitably because there was only so much to go around.

This false but powerful idea is enjoying a frightening resurgence upon university campuses and in society in general. The seductive allure of socialism is spreading with virus-like contagion. One reason for the newfound enthusiasm so many people have for a socialistic view of money and the economy is that it flows almost inevitably from secularism. Once we adopt a materialistic view of reality in which nothing that is not tangible exists, then money must also be material and tangible and therefore, like all physical things, it is limited. If there is only a certain amount to go around, surely it is moral to distribute it equitably? This is one of the ways that secular materialism corrodes the vitality of a culture and contributes to its eventual decay.

Those seduced by secular materialism and by its economic consequence, socialism, don't readily appreciate what both free-market capitalists and ancient Jewish wisdom understand to be the fact: that there is no reason to quibble about dividing up the pie when you can simply grow the pie and make more for everyone. As Grandpa Lapin and the free and ethical market economy show us, you do not have to rob anyone to make yourself richer. In fact, by making yourself richer, you will usually benefit everyone. But for this to be true, you must know that money is spiritual and thus infinite. Believing that money is physical is a terrible, fatal handicap to any decent person or society. Such a belief robs you of the ability to participate in business while thinking of yourself as a moral person. Thankfully, you need not believe this. Money is not finite.

Money is not interchangeable with products and services. They can be exchanged, but they are not interchangeable. This is because cost and value are not the same thing. Let me give you an example. Suppose I buy a pair of shoes from a local shop for $25. I have been looking for these shoes for weeks, and I finally have them. A friend compliments them and wants to know how much they cost. I tell him how much I paid, and he offers me $25 for them. I say no, I want to keep them. That's why I bought them. But is this logical? Aren't they *worth* $25? No, they *cost* me $25. But they are worth more than that to me. He offers me $30, but I say no because I don't want to have to go to the trouble of tracking down another pair for a profit of only $5. Now suppose my friend offers me $50 for the shoes. That is an offer I might take him up on. I would be $25 better off than I was before I bought the shoes, and I could still go look for some new, fancier shoes. If I were drafting a balance sheet, I could post a $25 profit. How about my friend? He paid $50, so clearly the shoes were worth more to him than me, and so he too is happy. As for the shopkeeper, he has posted a profit as well; he collects his margin on the shoes, which is the profit of the shoes after subtracting their cost and his costs of doing business from the net revenue of his sales. Everyone wins. The economic pie is larger, and we are all better off for the transaction. This may seem mundane because we never stop to think about the miracle of such transactions, but such win-win economic transactions are miraculous. They literally create wealth from thin air.

The Hebrew word for a store, the quintessential place where transactions take place, is *CHaNuT*, which is based on the Hebrew word CH*e*N, which translates to "God's grace." This suggests that God smiles on human economic interactions and business enterprises. As long as an economic interaction is ethical and isn't coercive, we can be certain that it will make all parties to the transaction happier and richer than they were before the exchange. Engaging in economic transactions literally creates money.

This is why the stock market can continue to go up and up and up. Yes, there are market corrections, but the trend is endless economic growth. It is also the reason that a central bank must mint new physical money. Because wealth is spiritual and endless, the physical markers of money must be created in an amount that matches the growth of wealth that occurs from these spiritual transactions. Governments everywhere struggle to mint a physical amount of legal tender that is equal to this growth in wealth. Too much physical money leads to inflation. Too little causes deflation. Striking a balance between inflation and deflation is difficult because physical money is just a marker for the creation of spiritual wealth, which grows at fluctuating rates. The spiritual growth of money is perfect and absolute and represents all the good created by all economic interactions. But physical things, including bills and coinage, don't work that way, only spiritual things do. So, inflation and deflation are observable proof of the difference between the physical and the spiritual aspects of money. They are proof that the creation of money is spiritual, even though its markers are not. You can literally observe the tension between the physical and spiritual in quantifiable terms.

Here is an analogy. A musical tune is a spiritual creation. A saxophone is an instrument, which is tangible and physical. If you take my saxophone, I am down one saxophone and very sad. But take a tune from me, and we can both enjoy it. You haven't hurt me. You're not taking anything away from me. This is why a good tune is so valuable to the creator. It can be rebought and resold infinitely. Money can also be re-traded infinitely. You must divorce the physical markers of money from the spiritual concept it represents. Think of money as a certificate of performance to prove that one human being benefited another human being. Such benefits are infinite and exponential in their effects. We need to print more and more markers to keep track of this growth, but they are just representations to facilitate transaction. The creation of wealth is the true miracle.

One Hebrew word for money is spelled *KeSeF*. The structure of a word in ancient Hebrew is based upon the meaning of the letters. The spiritual meaning of a word can be understood by analyzing the meaning and order of the letters. The first and last letters of this word, when combined, spell *K-F*, which is Hebrew for both the palm of the hand and/or the sole of the foot. What does this tell us? Well, the back of the hand is primarily used for punching and hitting, for defense and offensive combat, but the palm of the hand is different. The fingers curve and bend toward the palm so that we may use them to do work and to create things. Palms are therefore related to creation. The sole of the foot is used for movement and for transporting things. When we use our palms to create something and our soles to carry our creation to market, we create value. A bucket of sand is not worth much. But if we use our hands to turn that same sand into glass or silicon chips and our feet to carry it to market, we create value and thus money.

Creation and transport are the two primary ways of making money in this world. Like a bucket of sand in the Sahara, an iceberg in Alaska isn't worth much. But, prior to the creation of freezers, humans made icebergs valuable by breaking them into small blocks and transporting them to warmer locales where the ice could be used in iceboxes. Leave an iceberg where it is, and you have an iceberg. Float an iceberg down to the desert and you have valuable fresh drinking water. By transport and creation, we can create value from the natural world.

The middle letter of *KeSeF*, the Hebrew word for money, is notable for its circular shape. This letter first appears in Scripture in Genesis 2:11, a verse describing a river that encircles a land of gold where God declares that "the gold of that land is good." This first mention of that circular letter appears in a mention of a waterway encircling a land of money, the whole land of Havilah. A circle here indicates movement that goes around with no end, and we can see that movement must circle money through the economy. Gold, money—it must move through the economy to be of value.

Money must be kept circulating. Saving money is good, but an economy requires spending too so that money may circulate and multiply. If everybody in a specific society decided to put all their money under their mattress, the economy would collapse. There would be no more business transactions, and no wealth would be created. The whole economic system depends upon the circulation of money.

You can do your part to keep money circulating by allowing other people to serve you. I could mow my own lawn if I wanted, but doing so would be hours of tedious, backbreaking drudgery. Alternatively, I can pay $20 to an in-shape teenager who can have the whole thing done in an hour. Have I lost $20? No, I have gained three hours, and I have employed someone. By allowing someone to serve me, I have bettered my condition and theirs. We must keep money circulating by looking for opportunities such as this to let other people serve us. This increases the time that we ourselves can spend serving others in our own specialized profession. This allows each person to do the most serving and the most good for others, which will grow both the economy and their own personal wealth faster than anything else. Do not waste time doing that which you can better employ someone else to do. This is an important secret to good business sense: pay others with specialized skills and occupations to serve you so that you can better specialize and focus on serving others.

In Genesis 32:23–35, Jacob transports his family over a river and then goes back to the other side alone to check in on a few minor possessions. A strange messenger confronts Jacob on the far side of the river, and they wrestle all night. You may wonder whether or not this return trip was worth the effort. It was. The possessions may be minor, but they were Jacob's. Our possessions represent our money. Someone stealing your car or wallet is a serious matter because they are actually stealing part of your life. Accumulating wealth takes time. The time you put into earning a car are moments in your life that could have been put toward something else. When somebody steals that car, they are effectively stealing some of your life, and the legal system should treat an act of theft as such rather than ignoring it or with a slap on the wrist!

California's Proposition 47, originally passed in 2014, signaled a social trend to the rest of the United States. It announced that theft of personal property in amounts under $950 would no longer be prosecuted as a felony. Instead, it would be viewed as a misdemeanor and, in reality, seldom prosecuted at all. Other states rapidly followed this lead, implanting the idea that an individual's right to his property is tenuous. This evil doctrine spread rapidly. Today, in the United States, 38 states do not regard shoplifting objects with an aggregate value of less than $1,000 to be a felony. Not surprisingly, employees are demoralized, stores are closing, and violence is increasing.

Theft is seen as a minor offense because we do not, as a society, respect money and property as we should. This translates into not respecting people's work and, eventually, not respecting people. People would revere money more if they understood its important role in our lives and the economy. Money is our lifeblood. Steal someone's money or possessions, and you are stealing a part of their life.

Let us solicit your legal opinion on a hypothetical scenario. Imagine a man sees someone falling from a skyscraper. This bystander enjoys shooting, and he loves target practice—shooting skeet is his hobby. When he sees this falling man, he thinks that since the falling man is not going to survive the fall, he might as well shoot him for target practice. What should the legal system do? The intent of the man who gets shot was to take his own life, and he had maybe a second more of life at most. It's true: he was a goner. But this does not change the fact that, before he hits the ground, our shooter murdered him. What do we as a society do? We take the trigger-happy man to court, charge him with murder, and put him in jail like any other murderer. Every moral legal system in the world would imprison or execute someone for such an act. Murder is murder, whether it robs the victim of years, decades, minutes, or, in this case, a mere second.

Why then do we punish theft so lightly? If I spend a year's worth of my waking hours saving up to buy a luxury car that someone then steals from me, the perpetrator has stolen far more of my time than was stolen from our hypothetical jumper. And yet, we punish the man who steals a few seconds from someone far more harshly than we punish the man who steals a year of my time from me. This is a miscarriage of justice.

We are not saying we should throw people in jail forever for a small theft, but we should recognize it as the heinous crime it is. Theft is akin to murder. The difference is a matter of degree, not type.

Our money is our life force. Our money is part of who we are. Money represents everything we create. Your money represents the entire aggregate of your time, experience, effort, diligence, dedication, and persistence. We must respect money as this holy, spiritual thing that it is. Understanding and respecting money also has the salutary effect of making us better able to attract and create it.

To quote the great eighteenth-century British man of letters, Samuel Johnson, "Seldom is any man more innocently engaged than when he's trying to increase his own income." Somebody who is trying to increase his own income is not hurting anybody. Such a person is going to be racking his brains trying to figure out a way to make my life better so that I will pay him for his troubles. This is why I don't get worried when people tell me their goal in life is to make money. On the other hand, I get very nervous when somebody tells me they want to go into public service, a euphemism for government work. That concerns me because I know that this means another pair of hands reaching for my wallet. But when somebody just wants to make money, I can rest assured they will be doing something to help other people. Otherwise, they aren't going to get very far with making money.

Helping and earning necessarily go hand in hand, as we have discussed. This fact is, at the end of the day, the source of money's spiritual nature. And it is a wonderful thing that makes the world go around.

How You Feel About Yourself Is How Others Will See You

Because other people can so naturally intuit your feelings, how you feel about yourself is one of the main influences on how other people view you. Others will see you largely the way you see yourself.

In the musical *West Side Story*, there is a scene in which the character Maria sings the following song: "I feel pretty, oh, so pretty. I feel pretty and witty and bright. And I pity any girl who isn't me tonight." With these lyrics Maria hints at the principle behind this biblical business secret. While Natalie Wood, the actress who played Maria in the movie, is beautiful, she shines when she sings this song. Because Maria feels pretty, she becomes even prettier. Most of us can relate to feeling this way at times.

The opposite is true as well. Maybe you have had the experience of your spouse telling you that you look beautiful or handsome, only you don't really feel that way at the time. Maybe you are self-conscious about the outfit you are wearing. Or maybe you feel like your stylist or barber gave you a bad haircut. When we don't feel attractive, there is nothing our spouse or anyone else can say to change the way we feel.

The thing of note here is that this feeling is not entirely delusional. We may, in fact, be right. This is because thinking you look bad can be a self-fulfilling prophecy. Maria looks pretty in *West Side Story* because she feels pretty. If she felt unattractive, others would see that she was glum or unconfident and would probably find her less attractive, too.

The way you feel about yourself dictates how others see you. This includes customers and business partners. Subtle spiritual emanations that betray how you feel about yourself radiate from you and other people pick up on them. If you feel unworthy of wealth or undeserving of good, people will think these things are true. These will become self-fulfilling prophecies as they alienate potential customers and partners.

If your children are anything like ours were when they were young, they frequently ask for cookies. Even with those big innocent eyes, they're not very naturally persuasive. The answer just rolls off your tongue—no way. Saying no to such a self-interested request is the easiest thing in the world. But a child who has grown a little older and is a little more aware of negotiation might remind you that he has done a terrific job looking after his baby sister and keeping his room clean, and then look at you and ask, "Could I please have a cookie?" Such a request is much harder to turn down. He really feels as if he deserves a cookie. The parent perceives this and is wont to agree, even if the child has had way too many cookies already.

When you really feel you deserve something, you will be far more confident in your pursuit of it. Imagine three individuals asking for an increase in salary. The first person is asking for a raise because he is having trouble making ends meet. He doesn't see a correlation between deserving a raise and asking for one; he is focused on his own money woes and is barely able to meet his boss's eyes. The second individual, and unfortunately this is increasingly common among young college graduates, has been given the false impression that the world owes him money. He mistakenly thinks that he is entitled to an ample salary simply for existing. The third person has worked hard and knows that he is contributing to the company's bottom line. He confidently looks his boss in the eye and makes his case. Which of these three people do you think will most likely get a raise?

To succeed in business, you must hold a strong and confident conviction that you are a good and moral person and that what you do in the business world is good and moral. You don't need to be pompous, smug, or self-righteous. We merely hope to engender in you a deep conviction that you are not a selfish and loathsome human being because you are earning money. Making money is not shameful—it speaks to the highest of morals and is something to be proud of. The power of such an understanding is incalculable. Be confident in your successes, without bragging. Your own strong character and self-esteem will naturally radiate from you.

In our experience, it is not unusual for women who have a solid foundation for asking for a higher salary or a raise to have trouble presenting their case with confidence. Whether male or female, making an honest assessment of your request and making sure that you deeply feel a sense of harmony with yourself, with God, with the world, and with your money will lead the world to judge you more favorably.

We see this idea that others see you as you see yourself in the book of Numbers, chapter 13. Moses has sent out 12 of the nation's most prominent men to scout out the Promised Land. These spies have come back with a terrifying report: the inhabitants of the Promised Land are frightening, warlike giants. They are made up of terrifying enemies of the Israelites. Whether you regularly read the Bible or whether you have never opened its pages, pay attention to this verse:

> And there we saw the Nephilim the sons of giants from the Nephilim, and we were in our eyes as grasshoppers and so we were in their eyes. (Numbers 13:33)

The spies were not spotted; they did not speak with any of the land's inhabitants. How could they possibly know how the giants thought of them? These men saw themselves as tiny insects compared to those they observed, and understood that if this is how they saw themselves, then this is how others would see them.

This biblical business secret is directly applicable to your professional life. If you perform a service for someone, let's say fixing a leaky sink, but you hesitate uncomfortably when telling them your fee, they will feel that you are cheating them, that you are overcharging. If you need to raise your prices and are confident that this is a change based on a realistic assessment of your costs and the prevailing wage for your service, you will present your new fee with poise. If you can look yourself in the mirror and know that you are making an honest wage for an honest job, your customers will see you in the same way.

When we are too emotionally involved in a transaction, we can find it difficult to make sure that we are, indeed, looking for a win-win situation. While it is clear that if I own a candy store and someone pays the price listed for a bag of chocolate-covered pretzels, we both benefit, that understanding can get muddy when the stakes are higher or there is an emotional attachment to what is being sold.

Have you ever noticed the number of things for which we employ agents? We use real estate agents or realtors to help us buy or sell homes. You may think to yourself, "Why do I have to waste the money on an agent's commission?" Typical commission for a real estate agent is in the range of 3% to 6%. If you are a buyer, you may be tempted to deal directly with a seller to save that money. The seller might make the same calculation. And why not? One is selling. One is buying. Who needs a middleman? You could each save significant money!

The reason real estate agents are so popular is because many sales fall through without an agent to broker the deal. When the buyer and seller deal directly with one another, often too much emotion is involved, and the deal is likely to sour. Neither the buyer nor the seller wants to get a bad deal, and they are both too worried about getting the short end of the stick to come together and be comfortable negotiating.

Each side has too much at stake. Emotions run high. Realtors are necessary because they act as arbitrators. They earn their commission every single time because they serve as an emotional buffer between buyer and seller. A good realtor acts as a go-between and is able to camouflage both the concerns of the buyer and of the seller. When she looks at the living room she sees the stained carpet, not the owner's children roughhousing. She objectively sees price values in the neighborhood, not the desperation of the buyer whose new job is starting in a month.

Using a middleman keeps emotions out of the deal. The realtor does have skin in the game, though. She wants to close a deal and earn her commission. She does this by getting a fair offer on the table that both the buyer and the seller can be happy with and commit to. If she does this often enough, she acquires a reputation that leads more people to want to work with her. She understands that her services are valuable and conveys that message to future clients.

I'm sure we have all had the unpleasant experience of working with desperate salespeople. The experience is uncomfortable and unpleasant. Such salespeople come off as greedy and needy because you can tell they absolutely have to make the sale. In fact, they seem more concerned with making the sale than serving you. This is putting the cart before the horse—making money is the result of caring for others, not looking for others to care for you. Such a salesperson has only his or her own interests in mind and you can tell. That doesn't mean they are bad people, necessarily, but it is off-putting. They seem desperate, like they need to make the sale in order to make rent and buy food. They're so desperate that it's uncomfortable. We don't like that kind of emotional pressure when we're trying to conduct business. Most people, ourselves included, would rather do business with someone who radiates confidence. A confident salesperson makes customers feel like they have the customer's interest at heart, not just their own.

There is another important ramification to how we see ourselves. Today's society stops people from being successful and happy by promoting the idea of victimhood. If you can supply a college admission officer with a hard-luck story, your chances of getting admitted increase. If you can find someone to blame for your failure, you can be excused for failing. This is absolutely antithetical to being successful and living a fulfilling life.

Do not ever think of yourself as poor. You may not be making ends meet, you may have been laid off because your company went bankrupt, or you may be facing difficult financial times. Many of us have been down on our luck at one point or another. We all hit speed bumps in the road.

You are a person with potential and dreams who is in a tough situation. But that does not make you a poor person. This is an incredibly important distinction to make. When the government defines you as poor because your income is below a certain point, that may facilitate bureaucratic needs. But if you accept that definition, you are denying your humanity and obstructing your unique ability to bounce back.

Animals have predictable physical requirements. Depending on a dog's breed and size, it needs a certain amount of food each day. If a dog doesn't get the four scoops of kibbles it needs, the dog could be called poor because it's not getting its daily sustenance. Yet many of the world's greatest leaders and thinkers, many of the most successful entrepreneurs and innovators, chose at various times to skip a meal in order to buy a book or afford a class. That agency, that decision to choose how to behave, is a hallmark of being a human being.

Consider two people, each of whom has the same amount of money at his disposal. One of whom uses his discretionary income to send his children to private schools while living in a cramped apartment, while the second uses the same amount of money to buy a custom home, one that can house many worthwhile events and welcome guests. One woman chooses to devote herself to her husband and children, earning no salary, while another woman forgoes marriage and family to build a well-paying career. Can anyone say that one of these individuals is poor while the other isn't? Their bank accounts will not reveal the most important things about them. Human beings have their own dreams, aspirations, and desires. Wealth is relative for human beings, not for animals.

Deuteronomy 15:4 tells us that a society that follows all of God's rules will have no poor people. Almost immediately after this, Deuteronomy 15:7 tells us that we must open our hearts and hands to take care of the poor among us. This is followed by Deuteronomy 15:11, which reads: "The poor shall never cease out of the land." How can Scripture tell us that we will not have poor people when at almost exactly the same time it tells us that we need to give money to the poor and that there always will be those in need?

What is going on here? Ancient Jewish wisdom tells us that if we, as a society, follow God's instructions, we will merit a society of economic abundance. Even so, a biblically run society must, by definition, recognize that different people make different choices and take different risks. External factors affect our lives. There will always be individuals who have more or less than others. That in itself does not mean that anyone is poor, but for reasons both in and out of people's control, there will be people in need.

Poor is subjective. You should not think of yourself as poor, but that does not mean you should not recognize others who are less fortunate than you. We must always look out for someone who can use a hand. If we notice that someone needs help and we can stop and render aid, we should.

So what we originally see as a contradiction in Deuteronomy, chapter 15 is not a contradiction at all. It is merely a paradox of life—one of the many paradoxes that speak to God's mysterious, but magnificent plan for our economic interaction.

The Surprising Benefits of Charity

We hope that by this point in the book, you intellectually know and emotionally recognize that, for most working people, making money is a moral and upright activity. No one needs to apologize for wanting to accumulate wealth. Making money is another way of saying that you are creating value. Making money is entirely different from taking money. Unlike the old-time pirates of the Caribbean who rampaged and raped, pillaged and plundered, only to build cathedrals at the end of their careers in hopes of expiating their guilt and buying their way into respectable society, business professionals owe no apologies to anyone. In creating their wealth, they have been contributing to their communities and bettering society. The notion that successful people who earned money by honest and ethical means must "give back to society" is wrongheaded and pernicious because it implies that while making their money in the first place, these people were taking from society. On the contrary, these individuals have been giving to society all along, not taking anything from it.

If that is so, where does charity fit into the picture? After we understand, deep inside us, that charity is giving—not giving back—how should we relate to it? Charity is a biblical obligation. Ten percent of what we earn never belonged to us in the first place. God is that rare boss who allows us to work on a 90% commission and, what is more, allows us to decide where the 10% that does not belong to us should be distributed. What a deal! However, this book is not a book of religious instruction. Let's explore charity in an objective way, not as a vital part of including God in our lives.

Giving charity is good for both your physical and psychological health. A 2022 study from the Cleveland Clinic correlates the giving of money and time with lower blood pressure, longer life spans, and less stress.[1]

While we are not surprised that a loving God built our bodies in a way that taking care of His other children should benefit us, one doesn't need to believe in God to reap the benefits.

Focusing more on how being a giver helps you build wealth, let's zoom in on a correlation between the two. Giving to charity reveals that you understand a fundamental truth: Successful people are givers. This is an essential principle of business. In business, you must give something before you receive any benefit. Maybe you need to enroll in classes to learn a skill, perhaps you invest in renting a location and purchasing inventory or, if you haven't established a reputation yet, you might need to offer a customer or an employer your work for free, asking them (and trusting them) to pay only if they are satisfied.

At the most basic level, a shopkeeper usually puts your purchase in your hands and only then does he take your payment. When it comes to credit, you see this same principle amplified. Once you have proven yourself responsible and trustworthy, people will be happy to advance you whatever you want, confident that they will get your payment later. But first you must earn the trust of lenders by working on your credit score and establishing a track record as a dependable person.

Internet and e-commerce gurus stress the importance of giving products away for free. Giving out freebies encourages customers to get to know you. If they are happy, they will return for more. And it's not just products. Many businesses today, even small businesses, run blogs

---

[1] Cleveland Clinic. (2022). *Why giving is good for your health* [online]. Available from: https://health.clevelandclinic.org/why-giving-is-good-for-your-health/

doling out insider knowledge for free. By giving out valuable information, they know that many customers will return later to purchase products and services. When a customer sees that a business is giving them value without expecting payment, they trust the business and then return to patronize it. As you can see, giving before you get is a fundamental principle in business. You need to train your mind and soul to be comfortable with becoming a giver.

Giving charity flexes this giving muscle. You freely give of yourself. Charitable people find it easier to make investments because they are conditioned to hand over some of their money. People who don't give charity tend to find it troubling to part with money even for investment purposes. You need to develop the mindset of the giver if you want to do well in investing or business. You may have thought that the most surefire way to get wealthy is to hold your money tightly in your fist. That is not how it works. The adage, "It takes money to make money," is true. Being a charitable person is wonderful training for this concept.

On the surface, this principle is counterintuitive, which is why so many people have a problem grasping it. Charity demands that you focus on others rather than just on yourself. You take something valuable out of your pocket and kiss it goodbye. That money is beyond your absolute control. This can be scary and uncomfortable if you are not accustomed to making such an act of faith. For this reason, those who are comfortable with giving to charity have a leg up when it comes to business.

When you spend money on your professional life without knowing exactly where the return will come from, you are expecting the money to come back to you. And generally, it will. Maybe not on each expenditure. Not every investment succeeds and not every class pays off. Sometimes the connections will be tenuous. If you train as an electrician and someone pays you to wire their house, you can draw a straight line between your training and your earnings. Other times, connections are more hidden. You don't always know why a certain client knocked on your door. You cannot know for sure when looking at any one client or one customer. But, on average, you will get back more than you put in—you can have faith in this idea. But you have to play the game. You have to give of yourself first.

If you were not raised in a home where charity was part of the ethos, giving may be an uncomfortable experience initially. Don't let that stop you. Training yourself to give on a regular basis, whether weekly, bi-weekly or monthly, will trigger your brain and soul to see yourself as a person who is a giver. This will yield unimaginable results.

As young children quickly discover when they learn to drink from a straw, tubes that are meant for sucking liquid into their mouth also serve as tubes that allow them to blow bubbles into their glass of milk. A mother may have hoped that the straw would be used in one direction only, but once it is in place, movement can go in both directions.

Pneumatic tubes at the drive-through lane of banks function similarly. You can send a request for cash through the tube, and the teller sends the cash to you by reversing the direction of the flow. Visualize giving charity in that way. When you give out from yourself, you are building a pipe to the world. Once that pipeline is in place, it is far easier for money to flow in the other direction as well. In the next chapter we will explore some further reasons that this can happen even when we leave Divine intervention out of the picture.

Giving Money Away Connects Us with Other People

If you have read this far, you understand that making connections with other people is crucial to your career and the health of the overall economy. Here is another, very important feature of being charitable. Charity is an incredibly good tool for connecting with others, perhaps the best.

In Secret #33 we discussed that others see you largely as you see yourself. How does this intersect with being charitable? We have a friend named David who is a well-known entrepreneur in the medical industry. After a serendipitous meeting on an airplane, David was so entranced by the vision of his seatmate, a pastor, that David gave the initial commitment of $2 million to help fund the construction of a major church in his native Southern California. He promised to pay the donation within two years. It might surprise you to learn that he made this commitment before he had ever come close to earning enough money to pay that pledge. When David promised that money to his pastor, he didn't see the direct pathway to meet such an obligation. Yet, after sharing his vision with his wife, they both agreed to put aside their tithe for this new building. They put into the universe their belief that their business was going to succeed, and that success would benefit others as well as themselves. No sooner had David made this promise, than his business began to take off. From that moment, everything seemed to turn around for him financially. He was able to pay the full $2 million donation within the two years, and he still came out with a huge profit. This may seem far-fetched, but it is a true story.

This is not what is popularly known as prosperity gospel. Personally, we are perfectly comfortable saying that God blessed David. We know so many stories like this where it is clear to us that God often blesses those who generously give with economic largesse (though not always—that would turn giving into no more than a roulette wheel that always pays off). But let's look at this in another way. In making that commitment, David imprinted his view of himself as a successful entrepreneur upon his own soul. Almost subconsciously, he began coming across to potential investors and clients as a wealthy man of achievement. He believed in the morality of his enterprise and deeply exuded the idea that he was a good person. This helped to make others comfortable partnering with him. (Please note as well that David and June did not mortgage their home or behave irresponsibly. By committing to a tithe, in effect, they put the burden on God to make sure that they could pay their pledge.)

Spending money makes us feel good. This is why people engage in what is known as shopping therapy or retail therapy. There's no question about it: you do feel good when you spend money. However, this is a short-term feeling. When the credit card bill arrives at the end of the month, if we spend beyond our means, the happy feeling dissipates quite rapidly. Even before the bill comes due, it is frequently true that the pleasure we get from a new item is fleeting. We are not discounting the benefits of having a lovely home and beautiful possessions. What is important is that each of us recognizes when we reach the point of negative return. At some spot, more material belongings stop adding to our lives. Viewing ourselves as wealthy and successful doesn't mean spending money on overpriced cars, suits, or jewelry. You don't need the biggest, flashiest house. You don't need any of the trappings of conspicuous spending. On the other hand, being charitable and generous gives you a whole new outlook on life. You also will appear more positive to others, who, as we have discussed, view us as we view ourselves.

Charity is a wonderful act that makes us feel better about ourselves. It is also an act that makes other people view us more favorably, which is always good for business. Every act of making money involves human interaction. As we have seen, these interactions frequently create wealth. These interactions can make us come across as generous and high-minded or as selfish and venal. Many of us end up somewhere on the continuum between these two extremes. Human beings are sensitive and finely tuned creatures when it comes to evaluating other people. We are good at intuiting each other's motivations and intentions because we get constant practice. We interact with other people all day long, and as such, we get very good at reading each other. In fact, we get so good that we tend to become confident in our ability to make snap judgments about others.

This is why first impressions are so important. Perhaps you used to roll your eyes when your mother or a schoolteacher repeated this axiom to you: no one gets a second chance to make a first impression. It may be a cliché, but it is absolutely true. People form rapid assessments of you within moments of meeting you. These assessments are based on many things, but one of the most important is your countenance and demeanor. People who are selfish and possessive and who care only about their own welfare tend to project this negativity wherever they go.

On the other hand, if you walk around with a beaming smile and sense of generosity for your fellow man, others will detect your positivity and view you positively. As customers and business professionals, we tend to make our choices about where to patronize and whom to do business with based on these intuitions about other people's personalities. If you come across as a good and generous person who is concerned about others, then people will want to do business with you. Much of that goodwill tends to flow from the very first impression you make. This may not be fair, and it may not be accurate all the time, but the truth is that it is hard to blame someone for not wanting to work with you if you seem like a selfish and negative person.

There are sociopathic con men who are good at fooling others, but for the most part, the overwhelming majority of people project their true inner selves loudly enough that others can tell what a person is thinking and feeling immediately. People read us very, very quickly.

It's not hard to spot a whiner or a miserable individual. They are usually whining, and they look miserable! Likewise, spotting a positive and generous person is also fairly easy. They are probably trying to serve you from the get-go.

Living only for ourselves as well as living beyond our means causes us to radiate subtle signals of selfishness. But when we give beyond our means, we tend to beam with confidence, courage, and compassion. If you have an important interview, one of the best ways to build up your self-confidence and pep yourself up beforehand is to write a check to a good charity and drop it in the mail on your way to the interview. You will walk into that interview feeling like you are the kind of person who knows how to serve. And this will radiate from you.

We have stressed in this book that connecting with others and belonging to a group is a powerful thing. There are many ways to do this. Thoughtfully belonging to a group whose purpose is supporting a specific charity is an especially good way of making connections. It links us to a group of those whose values mirror our own. Joining a charitable group whose mission statement resonates with you allows you to self-select virtuous peers. Surrounding ourselves with moral and upright people helps keep us honest and ethical. Peer pressure can be a wonderful thing. Having friends who will hold us accountable is a gift we give ourselves. Making these connections through charitable organizations connects you to a wider philanthropic, social, and business community. Give to several charities, and you can count on being invited to formals, galas, fundraisers, and other events. Your circle of acquaintances will naturally expand. Giving money makes you a desirable person and others will want to be around you. They will want to form communities with you, making this effect exponential.

This is extremely important in business because your professional network is the lifeblood upon which your career depends. Now, we understand that saying this may sound vulgar. Indeed, occasionally we hear sad stories about religious groups that are infiltrated by a con artist who takes advantage of the natural trust and friendship extended within the group. We are not talking to that type of dishonorable person. However, if you truly work on yourself to be a charitable person and to think carefully about what charity speaks to your soul, then being involved in charitable organizations will have consequences that flow toward the giver. First and foremost, when you associate with other givers, you connect with like-minded people and establish relationships.

There are other ways to do this, of course. You could join business development clubs. But most working professionals have limited time, and if this describes you, consider passing on joining a business development club. In case you are not familiar with them, business development clubs are groups formed by people from different professions who get together regularly to meet and exchange business cards. The idea is to network with people in other professions with whom you would not normally spend much time. This way you benefit from a diverse community of working professionals you already know personally. In theory, this sounds like a great idea, and these kinds of groups can be helpful, but they are not ideal, and you have better options at your disposal.

Business development clubs have no real advantage over networking through charitable organizations and groups, but the former does have one significant disadvantage over the latter. People join business development groups primarily to further their own interests. People who attend these groups are there to hand out business cards because they are looking to encourage business. There's nothing wrong with this, but everyone's motives are perfectly clear and obvious—they are in it for them. Business and networking that is done at churches, synagogues, and other religious and charitable institutions rather than at these artificial business development clubs, tends to be more sincere and long-lasting. Giving charity connects you to the best possible people in the best possible way. Charitable groups and spiritual congregations are not just about exchanging business cards once a month. You attend church or synagogue often enough, and you are going to really get to know people. Genuine connections are formed, and you will make friends, not just acquaintances.

Some pastors and rabbis may be sad to hear that parishioners are motivated in part to attend services for the networking advantage, but we don't agree. We think it is a wonderful thing that people come to synagogue, in part, to meet other virtuous and charitable people who genuinely care about other people. This extends beyond religious congregations. Rotary Clubs and other civic organizations are another great vehicle for this type of networking. Lots of business is conducted at Rotary Clubs. Knowing that anyone you meet at a Rotary Club is likely to be there to do good for the community is a wonderful calling card. It is natural for two virtuous people in close proximity to conduct business with one another. That's the sort of thing you don't always get at business development clubs, which create an artificial community of people who are mostly in it for themselves. Those kinds of groups aren't self-selective the way a charitable group is.

The Hebrew word for "tithing," for giving a tenth of your earnings to charity, is A-S-R. Since, in Hebrew, the S and SH are the same letter, the word for tithing is inextricably linked to the word for wealth, A-SH-R. For those who do not understand, this connection may seem counterintuitive. On the surface, wealth is about making money while being charitable is about giving money away. Yet, when we look at the ideas in depth, we understand that transforming ourselves into charitable people is one of the greatest tools we have for making money.

It should not surprise you that your fellow man will respect and listen to you if you are and feel wealthy. In the book of Proverbs, King Solomon said: "Wealth is a crown upon the heads of the wise." We tend to listen more carefully to people who are financially successful. We tend to give more deference to the opinion of a wealthy person. If that person is wealthy because they gamed the system (many politicians come to mind) or because they inherited great wealth, then this adulation may be a flaw in our character. However, when it is our neighbor who worked hard and built a large successful business perhaps becoming the proverbial "millionaire next door," it is an honorable sentiment. Deep in our hearts, we know that this individual successfully interacts with others. Successful people like these tend to be good communicators and good people. For someone to have made substantial money ethically and honestly, a large number of other people must have trusted and liked this person. We recognize this and want to be their friend. We also correctly assume that there is a great deal that we can learn from such a person. This doesn't mean we act smarmy. We don't have to approach them in a fawning, obsequious way. It just means we are generally interested in a person who is successful, a person who is good at serving God's other children. This is only natural and to be expected.

You want people to view you in this way, too. If you are successful, which should be your goal, you want to project that to others because it will attract them to you. The best way to communicate your own wealth is to be generous with your money. You will appear confident and more positive to people, who are, as we have discussed, very astute in reading other people. By being charitable you can feel wealthy, rather than merely acting as if you were.

Do you know why the origin of the handshake is a universal symbol of friendship? The reason might surprise you. The Hebrew word for hand is *yad*, spelled *Y—D*. The Hebrew word for friend is spelled *Y-D-Y-D*. *Friend* is spelled by spelling *hand* out twice. In the Lord's language, two hands together mean friend. This is the reason that clasped hands are the universal sign of friendship.

An outreached hand with the palm up signals that the person needs or is taking something. We put out our hands when we are asking for help. When I put out my hand, I'm asking for something. And, in contrast, when I put out my hand with the palm forward, this means that I do not need something, that I already have enough. It might interest you to know that the Hebrew word for "enough" is "hand" spelled backward.

So, an outreached hand in one direction indicates taking and an outreached hand in the opposite orientation means giving. And two hands clasping is a symbol for people giving and taking from one another. Another word for this is, of course, a transaction. What is a transaction other than two parties giving each other things? One gives a good or a service. The other gives money in return. The clasped hands of a handshake are a symbol for coming together to make a transaction. This is why we shake to seal business deals, too.

Shopkeepers take care of their loyal customers. Regular patrons of dining establishments care deeply for their proprietors. This is no surprise; these people regularly do business that benefits one another and that leads to the formation of spiritual bonds between customers and business professionals. But there are other surprising ways in which people who do business together help each other.

A number of years ago, a friend of ours from Los Angeles owned a factory that burned to the ground one night. He was devastated and distraught because his customers depended upon him to refurbish their goods. He would be unable to fill their orders in the morning. He knew that trucks would start dropping off electronics for servicing in the morning, and he would be unequipped to take them. He didn't know what to do. Then, he started getting phone calls from his competitors. They offered to take care of his customers until he got the factory up and running again. Keep in mind, these are his *competitors*. But they are also people who do business together from time to time. They let him divert his customers' trucks to their factories where they did the work and then returned the merchandise to their competitor's customers. These competitors took care of him and helped him back on his feet. And when he had his factory up and running again, they went back to being competitors. That's what business is really all about. Shaking hands. Clasping hands. Real friends giving and taking, exchanging and trading. This is the most reliable form of friendship that there is because it is reciprocal. And it starts with two clasped hands, giving and taking from one another.

Ideas Hit Reality

Have you ever heard a tune being played by an amateur band or group in which one musician is way off key? Regardless of how well the others play, the piece is ruined. All you hear are the discordant notes and jarring dissonance. It might be only one mediocre musician out of, perhaps, six or seven virtuosos, but one is enough to demolish the efforts of many. Your business plan and operation are similar. Regardless of how well you do your work, and regardless of how well your employees or associates do theirs, one bad idea can ruin the entire endeavor.

You might have thought we were going to say, "One bad person can ruin the entire endeavor." No, we assume that you by now have learned to hire slow and fire fast. We assume that you have learned how to find top talent and recruit the right people and to be such a person yourself. We're talking about the damage that can be done when a bad idea infects one, some, or all of your people.

Remember that you yourself are not only "one of your people," but you are the most important person on your team, and what is more, you are the person over whom you have most control. It goes without saying that guarding yourself against the infection of bad ideas is one of your most important tasks. You might well think to yourself, "Oh, no worries! Ideas are ephemeral; they're airy things without enough mass to impact the realities of my world." However, this is a common mistake made by, probably, most people. Even only one bad idea is like a small vial of acid poured into an exquisitely delicate and complicated mechanical watch movement. That is all it takes to undo the year-long work of a team of dedicated and talented Swiss watchmakers.

We don't think that comparing bad ideas to a corrosive acid or to some dreadfully toxic pesticide like paraquat dichloride is an exaggeration. Like a really bad idea, paraquat dichloride is fatal, and there is no known antidote. Yes, even a tiny drop of it in an otherwise outstanding glass of beer turns a celebration into a tragedy. That is just what bad ideas can do. The only difference is that they take a little longer to destroy, but the destruction they wreak is just as deadly. We do not exaggerate when we insist that a bad idea fed into the bloodstream of a business can do the same damage to the business as an air bubble injected into the bloodstream of a fragile patient.

My [RDL] late father and teacher, Rabbi A. H. Lapin, used to tell the following story. I remember enjoying each retell. As a boy, I laughed hilariously at the word picture, but it effectively illustrates the danger of a bad idea. I had no idea that one day I would be privileged to be the father of six incredible girls and I would encounter my own share of real-life instances of this story.

Apparently, a matchmaker approached the girl's father and began to extol the virtues of a certain young man. He has such a wonderful sense of humor. So good looking. He comes from a lovely family. Passed all his examinations at school with good grades. The matchmaker described each attribute more lavishly than the previous. Just as the potential father-in-law was about to agree to the young couple meeting, the matchmaker added, "There is perhaps one small flaw I should mention; after all, nobody is perfect." The girl's father waited expectantly for the matchmaker to continue, "Yes, one small flaw," he allowed. "The young man is a bit foolish."

The prospective father-in-law, who was clearly no fool himself, explained to the matchmaker that his mistake was viewing this linearly.

"You gave me a list of positive qualities and at the end of the list was one negative quality. You think that if we add up the five or six positive qualities and we deduct the single negative quality, that leaves us with what is still a nice positive number."

In reality, we must place the positive qualities on the circumference of a circle. The negative quality, in this case, being a fool, doesn't take its place on the circumference but right in the middle of the circle. Then we join it with a line to each of the positive qualities, and we evaluate each link. How important are his good looks if he is also a fool? How important is his success at school if he is a fool? School smarts and perhaps native intelligence are not much good when coupled with an utter lack of wisdom—in other words, foolishness. The man demonstrated to the matchmaker that the "one small flaw" diminished each of the other positive qualities.

Bad ideas are almost always also foolish ideas. The only problem is that as we noted earlier, acid almost instantly destroys the miniature mechanical miracle of a wrist chronometer. Paraquat dichloride almost instantly kills its victim. Bad ideas can take years to inflict their ultimate destruction. This makes them far harder to detect and thus more dangerous to your life.

Consider the case of a healthcare industry startup that held a series of strategy planning sessions about recruiting, staffing, onboarding, and other human resource concerns. These meetings yielded a set of guiding principles for their startup. Guiding principle number four, one of their really bad ideas, was that the highest paid employee should never be paid more than 10 times the salary of the lowest paid employee. As a group of fervently religious business professionals and investors, they felt that 10 was an important biblical number, and they thought this was an ethical and compassionate idea. They wished to express their values in their business. No sooner had they adopted that compensation plan, than their experienced chief financial officer and chief executive officer both responded to the projected pay cut by quitting. No matter how good the intentions, that ratio was not rooted in any biblical principle and made little sense.

Morale plummeted and, with no leadership consistency, so did revenue. This one bad idea nullified almost every part of their business model, which was otherwise quite good. After eventually abandoning that bad idea, they were able to attract seasoned management, and they again began to grow successfully.

Of course, none of us exist in our own, closed society. We are affected by cultural trends and government fiats. Because of the complexity and large-scale interconnectivity of an economy, general prosperity and the conditions for growing wealth are usually contingent on size of population, shared moral matrix, effective communication, and optimistic culture. Almost anything that interferes with these factors will have a detrimental effect on the economy. In other words, any cultural or political forces that damage the ability of a large number of people to function almost as one massive organism is going to impact your bank account. Understanding these phenomena and the trends they manifest will greatly enhance your money making potential.

We know that World War II is almost ancient history; after all, it was fought about 80 years ago. It is tempting to try and draw examples and insights from more recent wars. Yet, we aren't going to bring examples from more recent wars like Korea, Viet Nam, Kuwait, Iraq, Afghanistan, Israel's Yom Kippur war or their Hamas war of 2023. One reason is that World War II was the last war that was decisively won by unconditional surrender. Another reason is that it involved so many countries. Finally, no other war has been more studied or had more books written about it. The more than five years of World War II provide so many important lessons.

When Germany attacked France in May 1940, France was defended by far more men under arms than the German army was able to deploy. France possessed significantly more tanks and artillery. Including the British Expeditionary force, France had more airplanes than the German Luftwaffe. Finally, France had many more miles of railway and far more rolling stock than German Federal Railways. Yet, Germany completely conquered France in about six weeks. The word *Blitzkrieg*—lightning war—was applied to the unprecedented defeat of France.

What is the explanation behind an inferior force defeating a superior force so quickly? The answer is near-perfect organization, meticulous planning, and super-diligent execution. It is true that

German tanks were outnumbered by the French armored corps. However, German tanks were commanded and controlled by radio communications. By being able to focus their fury in carefully coordinated assaults, they went through French defenses like a hot knife cutting through Camembert cheese.

Similarly, German railways were far more dependable on delivering troops and materiel where they were needed exactly when they were needed. This is probably not entirely disconnected from the reason that Mercedes and BMW tend to be far more reliable car brands than Citroën and Renault.

We describe all this in order to try and emphasize the importance of systems in which all the component parts work together in synchronized harmony, all working toward a common purpose. The fact that French airplanes were superior both in number and quality or the fact that France had a bigger railway system didn't matter in the face of German forces acting as one large perfectly unified system.

What this means is that a commander of a German platoon, say, knew he had to get his men to a specific destination by a certain time. His directives would have included what railway station to use and what train to board at what time. And that is exactly what would have happened. When he took his platoon off the train, and they began marching to the hill they were to attack, they found that ammunition, fuel, and food had already been delivered to await their arrival. When they called for aerial support, it came because the infantry and the air force were coordinated by central command. Projected onto a large screen, this would describe the German assault on France.

Now, imagine a similar leader arriving with his platoon at the railway station and being told that the station has been changed and he has to march several miles to another railway station. When he gets there he is told that the train left long ago, and it will be a day or two before the next train arrives. Later he finds inadequate supplies and no aerial support. If any airplanes do arrive, they frequently bomb the wrong target. It also turns out that most of his soldiers have not received adequate training so the enemy overruns their position. Actually, you don't have to imagine this baleful scenario. It is exactly what happened to French defenders in May 1940. Systems are not easy to build, maintain, or operate but they are indispensable.

During the nineteenth century, it used to be said about the navy that built and defended one of history's greatest empires, the Royal Navy, that it was a system designed by geniuses to be operated by idiots. A system does need to be carefully designed by thoughtful people, but that old aphorism is an exaggeration. Actual idiots can probably destroy a system.

But a good system can be operated effectively by people who are not consciously focused on the *hows* and *whys* of the system. For instance, we drive a car to the market with our minds probably busy planning our intended purchases. We give no thought to the smooth and silent changes occurring in the gearbox and transmission. We give no thought to the rapid movements of the pistons in their cylinders or the fuel pump injecting microscopically calibrated droplets of fuel into the cylinders. A modern automobile is a marvelous system.

Now we arrive at the point of this discussion: the economic system of a society is a brilliantly contrived, incredibly complex, system of human interaction involving countless individuals engaged in countless and unpredictable transactions, involving a countless array of goods and services. Every occasion in history in which governments attempted to assume command of the economy by means of centralized control has failed. It has failed because the economic system was designed to operate, not in conformity with the utopian dreams of tyrannical regimes but in conformity with how humans would conduct themselves within the framework of a commonly adhered to moral system.

A viable economy operates largely on the basis of people seeking to improve their own stations in life while not impinging on anyone else's ability to do the same by virtue of an overarching Judeo-Christian, Bible-based worldview. Very few of us participating in our economy are thinking about money supply or inter-currency convertibility. The economy is a system and as such it does not require its "operators" to be consciously focused on its internal mechanisms. But it does depend upon those in power not exploiting their power for their own benefit and not corrupting civic institutions such as the judiciary or the currency.

We are slightly uneasy about giving you some of the most egregious examples of really bad ideas. That is because many of them sweep through a population like a covid virus; they colonize hearts and minds until anyone who rejects the bad idea is made to feel like a pariah. What is more, those who reject the bad idea are likely to be canceled or to suffer other even worse consequences of being shunned. Since our goal in this book is to help you increase your revenue, the last thing we want is to introduce a political symposium of controversial doctrines. Nonetheless, because politics is really nothing more than the practical application of deeply held ideas and values, we must proceed to provide you with some more examples in order to help you develop the skills to identify the culprits and reject them. Yes, most political decisions are the result of deeply held ideas even though many of them are not our ideas.

Consider how widely spread is the notion that diversity is a company's biggest asset. Now, *diversity* is a broad word. There are many companies where getting input from both men and women makes sense and other companies where having geographic diversity would be beneficial. Certainly, having people with different strengths and ways of thinking is useful. But in most countries where diversity is preached, what is meant is only diversity of race, gender, and sexual orientation. And those are meant to take priority over the skills that are needed to fill a position. We aren't so interested, for the purpose of this book, in where this comes from or why people believe it. Our only concern is whether you believe it and consequently make bad choices in your finances. The truth should be clear: a company's biggest asset is its financial performance. Drilling down, that means that the biggest asset is how productive are all the people who work for that company. We really don't care what they look like (unless we are a model agency or something similar; we only care about their skills, integrity, resilience, resourcefulness, and other basic indices of productivity. Diversity as an overriding operating principle is a bad idea. We think this will probably eventually self-correct after this particular bad idea has destroyed too many businesses. Just don't let it harm yours.

The government-driven mania for electric cars is another example. Not that there is anything intrinsically wrong with a battery-driven car, just as there is nothing wrong with a low-slung, high-powered, hard-suspension sports and track car. It is just that a middle-aged family man with a bad back really shouldn't be forced to purchase that howling head-turner of a car by putting all other options off the market. There are certainly customers and conditions for which an electric car or truck works very well. A forklift working inside a closed warehouse comes to mind.

On the other hand, powering the vital channels of commerce crisscrossing the country by battery-driven 18-wheeler truck rigs is a really bad idea. Yet, in California, starting in January 2024, all new trucking rigs have to be electric. A diesel big rig can fuel up in 15 minutes and then drive from say, Los Angeles, California, to Reno, Nevada, and back again without having to refuel. By contrast, according to IMC, a Tennessee-based trucking company, making the same trip in an electric truck would require at least six recharging stops, taking at least an hour and a half each. What is more, electric trucks weigh considerably more than their diesel counterparts, which means that their carrying capacity is much less since the total all-up weight of trucks is regulated.

For instance, Ford recently canceled plans for a huge battery factory they had started to build in Michigan because they were not selling nearly as many electric vehicles as they had projected. Along with other battery car builders, Mercedes is offering dramatic discounts to try tolure customers into the showroom. The American public has already made it clear that it is not ready to abandon gasoline-driven cars, yet government rules mandating how many e-cars each builder must produce remain unaltered.

Much the same calculus applies to other industries. Car manufacturers have cut back significantly on their electric car production as inventory piles up on dealers' lots. Even heavy discounts from prestige brands like Mercedes added to government rebates have failed to move these vehicles. American drivers do not want these cars, but the government taxes hard-working farmers in Kansas in order to underwrite electric car purchasers in Beverly Hills. We don't have a horse in this race; go ahead and buy any car that makes sense to you. But in terms of running your business affairs, don't make the mistake of confusing government pressures with market realities. Cars are not the only products that governments feel tempted to foist onto consumers in the name of one fad or another. Government actions like determining what sort of appliances citizens should have in their homes, what sort of light bulbs should light their homes, or how much water their showers and toilets should use are ways of distorting the economy. What all these initiatives have in common is that decisions are not being made in terms of what makes most economic sense. Ideologies are being made to masquerade as policies. We are reminding you that the culture is full of bad ideas and identifying them correctly presents you with the advantages of knowing how the world really works.

Here is the final example we will give you, though there are many more to be found.

One of the requirements of a successful economy is a dependable system of justice. I might well risk engaging in a transaction, particularly one that involves credit as most do, with someone who might be a trifle unreliable as long as I know that I can depend upon a justice system that will enforce a contract. In the absence of such a system, the volume of transactions in which I will engage drops dramatically.

How does a judicial system corrupt and deteriorate? Often through well-meaning officials. For instance, imagine a civil court case between two litigants, one rich and the other poor. According to the laws of the land and the requirements of justice, the poor man must pay the rich man $100. The judge, a kind and compassionate man, says to himself, "The rich man doesn't need the $100, while for the poor man $100 represents a significant chunk of change." Surely the truly just thing to do is rule that neither litigant needs to pay anything. Case dismissed. This is a calamitous milestone on the road to social dissolution.

Along similar lines, as emotional appeals of victimhood and identity politics gain cultural credibility, landlords are designated "rich" and tenants, "poor." Thus, when a tenant ceases to pay rent but remains firmly ensconced in the property belonging to the landlord, the court obstructs every attempt by the landlord to dislodge his freeloading squatter and in the name of compassion rather than justice. It matters nothing that the landlord is a retired couple trying to subsist on the income of the little fourplex they invested in many years earlier and that the tenant may drive a fancy imported sports car. Throughout the United States, in 2022, a contested eviction for nonpayment of rent could take from 6 to 17 months. When society then discovers the inevitable housing shortage as fewer investors wish to put their savings into rental housing, few connect the dots.

The Bible warned against these very dangers in Leviticus 19:15.

You shall not render an unfair decision: do not favor the poor or show deference to the rich; judge your kin fairly.

When the emotions of judges begin to determine what passes for justice, justice ceases to exist. When justice ceases to exist, society ceases to thrive. What we are trying to demonstrate is how small and subtle damage to the system's machinery will eventually result in the system grinding to a standstill.

The system works on each participant's sense of wanting to do what is in his or her best interest, but also self-policing and self-evaluating each behavior according to the shared moral framework. An individual may have a wrong sense of his own self-interest but in most of such instances, the system will self-correct.

While it is certainly true that short-term profits can be found in riding the wave of short-lived fads, it is not the way to build a lasting, legacy business. By allowing yourself to be caught up in a bad idea that is having its moment, you could end up distorting much of your business model to the point of no return. It can require courage to avoid joining the crowd rushing toward the new bad idea like moths rush to the flame that will ultimately consume them. Think critically and courageously as you evaluate your business course and try to avoid the bad ideas that will inevitably lie in your path like barely awash rocks that lie in wait for the unwary navigator.

If There Is No Hebrew Word for Something, Then That Thing Does Not Exist

A few years ago, I [RDL] had the fortunate experience of sailing across the Pacific, a lifelong ambition of mine. After a year of preparation, my wife and I loaded the sailboat up with our (then) three children, with a few friends as crew, and with provisions. We set sail from the West Coast of California to Hawaii on what became a 22-day voyage. While the Pacific Ocean is vast, you do have to stand watch around the clock to ensure that you don't hit other ships or run into cargo containers that have been washed overboard. We took shifts, and the nighttime watches, in particular, were both exhilarating and exhausting.

On one particular night, about halfway into the trip, I began to worry about our freshwater supply. Were we consuming water too quickly? While I normally checked the water tanks every day or so by measuring it with a dipstick, I took it into my head that I needed to perform a middle of the night check. To my dismay, I found that there was nothing left. The water was all gone. My first instinct was to panic.

Maybe we had sprung a leak or perhaps a pump had gone haywire and pumped all our water up out of a pipe. Whatever the reason, I was responsible for the safety of my family and friends, and we were out of water! Completely inappropriately, I started laughing hysterically.

What was I laughing about at this inopportune time? My mind jumped to thinking about the United States Declaration of Independence, that states that Americans have a right to life, liberty, and the pursuit of happiness. My dire situation exposed this promise for the absurdity that it is. It was the middle of the night, everyone else was asleep, and here I was sitting on the floor of the boat laughing manically about the fallacy of this guarantee. Does the Declaration of Independence actually guarantee me life? What if I want to draw on that right when I'm a thousand miles out in the Pacific Ocean? I was laughing because I was thinking, "How in the world would anyone find us? And why should they? Nobody told us to go out into the ocean on a sailboat. What does this 'right' to life really mean?"

I realized then and there that the word "right" is completely meaningless. Anytime somebody tells you that you have a right to anything, be very suspect. If there isn't anybody who accepts the obligation to deliver on that right, that right is absolutely worthless. The word "right" is, on its face, nonsensical. It doesn't mean anything. How can something be guaranteed to you if there is no guarantee that someone can and will deliver it to you?

Granted, I was overtired and overtaxed. There was nothing humorous in the situation. Once the dawn broke, I rechecked the water supply and to my amazement and relief found that there was plenty of water. In my exhaustion I had somehow misread the dipstick that gauged how much water was left. Embarrassing, yes, but what a relief to know we were going to live! Everything was going to be fine. Nonetheless, the ordeal had taught me a lesson. It reminded me that the English language is full of words that are pure nonsense. These words define concepts that do not exist.

There is no word for rights in the Lord's language. There is no Hebrew word that translates to even roughly the same thing. And you can be sure that, if a word doesn't exist in the Lord's language, that thing does not exist at all. It is not real. Otherwise, God would have named it.

Naturally, this doesn't apply to words describing modern technology. There's no word in biblical Hebrew for helicopter or telephone, of course. Yet helicopters and telephones are real. There is a word in Modern Hebrew for telephone—it is *telefon*—but there is no such word in biblical Hebrew. This is not what we are talking about. Helicopters and telephones fall into the realm of things that do change, which we discussed earlier, which include technology, medicine, and science. We are speaking here strictly of those things that do not change—man, God, the spiritual, the earth. When it comes to spiritual ideas, if there is no ancient Hebrew word for a thing or concept, that thing or concept does not exist.

Nowhere in the whole Torah does it ever mention a right to anything. Not once is a right mentioned anywhere among the 613 commandments. There are only obligations. Do poor people have a right to charity? Absolutely not. Instead, each of us has an obligation to give to charity. No one may claim that I must give to them. The result, where those who are needy are helped, may be the same, but the difference is meaningful. We all have obligations, but nobody in the Bible has a right to anything. The word doesn't exist in Hebrew because it doesn't exist in the world. When anyone coerces you to provide such a right, it is not charity by the very definition of charity, which is voluntary giving. There is also no word in Hebrew for coincidence. The concept of a coincidence is contrary to God's plan. Calling something a coincidence is a fallacy because it conceals God's involvement in the world. There are no accidents or coincidences, only design that we fail to see. Just because we fail to take notice when God is conveying something to us does not make His message a coincidence. What we think of as coincidence is usually nothing more than God camouflaging His purpose. There is a reason for every single thing that has and ever will happen. We do ourselves a favor by spending a few minutes trying to figure out what we can learn from seeming coincidences rather than chalking them up as random.

There is also no Hebrew word for "fair." This is another nonsense word that the Lord's language does not recognize. Some people invoke fairness when they see inequality. They see you with two of something when they have none, and they call it unfair. But why should we all have the same amount of something, especially when you might have worked for something that I have not? Children internalize this nonsensical notion of fairness from a very young age. The parents reading this will know what I mean. How many times have you heard your children say, "But, Mommy, Daddy, it's not *fair*." Perhaps you feel the same way sometime when things aren't going your way, or you find yourself coveting what someone else has. That type of thinking leads to misery; there is no such reality as fair.

Another modern word for which there is no ancient Hebrew equivalent is "vacation," which again tells us that the thing does not exist in the eyes of the Lord. This should be obvious: the Lord wants us to serve each other, which requires that we work, and a vacation precludes working.

There is very much a concept of rest—in fact our week is meant to revolve around six days of work and one day of ceasing to impact the world. There are days that are meant to be special, either as holy days or as days with special qualities. But vacation? Vacating our existence? The British go on holiday rather than vacation. *Vacation* focuses on what you are leaving behind. You are vacating work or school or your daily routine. *Holiday* is full of mystique and charm, focusing on thrilling activities that will take the place of everyday life.

There is another dimension to this seemingly minor vocabulary difference. When you vacate or take a break from something, there is an implication that it is a burden you are happy to shrug off. In contrast to that, a holiday means that there is a fleeting (after all holidays can't last forever) opportunity on the calendar. A subtle point, perhaps, but subtleties can have a big impact.

Expanding on this idea, it probably won't surprise you to know that there is no ancient Hebrew word for retirement. The concept is a relatively new development. People did not retire in the Stone Age. They did not retire in medieval times or even during the Renaissance or Victorian times. The first mention of retirement came in 1883, when Otto von Bismarck, the chancellor of Germany, instituted a retirement age of 65. This was a fairly safe age for a society to pick back then, as most people didn't live this long—infant mortality was high and penicillin didn't exist yet—but the precedent was a bad one. People are living well past that age now, but the precedent took and now societies across the Western world observe this cutoff. But before 1883, it was unheard of. This was the first time a society had instituted the strange notion that the government would pay people not for working, but for simply growing old. Entitlement programs for retirees, such as Social Security in the United States, are bankrupting whole nations today. And for what? So we can stop working? We are bankrupting society so that we can help people stop serving each other? Sometimes the case is made that retirement is a social obligation. Retirement is framed as a way for the elderly to make room for the next generation to enter the workforce. This argument is fallacious. Think about it: if it is such a good idea to retire people at 65 so that younger people can easily find jobs, then why not retire people at age 50? Why not retire everyone at 30 so all of the 21-year-olds can find work? This makes no sense because there are no hard limits on human wealth. When people stop working, they stop producing, and often become less healthy as a result.

In a properly functioning system, everyone who works produces vastly more than they consume. You can verify this fact by looking around your own neighborhood. Sewage does not run down the street because someone put in sewer lines. You live in a house and not a field. You eat food from the supermarket, not food from the woods. All of these things required a surplus of production for you to be able to enjoy them through trade. Modern conveniences and discretionary income are proof that we produce far more than we consume. This is true for almost all people around the developed world.

Why then should we put productive people out of work? How does this help anything? There is no point at which somebody automatically becomes useless. Everyone has something to contribute—yes, some more than others. But everyone can contribute. We are never too old to contribute. Our ability to contribute may change or morph, but every person has something to give, some way to serve.

In the book of Numbers, we are introduced to a set of priests with less than desirable job duties. They must drag animal carcasses, perform sacrifices, and deal with recalcitrant customers or worshippers. In Numbers 8:25, God tells Moses that these priests over the age of 50 should withdraw from the service in the Tent of Meeting. Is this a biblical reference to retirement? No. The next verse tells us that these men should work in a different manner than previously. They are still doing a very important job and getting paid for it. It's just a different job.

God recognizes that the physical labor of dragging around heavy carcasses is no longer suitable for a priest at the age of 50. The work is beyond them physically and beneath their dignity. These older priests are moved into an elevated advisory position. They become the boss priests. But they are still working. There is no point in the Bible that espouses the notion that we quit working altogether at any age. Retirement should not be a core principle of the working life. We must get away from the notion that the point of working is so that one day we can retire and do whatever we want to do and never serve anyone ever again. If God had planned this, He would have named such a thing. There's no Hebrew word for retirement, and so we know He did not.

Retirement Is Unhealthy

We know many people who could not wait to retire. They worked their whole lives and were at the peak of their physical and mental health. Then they hit age 65 and immediately stopped working. They said goodbye to their coworkers, perhaps enjoyed a piece of cake at a retirement party, and quit working. They received Social Security and drew down their savings. Almost instantly, their health began to decline. Sometimes, they fell into a deep depression. A few retirees go back to work just to have something to do, to have a way to meet and connect with people as they did when they were working. Suddenly, they feel good again.

The bottom line is this: retirement is unhealthy, physically, emotionally, and spiritually.

The *New England Journal of Medicine* has published many articles over the years that correlate faith and prayer with good health. There is an observable connection. Might this have any correlation with retirement? If we accept the premise of this book, that our work is largely about serving God's other children, then on what basis do you ask God for help and good health when you are not out there every day helping His other children? It is certainly more difficult. This is one reason why so many people's lives deteriorate when they quit working and they no longer have the structure and discipline that working provides. People stop working, and they lose their drive and the thrill that comes from producing and being helpful. They begin to decline not only physically, but spiritually too.

Many people replace work by volunteering, which is better than doing nothing, but less healthy than working in a paid career, if that is at all possible. There are many worthy organizations that depend on volunteer work, and everybody should put in some volunteer hours. It is noble and good. But ideally, you should do it in addition to actual paid work, not as a replacement for work. The problem with volunteering is that it is too easy to fall into the habit of doing only when we feel like it. There is (often) no accountability and thus no discipline involved. Say you promised the Helping Hands where you volunteer that you will come in on a Sunday, but then when Sunday morning rolls around, you notice that the weather looks perfect for a day of hiking. What is to stop you from calling in your regrets and going to the trail instead? It's not as though the place where you volunteer can fire you. You can come and go as you please. For most people, volunteering is a case of doing what you feel like doing, even if it's lovely that you feel like doing something worthwhile. While some wonderful souls treat volunteering like a job and show up day in and day out whether they feel like it or not, these are a rare few special people. They show up no matter how they feel and no matter what unexpected things happen in their lives, just like people who have a job for which they get paid. But this is a tiny minority, a small fraction of a fraction of all people.

Most of us need economic incentives and administrative oversight. We do much better in situations that force us to overcome our personal wants and desires. Too often, retirement means that all of a sudden, we can do whatever we want whenever we want. We can lie in bed when we feel like lying in bed. We can go fishing or hiking when we want. These are all very nice and fine pursuits, but it is not healthy to pursue them, or any personal pleasures, to exclusion. Without a job, we have no accountability or discipline. Human beings thrive when they are growing and developing, and this requires discipline. Discipline and accountability keep us alive. Working engenders a growing, strengthening willpower that ensures that we go into work to serve our fellow man each and every day. This is a good thing because working means you are serving. Do that and you will find that you are more likely to stay in good shape, physically and spiritually. It's not that you haven't missed a day of work because you're in good shape. It's the other way around. You are in good shape precisely because you haven't missed a day of work.

Another problem with volunteering in lieu of doing paid work is that we can never be totally sure that we are actually doing something that is necessary. Organizations want to keep their volunteers. Many organizations depend on volunteers for their continuation. But sometimes there just isn't enough to do or the skillset of the volunteers doesn't match the jobs that need doing. One of the great things about being paid, aside from the paycheck, is that you know you are doing some good for somebody. This must be true, or no one would pay you. Being paid ensures that you are delivering value. This is, ultimately, why you must keep working.

Retirement is so unhealthy precisely because it leads to a sense of worthlessness. If we don't think we are serving, if we don't think we are adding value, we feel worthless. When people only do what they feel like and do not have the opportunity and luxury of serving others, they begin to feel as if their life force is being eroded. Our spirits will feel damaged and defective, which translates into mental and physical health problems.

When the prophet Samuel was still a young boy, his mother took him to Jerusalem so that his life would be devoted to God. Early in the first book of Samuel, we are told: "And the lad served the Lord and Eli the priest" (1 Samuel 2:11). Note that Samuel is not even named here. This is a man who will one day grow up to be a prophet, but right now he holds a lowly status. He is at the beginning of his career at the Tabernacle. It is not until later that we are told: "And the lad Samuel served the Lord before Eli" (1 Samuel 3:1). Here we see that he is named. He is still referred to as a mere lad, but he is named because Samuel is beginning to take over and advance in his career.

These verses are linguistically marked in the Hebrew text in a way that is lost in translation. The Hebrew word *ET* is made up of the first and last letters in the Hebrew alphabet, which suggests an embrace and parentheses. *ET* is often used before a name to signify tremendous emphasis and importance. In the Hebrew text, Samuel 2:11 reads: "And the lad served *ET*, the Lord and *ET* Eli the priest." The word *ET* here indicates that Samuel is splitting his focus between God and his master, Eli, both of whom he is serving. But in 1 Samuel 3:1, the text reads: "And the lad Samuel served, *ET* the Lord before Eli." Eli is no longer referred to as the priest. Furthermore, unlike in 2:11 there is no *ET* preceding Eli's name. The focus has now shifted away from Samuel serving his master to serving his God. This is a normal and natural shift for Samuel. It is the natural development of a career at the Tabernacle—first you apprentice and then you move to serving God. One's method of working does not stay the same through a lifetime, but being a contributor is a need that remains.

(There is one caveat we would like to make, though we are not going to attempt to explain it here. There is a difference between men and women when it comes to the need to be paid in order to know for sure that one's work is meaningful. We explain this concept in detail in our book *The Holistic You: Integrating Your Family, Finances, Faith, Friends and Fitness*.)

A person's skills, abilities, and experience develop and change over the course of a lifetime, but that does not mean that they should be put out to pasture when they are no longer well suited to a particular job. You are still useful, just in different ways. The idea that older people are no longer useful is a terrible and destructive modern idea that hurts both individuals and the larger economy. Forced retirement is a strange and unnatural thing. Many companies have policies of a mandatory retirement age, and this is a total mistake. Older people have so much to give still. If you want to make room for young people, expand the company. Expansion is what leads to growth, and economic growth is good for everybody. Forcing people to retire is good for no one. The business suffers, the retiree suffers, and society suffers. Everyone suffers a loss of potential wealth and fulfillment.

How You Think About Tomorrow Affects How You Behave Today

W e are not golfers. In fact, we know very little about the game. But one thing we do know is that the swing and subsequent follow-through is one of the most important parts of the game. Before you take a swing, you walk up to the ball, plan your swing, maybe wiggle yourself a bit like they do on TV, and then you bring club back and crack the ball. What happens next? The ball either goes the right way or it doesn't. Once the club has connected with the ball and sent it soaring down the fairway, what you do afterward should be irrelevant. Once the club has hit the ball, it makes no sense that what you do next should sway the ball's path. Whether you move the club sideways, or do a dance, or lean in hopefully while reciting a poem, the ball is already on its way. That sounds sensible, but it isn't accurate. It turns out that the swing of the golf club *after* it has contacted the ball and the motion of the ball in the air are part of the same smooth movement. If a golfer doesn't properly plan the swing the entire way through to the end, the ball doesn't take the correct path onto the green. Pro golfers focus on the swing and the follow-through movement as one continuous movement. It turns out that if the ball doesn't go where you intended it to go, the problem might lie in not having properly planned through the entire movement, from beginning to the end. The beginning and the follow-through are inextricable from one another. They are one smooth motion.

And so it is with life. When we plan our careers looking at earning money as a discrete entity that belongs to only a few years that are separate from the other parts of our life such as our families, friends, our physical well-being, and our relationship to the spiritual, we should not be surprised if that discrete entity, the years we accord to earning money, does not end up where we want it to go. When we think of the years spent earning money as a penalty we must pay to get as quickly as possible to a life of indulgence and free time that is our goal (otherwise known as retirement), most of us will neither make as much as we could have nor will we obtain the benefits that come from working hard and being productive.

As our society becomes more secularized, this shattering of the connection between different stages of our lives becomes more acute. At a simple level, individuals used to live in multigenerational families, which might include a newborn baby and an elderly great-grandparent. The panoply of life was evident. Today, age groups tend to be more segregated and, not unrelated, seriously more isolated and lonelier. We cannot discount the effect of secularization on our attitudes toward business.

A protracted period of freezing weather can cause quite a few different consequences. Cars whose owners neglect to put the correct antifreeze solution into the cooling system might suffer cracked radiators. Roofs can be damaged by the weight of snow. Driveways can crack on account of the rapid freezing of water and the subsequent expansion as it becomes ice.

Similarly, a once healthy society can suffer a variety of damage as it enters a protracted period of secularism. Without us even realizing it on a day-by-day basis, a Judeo-Christian Bible-based cultural matrix provides a preventative against several problems that we may not even see coming.

Ancient Jewish wisdom speaks of an observer confronting a rather elderly looking man who was engaged in planting a variety of carob tree known for producing fruit only after 70 years. "What is the point of planting trees whose fruit you will never see?" asked the bystander.

The wise old man responded, "Had those who came before me not planted carob trees for me, I wouldn't be eating today."

While a culture is still anchored to the fullness of time, its entrepreneurs dream of building businesses that their children and grandchildren will operate and from which they will benefit. They build for the long term. In societies with that perspective, people willingly work hard in the dream that their businesses will one day boast the accolade, "a family business for three (or four or five) generations."

However, once a culture secularizes, the time window shrinks. Entrepreneurs dream of the quick exit. They design their business plans for an early exit event, such as "going public," planning for the founders and initial investors to get out fairly quickly. It is hard to imagine that this trend produces a healthier economy than one built by individuals whose timeline runs far into future generations.

You cannot disconnect the future from the present, and you cannot disconnect the present from the past. That's not how time works. Time moves in a continuous motion.

Planning for the quick exit, or for being able to retire at an age when one's physical and mental capabilities are still strong, corrupts one's entire career. Viewed through that lens, retirement is the idea that, once you have earned enough money, you drop out of the system. If you focus only on the monetary rewards of working, you lose sight of the true goal, which is to help other people. If we are working only with retirement in mind, clearly we are only working for the money, not for the serving. There is no such thing as having "served enough." As we have stressed repeatedly in this book, we work in order to serve other people. The joy of work is serving God's other children. Money is the inevitable consequence of that. We don't chase money. We don't love money. We love the opportunity of serving other human beings. The fact that God has set up a world in which serving others results in earning money is just icing on the cake. Bountiful prosperity is a huge blessing. But never lose sight of the goal, which is serving others. Money is the mere testimony to the fact that we have served many of God's children. It is not the end goal. In other words, plan the end of the swing correctly from the start.

Working to amass enough money to stop working is not God's plan for us. Working isn't about what you get; it's about what you give.

Working is about asking: "What can I do for you?" There is no reason you should stop asking that when you have a certain amount of savings or when you turn a certain age. The obsession, the preoccupation, the joy, and the exhilaration of work arise from serving other people. It so happens that the more you serve, the more money flows toward you. But do not get this backward. Your focus is the serving, not the money. The more you focus on the money, the less it flows toward you. This is the paradox of work. Not focusing on when one will "have enough" to stop work does not mean that we should be irresponsible and not plan for the future. Just as the priests in the Tabernacle moved to different work when they reached a certain age, welder and construction workers should recognize that they will need to transition away from physical labor. Every ballet dancer or athlete knows that there are limited years when they can push their bodies to the extent necessary to be successful in those jobs. During a visit to a major East Coast city recently, we had the pleasure of meeting an outstanding young man who has been a principal male dancer for that city's distinguished ballet company since he was seven years old. He had just retired from ballet at the age of 34. What impressed us was that he had also just enrolled in an MBA program at the local university's business school. This struck us as a perfect real-life example of what we teach. Even in jobs that are not physically focused, a shift in direction is often necessary as family, business, and personal realities change. Flexibility in how one serves God's other children is valuable; that is completely different from having as one's life goal the plan of caring only about oneself. Realistically anticipating the future is an imperative. We are saying that there are two paths to take. The first is to plan to make enough money in one's strongest years so that one can stop working at a young age. The second, the preferable way, is to recognize that contributing to society is a lifelong task and one should plan for different ways to accomplish that goal. Advising you never to retire does not mean ignoring savings and pretending that a 70-year-old body can compete with one that is 30 years old. It is nice to have the capacity not to need to work out of desperation.

Nothing throws the brakes on success like pointless worry about the future. Plan and act for the future, but don't worry about future events you cannot influence. You might be going about your day, meeting all of your obligations with aplomb, diligently serving other people and God, doing everything right, and you feel great, when suddenly this niggling feeling about tomorrow descends over you. This kind of nagging worry is a terrible form of spiritual gravity because it is so pernicious. Everything may not fall apart at once, but we can feel ourselves slowly coming apart at the seams. We start planning and fretting over what must be done the next day, or the next week, and we worry about what the following year holds, and suddenly we are not living fully in the present. Worrying about the future is troubling for humans. Bad thoughts about tomorrow can infect our spirits and performance today in noticeable and measurable ways.

In the same way that spending much of your professional career dreaming of retirement can be harmful, keeping in mind the nobility of work will help you. While dining at a kosher restaurant in Dallas recently, we eavesdropped on a conversation between a waitress and another customer. The customer asked the waitress what she did when she wasn't waiting tables. She responded that she was a recent immigrant and hadn't found any other work yet. The customer smiled and said, "You give great service. How would you like to help people enjoy healthier skin and better looks?" Her eyes lit up when he offered to hire her to do sales from a cosmetics kiosk in one of the largest malls in Texas.

Never mind hiring the waitress—we would have liked to hire that man! He knew not to ask his prospect, "How would you like to make money persuading passersby to try a hand cream?" Instead, he motivated her by appealing to a slightly higher purpose. He inspired her by suggesting how she could serve her fellow man.

One thing I [RDL] learned as a parent was that igniting a contagious enthusiasm for chores among my young children was easy, provided that I first spoke about how much we all owed my wife, their mother, before assigning tasks. Rather than lecturing on why clean dishes and swept floors were so important, I appealed to a higher purpose. Such tactics can light a fire in the hearts of humans.

Needless to say, just as fire can cook delicious food, heat our homes, and provide mechanized transport, it can also burn and destroy. The more powerful a tool, the more powerfully it can be used for both good and evil. Similarly, the ability to tap into the worthy human desire to strive for a greater purpose than merely our physical existence can also be used for both good and evil. Politicians win support for unpopular policies by explaining, for instance, that confiscatory rates of taxation are necessary to "give every citizen free medicine," to "help the children," or "to end poverty." They know better than to justify higher taxes by explaining that they wish to hire more of their cronies and provide them with lavish benefits.

Nimrod, who enslaved the populace to build the Tower of Babel, knew, as all tyrants know, that you cannot subdue people by telling them, "I want to enslave you. I want you to work for my aggrandizement." You have to find a way to appeal to their desire for a higher purpose. When, in Genesis 11:4, Nimrod said, "Come; let us build a city and a tower whose top will reach heaven," he was speaking to a spiritual need. The tower was a metaphor for appealing to a higher purpose.

In the Lord's language, Hebrew, the word for tower, *MiGDaL*, is closely related to the word for great, *GaDoL*. Not only is a tower a great building, but a tower is also the physical depiction of our own human yearning to find transcendent purpose in our lives. Often companies build enormous headquarters, not because they need the space but because they want a symbol of their vision. Every one of us yearns to reach for the sky. Similarly, by orating about his stairway to Heaven, Nimrod is saying, "Come with me, I will help you reach for your highest aspirations."

Knowing that on the deepest level most people are motivated best by a call to higher purpose is a practical and indispensable tool for managing a military, a business, or a family. A good leader takes the time to share his or her vision and the idea and passion behind it rather than simply relaying the task that needs to be accomplished. Mundane and often boring jobs lay the groundwork for majestic missions. Being able to envision the goal in grand terms makes even difficult tasks achievable. This is true for organizations and for individuals.

Secret #40

The Three Most Important Words: Relationships, Relationships, Relationships

Earlier in this book we looked at one of the Hebrew words for "friend," *YeDiD*. There are several biblical words for the concept because friendship and connection are so important in ancient Jewish wisdom. We now want to introduce one more Hebrew word for friend: *HaVeR*. The first two letters of this word form another word that describes the essence of friendship. *H-V* is Hebrew for "obligation." The message is that a friend is somebody to whom we have obligations. You may have thought that a friend is someone who gives to you, who is committed to you, and who makes your life better. There is certainly an element of truth to this, but that is a consequence of friendship, not a description. If you recall our earlier conversation that there is no word for "rights" in biblical Hebrew, you will remember that there is no such thing as a right. We get what we need when each of us focuses on our obligations. So, yes, we get a tremendous amount from our friends, but in a true friendship this comes about because each member of the friendship recognizes his or her obligation to their counterpart.

Relationships are intensified by a sense of obligation. On a practical level, you can use this principle to help make new friends and establish new connections. Doing favors for someone is a wonderful way to make friends, and not just because people like favors. Doing someone a favor is a subtle but powerful way of entering an "obligation relationship" with another person. When you do a decent person a favor, they feel obliged to return the favor. Doing favors creates bonds and reoccurring interaction between people. When we moved into a new neighborhood, we both extended and received Shabbat dinner invitations from our new neighbors. In return, our guests reciprocated by inviting us, and for those families where we were the guests, we reciprocated by inviting our hosts. The time spent together was a promising first step toward building friendships.

Treat this as a tool for making friends and business contacts. Do not approach this tool cynically or in a self-interested fashion. Don't grant favors or request them in order to manipulate people into liking you. Rather, do favors because you have a genuine interest in making connections. Though you must not be cynical about this, you may be pragmatic. Favors establish and reinforce connections, including business connections, and you do yourself no justice by ignoring this truth. Doing favors for someone obligates them to do the same in kind. Your goal is not self-interest, to force someone to feel an obligation to you. Your goal is to establish a "conversation" of favors. You are providing the opening for establishing communication and lasting connection. There is a joy in doing other people favors, and it is something both parties can and should engage in. It's a wonderful thing that brings people closer together and binds them. That is your goal. The side benefit is that the person you do a favor for feels an obligation to reciprocate the favor, and this establishes a cycle that intensifies the relationship. This is what friendship is: a set of reoccurring obligations that people fill. Two people that have and feel no obligations to one another are not friends.

Often people express happiness that they are married to their best friend. They may consider themselves lucky. But is it luck? Or is it a self-fulfilling prophecy? We contend it is the latter. If friendship is based on having shared obligations, is there anyone in the world you share more obligations with than your spouse? Of course not. It is only natural that married people identify their spouses as their best friends since marriage is one of the greatest obligations you can enter into with another person. Therefore, marriage begets deep and lasting friendship. In fact, the word for affection in Hebrew is based on the same root letters of *H-V* as is the word for friendship. Affection is dependent on obligation.

Words like *connection* and *relationship* suggest a two-way street. Occasionally you will meet a person for whom you simply cannot do a favor. You may want to become friendly with this individual for personal and professional reasons, and you know that friendship is based on obligation. So, you would like to do your best to engender a sense of obligation by doing favors, but due to circumstance, maybe your lack of ability to actually help them, you simply cannot find a way to do them a favor. There's absolutely nothing you can think of that you can do for this person.

What can you do in a situation like this? When you cannot offer someone a favor, you can try the reverse: ask a favor of them, instead. This is the same principle albeit working in the reverse direction. You might be astonished how often people will say yes. You shouldn't be. Good people like being asked for favors, so long as they are reasonable. Most people will go out of their way to do a favor that is within their reach, provided the request is manageable and doesn't harm them. For example, if you ask a person you admire and wish to know better to spend 15 minutes with you answering questions about their field of work, at a time that is convenient for them, most professionals will be happy to spend that time with you. An unreasonable request would be for them to put in a good word for you with their business's employment office, when they know little about you or your skills. That could damage their reputation. However, once someone does you a favor, the lines of communication are open. You owe them something and, at a minimum, you will write a letter expressing your appreciation for what they did. From there, the relationship can strengthen as favors and goodwill are passed back and forth.

Remember that relationships are a mainstay in your personal and professional life. They are the lifeblood of your career. This is one of the main reasons to shy away from retirement. Retirement severs, mutes, and precludes these deep professional connections. In doing so, retirement tends to isolate us. If our business associates recognize that we are only interested in a position for the short term, they will be lukewarm to us and less willing to invest in forming a meaningful relationship.

Because coworkers, professionals, customers, vendors, and the like depend on each other for their needs, the bonds they form can go very deep. Work is how we earn money, our lifeblood, and so the relationships we form there take on a deep significance in our lives.

If you are a good worker, you are probably indispensable to your boss. He needs you to show up every day, providing your unique know-how, skillset, and character. Chances are that you are very difficult to replace as a worker or colleague.

Unfortunately, some business management experts have adopted the modern notion that all workers are dispensable. These so-called experts believe that businesses run like machines and that workers are merely interchangeable cogs that can be swapped in and out at will. This is patently untrue. Anybody who has ever run a business knows enough to reject this notion. Nobody is dispensable. Every compensated associate plays a vital role.

This is not to say that losing an employee causes the system to grind to a halt. People quit their jobs for any number of reasons. Employees make lateral moves or take promotions to other divisions or employers. Layoffs and firings happen. People retire (although they should think carefully before doing so), and people switch fields. None of this means that a business must grind to a halt. Businesses find a way to carry on. But there is a cost associated with losing personnel. This is why companies strive for maximum retention rates. Having a high incidence of employee turnover is expensive and disruptive to workflow and customer satisfaction. High turnover of staff also makes it difficult for companies to build a brand. While huge companies like Google and Microsoft technically could fire and replace all their employees overnight, the resulting companies would not be the same even if all the positions were filled and they retained the same corporate structure. Individuals make all the difference in any company. Why do you think companies continue to pay high salaries to senior and upper-level employees when they could easily hire a newly minted graduate into the position for a third of the payroll expense?

The answer is that seasoned employees add value, far more than the sticker price of their higher salaries. Continuity of personnel leads to a continuity of business, which is good for the bottom line and good for brand building.

This is why researchers and employers the world over have devoted so much time and resources into figuring out how to retain staff. They understand that good personnel are not easily replaced. This only applies to excellent people, of course. Staff members who do not function efficiently and effectively and do not add value to the company or increase the bottom line are quite dispensable.

Think about how much of your daily interaction and human connections flow directly from your professional life. You have coworkers and customers. You may be part of a work association with fellow workers, professional groups, and self-improvement and development programs. One of the keys to this equation is that you see these people regularly. Forging human connections requires proximity and repeated unplanned social interactions. As a worker, you are an indispensable part of a larger operation. You are in regular contact with others. And you are serving people, which creates bonds of love.

In a healthy work situation, the people with whom you work really care about you. Of course, this demands that you are a good and considerate coworker. If you have ever had the unpleasant experience of working with somebody who regularly slacks off at work, if they show up at all, you will know what we mean. Showing up matters. Showing up ready to work matters even more. Being courteous, appreciative, and pleasant makes all the difference. Good workers are missed when they miss a day, change jobs, or retire. Their absence causes real problems and hardships for the company. Therefore, your connection with others at work is inherently significant. By filling your needed position as a hardworking, moral, enthusiastic, service-oriented worker, you ensure that your bosses, coworkers, and customers will appreciate you and recognize you as the valuable asset that you are. More than anything else, isolation destroys our ability to create money and build prosperity. Remember that your salary or wage is not just a measure of purchasing power. Money is a quantifiable analog for your entire life force. People with many strong relationships tend to be people with lots of money. Despite disproportionate headlines and attention paid to rogues, people who hold themselves to a high moral standard tend to be wealthier than those who fail to live virtuously. Those who live dissolute lives in which they fail to make and keep commitments and accept discipline do not tend to do well financially. If you live in such a way, you simply will not prosper. Only those who live by God's laws will truly prosper, spiritually, mentally, physically, and financially.

Money plays a central role in God's plan for creation and human economic interaction by forcing us to live a deliberate, purposeful, calculated life. This is the beauty of money and the economy. The particular placement of money at the center of all economic and social interaction gives us a vested interest in committing to mutual service. It keeps us from floating along, happy-go-lucky, doing what we want just because we feel like it. Money is not the goal, and you will not thrive on ill-gotten funds and goods. The result of this way of thinking has led many people to lead miserable lives of poverty. It has led them to lead lives in which they do very little to help those around them.

A purposeful, examined, deliberate life naturally follows from having the right perspective on money and its role within creation. Remember Samuel Johnson's sentiment.

Earning money is a good and healthy activity because it forces us to build and maintain relationships. It forces us to be good to one another. Earning money leads us to find ways, often new and ingenious ways, to serve one another. Earning money allows us to live a measured and reasonable life without excess, as long as we remain focused on earning money in the right way—by serving people. While this may sound counterintuitive to you if you have been indoctrinated to view the pursuit of wealth as a self-interested, immoral act, we hope that this book has challenged those preconceptions. You might have been told that money is the root of all evil. Money is actually one of the driving forces behind human interaction. You have probably been told again and again that money is not the most important thing in life. That is true. It is not the most important thing in life, but neither is it the least important.

Sometimes people accuse us of holding the belief that life is all about money. Our emphasis on making money makes them uncomfortable. They accuse us of thinking about nothing other than money. This is far from the truth. However, we freely admit that we spend much time thinking about money because money affects every area of our life. Being unable to afford what one needs is not a virtue; it is a sad state in which to be. Being married, raising a family, participating in one's neighborhood and faith community, staying healthy, are all easier when one isn't worried about putting a roof over one's head. We may enjoy hobbies, but we can survive without them. We, for example, love sailing. But it is not constantly on our minds. We do not engage in that activity every day, nor do we think about it every day. But other than on the Sabbath, not a day goes by in which we do not think about money and where it doesn't affect our lives. Are we doing our best to serve and earn? Are we finding the best opportunities to do so? We ask these questions of ourselves constantly. Doing so is as natural as breathing and just as necessary to life.

Making money and thinking about money makes not only for a better life, but also for a better society. The good that comes from wealth creation transcends the benefit of any one person. Making money isn't just about us and our bank account. It is about us actively helping to build a prosperous community, society, and nation. It is larger than just us. Focusing on earning money is the most natural and preordained mechanism by which we are best able to serve others and to build a society that reflects God's goodness. We focus on our career, you focus on yours, and together we build a better, healthier economy.

If you still harbor doubts about the virtue of earning money, perhaps harboring a suspicion that you would be acting more nobly if you devoted yourself to volunteer work, we encourage you to answer the following question. If the ability for each individual to earn his own money and build wealth wasn't a factor, how would society run? We used to live on a beautiful island in the Pacific Northwest. Our family was happy, and our needs were met with a little left over for luxuries. We were as comfortable and happy as can be and said prayers of gratitude every morning for being able to live where and how we did. We lived in the middle of the island, though. Around the perimeter of the island were about 300 waterfront homes. To be perfectly honest, we would have loved to live in one of these waterfront homes, with their magnificent views. Being right on the water is splendid. You get to have a private dock, and you can park your boat right outside your front door. That is something this seafaring family could get used to!

But we were not the only ones who wanted one of these waterfront houses. Millions of people in America would like a waterfront home on this enchanted island, but there are only about 300 here to be had. How should we decide who gets one and who doesn't? How should we make that decision? There are really only five ways to do so, some better and some worse than others.

The first way is to hold a lottery. The outcome is totally random. Three hundred lucky people get a free home, and everyone else is out of luck. You might think this is a terrible idea, and it is, but let's not forget that almost every state in the United States holds government lotteries. And, yes, they are terrible ideas, every last one of them. The lottery is like a tax on naïve and desperate people. Sometimes, the government will try to gussy the scheme up by painting it as for a good cause. Often lotteries are used to pay for education, for example. Education is great, but there are more equitable and moral ways to raise money for schools. The lottery cultivates a terrible culture of winning, not earning. Gambling tricks people into thinking they can receive the benefit of serving others without having to put in the work.

If a lottery turns you off, too, consider the second option: brute force and survival of the fittest. We could award the houses to whoever could take them by force. Anyone who wants a home could recruit and arm a hundred thugs. Now you might laugh at that system, but unfortunately in many parts of the world today this is the economic system. Property is divided based upon the use of force. Dictators do this. Tribes do this. Criminal thugs around the world do this. It is the system of tyranny and anarchy.

Maybe you are a strong and immoral person, and this sounds like a good way for you to take one of the waterfront houses for yourself. Just don't forget that once you get the house, you have to keep it under your control. You have to keep your army of thugs around to keep someone else from coming in to evict or even kill you. This scenario invariably leads to a brutish and unpleasant existence, even for those on top. Dictators, mobsters, and cartel owners operate in this world, and even those on top are at constant risk of being dethroned and dispatched. We would rather keep our quiet life and little house in the middle of the island than risk our neck for a waterfront home. So, this method has drawbacks, but it is certainly a way to assign ownership of the houses.

What some might consider a more civilized way to decide who gets the houses is to set up a committee to assign ownership. We would gather a few politicians, a couple of academics, and some bureaucrats all into the same room and form a think tank. They would be tasked with the job of deciding who should receive the houses. But how do they pick who is most worthy? On what basis would they make these decisions?

As it turns out they have no problem assigning ownership of the homes. What might come as a surprise is that all of the most worthy and deserving people whom they will identify as fortunate recipients just happen to be closely related to the people sitting on the committee. What a coincidence! Also, some of the people on this committee seem to suddenly be very rich, as if someone had just sent them large sums of money. If you have any idea of the net worth of, let's say, members of the United States Congress or heads of government bureaucracies, you will share our cynicism at this method of distributing property. But cronyism and nepotism certainly are one widely used method to allocate riches in many parts of the world. The problem with this system is that people are venal. Power corrupts. As Lord Acton said, "Absolute power corrupts absolutely."

None of these ideas sound too great, do they? The problem is that there always seem to be winners and losers. What if there were a way that we could all enjoy the waterfront? This brings us to the fourth option: give the waterfront houses not to a few people, but to everybody. How is this possible? By pulling down all the houses on the waterfront and turning the whole ring into a beautiful public beach that wraps around the island. This way everyone gets to be on the waterfront. Isn't that great? Even setting aside the destruction of wealth that pulling down the houses causes, this doesn't really solve the initial problem. Once the waterfront houses are gone and the land has been socialized and made public, what happens to the ring of houses behind the waterfront houses? These are now the best on the island. Not only do they have closest access to the water, they have beach, access too!

How do we decide who gets these houses? Unless we are prepared to tear down all of civilization, we are back to square one.

Clearly none of these methods are workable or desirable. There is only one other option we know of. If you think of another, please feel free to write to us about it, and we will add it to our next book. But we really don't think there's anything else. There are only five, and here is the fifth: we utilize something called money. Money allows each and every one of us to decide how badly we want that waterfront house. We have a limited number of these tokens, and the person willing and able to part with the most tokens gets the waterfront house of their choice. We each may decide if we want the waterfront house more than we want a vacation, a nice car, or a good education for our children. Do you want the house more than you want your current career? Because to get it, you might have to give up your current career and enter a more lucrative career field. You are welcome to bid as much of your money as you can spare. You get to decide how much to bid, and everybody else does the same.

Do you think this is a perfect system? Is this system without any drawbacks? No, we don't think so. There are obvious problems. But it is clearly a better way of assigning ownership of the houses, a very scarce resource, than any of the other four options. There's no brute force involved, no random chance, no opportunity for corruption, no wanton destruction of the very thing you were trying to divvy up. It's a straightforward direct system.

The best part of the system, of course, is that achieving a waterfront house, or anything else you want to buy, impels you to serve your fellow human beings with enthusiasm, passion, zeal, and dedication to earn enough money to make a high bid for a waterfront house. There is nothing wrong with that. Despite years of social conditioning urging us to think that there's something crass about earning money, despite indoctrination to believe that money is morally tainted and that we should turn our noses up at money and put on airs of a higher sensibility, the reality is that money is a miracle of God. Money is something that helps us live good, healthy, productive lives. Money is something that generates a deep desire in each and every one of us to serve our fellow human beings with energy and passion, without staring longingly at a clock or calendar, waiting for the hour and day on which we can go home and never have to help someone again.

Money is not evil. It does great good in the world. We live in a world where the greatest thrills, the deepest passions, and the most profound joy come from serving God's other children. Doing that from the moment we start working and not stopping until the day that the good Lord invites us home is the best way to live a fulfilling and meaningful life. And what a glorious and magnificent ride it is. We get to spend each day building our lives around the magnificence of making money, building not only lives in which we each do well, but also lives in which we do good for one another.

Final Thoughts

Now that you have come to the end of this book, we have one last lesson to impart. Taking in all of the knowledge contained within this book has probably felt like a long journey. But this material must make one more journey. It is not a journey from our minds to your brain—that has already happened. You now know what you need to do. The final journey is for the information and wisdom contained in this book to move from your head to your heart.

You have to now transition from knowing what to do to actually willfully doing it. And you have to want that. It is easier for us to do what our heart wants than what our heads tell us we should do. You must therefore move everything you learned from this book from your head to your heart so that you will actually *want* to employ the tips, tools, techniques, and principles previously discussed.

Do this, and these biblical business secrets will become not only a part of what you think and what you know, but also a part of who you are and how you live. Do this and making money will no longer be an unpleasantness to be endured for 40 to 50 hours a week. Making money will become your calling. You will integrate your soul and your body, unite your values with your work, and be filled with the delight of serving God's other children each minute of your working day. You will know that each and every dollar that flows into your bank account is yet another eloquent witness to the effectiveness with which you have served others.

May God bless your efforts and your diligence in following this biblical blueprint and may bountiful abundance be your lot for all your days.

About the Authors

Rabbi Daniel and Susan Lapin

Rabbi Daniel Lapin, noted rabbinic scholar, best-selling author of books like *Thou Shall Prosper, The Holistic You,* and *America's Real War* and host of *The Rabbi Daniel Lapin* podcast, appears live before more than 35,000 people in audiences around the world each year. He is famous for teaching life principles from the Torah, what he calls *Ancient Solutions to Modern Problems,* to people of all backgrounds in entertaining and practical ways.

Newsweek magazine included him in its first list of America's 50 most influential rabbis. With his wife, Susan, he hosted a daily television show, *Ancient Jewish Wisdom.* Through his books, broadcasts, and speeches, he has become one of America's most compelling and persuasive voices of practical biblical principles for both Jews and Christians.

He serves as the president of the American Alliance of Jews and Christians working toward restoring biblical values as the basis of civilization.

Before immigrating to the United States, Rabbi Daniel Lapin studied Torah, physics, economics, and mathematics in yeshivas and schools in South Africa, the United Kingdom, and Israel. He was the founding rabbi of Pacific Jewish Center, a now legendary Orthodox synagogue in Venice, California.

Rabbi Lapin is a frequent speaker for hundreds of trade groups, political, social, religious, and civic institutions, financial conferences, organizations, and companies. He speaks regularly at synagogues, churches, and universities throughout the country as well as in Europe and Asia. He appears on national radio and television shows.

His articles have appeared in the *Wall Street Journal, Commentary,* and the *Jewish Press*. He and his wife have published seven books, some of which have been translated into Chinese, Croatian, Hungarian, and Korean.

An enthusiastic boater who has sailed his family across the Pacific in their own boat, Lapin raised his family on Mercer Island, Washington. He and his wife recently relocated to the East Coast.

Growing up in the tail winds of second-wave feminism, Susan Lapin contemplated a variety of career options. She never considered being a rabbi's wife and partner as a possible choice, but then she also had no idea that marriage would entail sailing her young family in a small boat across the Pacific Ocean. God had different plans, and for 15 years, she helped lead the legendary synagogue, Pacific Jewish Center of Venice, California, with her husband, its founder, Rabbi Daniel Lapin. During that time, as well as lecturing to women around California on Scripture, personal growth, marriage, parenting, and education, Susan was busy with the Lapins' seven children and homeschooling over the course of 16 years. (Yes, those who wanted to did get into college, where they excelled.) She now lectures to both Jewish and non-Jewish audiences, writes a widely read column, Susan's Musings, and has cowritten many books, including *Buried Treasure: Secrets for Living from the Lord's Language,* with her husband. She also cohosted the daily Ancient Jewish Wisdom TV Show on the TCT television network with her husband. Now living on the East Coast, she finds time to hold an annual summer Grandma Camp for half a dozen little girls who look remarkably like her.

Did You Enjoy this Book?

Sign up to receive a FREE *Thought Tool* every week!

Thought Tools is a free weekly email from Rabbi Daniel and Susan Lapin. This short message brings you spiritual tips, techniques, and knowledge that you can use to improve your life in four areas: family, faith, friends, and finances.

Regardless of your background, *Thought Tools* offers you fascinating glimpses into the Lord's language—Hebrew—little-known secrets from Ancient Jewish Wisdom, information on Jewish holidays and customs, Bible secrets, and other mystical traditions with practical implications.

Expand your range of consciousness and spark conversation with family and friends by sharing these nuggets of wisdom.

Sign up for *Thought Tools* at
www.rabbidaniellapin.com

"The more things change, the more we depend on those things that never change. That's why you need a rabbi."

— Rabbi Daniel Lapin

We would love to stay in touch with you!

Websites:

- **www.rabbidaniellapin.com**

(for weekly blogs, books, audio teachings, e-books, and other resources)

- **www.wehappywarriors.com**

(for membership, online courses, and streaming content)

- **www.aajc.org**

(home of the American Alliance of Jews and Christians, and a way to support our ongoing ministry)

The RDL Podcast

Learn how the world *really* works, and how to trust in those things that never change.

- Listen here: rabbidaniellapin.com/podcast/
- Podcast page: https://rabbidaniellapin.libsyn.com/
- Also available on iTunes, YouTube, and a variety of podcast players around the world.

Social Media:

- Facebook: www.facebook.com/youneedarabbi
- Twitter/X: www.twitter.com/DanielLapin
- Instagram: www.instagram.com/rabbidaniellapin
- YouTube: ww.youtube.com/c/RabbiDanielLapin_ AncientJewishWisdom

Sign up for free weekly teachings at:
www.wehappywarriors.com/email-list-opt-in
or Scan the QR Code

We Happy Warriors
COMMUNITY

Memberships
Join the community and conversation!

Membership community led by Rabbi Daniel & Susan Lapin.

Happy Warriors are devoted to enhancing the five crucial areas of their lives: family, finances, faith, friends and fitness. Rabbi Daniel and Susan provide ancient solutions for modern problems extracted from over 3,000 years of Jewish wisdom in the areas that matter most to this community of like-minded, growth-oriented individuals.

SCAN THE QR CODE TO LEARN MORE

OR GO TO OUR WEBSITE:
www.WeHappyWarriors.com

We Happy Warriors
RABBI DANIEL LAPIN

Join the Community!

Get a Free 14-Day Trial of our Basic Membership
(Scan the QR code below)

https://www.wehappywarriors.com
/offers/wqVmhjRm/checkout

www.wehappywarriors.com

ONLINE COURSES

www.wehappywarriors.com/store

Additional Resources
Lifecodex Publishing, LLC

If you are interested in learning more ancient Jewish wisdom, check out our full catalog of resources

Additional Resources
Lifecodex Publishing, LLC

If you are interested in learning more ancient Jewish wisdom, check out our full catalog of resources

BOOKS & E-BOOKS

www.rabbidaniellapin.com

Index